Physics

for Cambridge International AS & A Level

EXAM PREPARATION AND PRACTICE

Kit Betts-Masters, Mike Follows & Phil McComish

Contents

How to use this series — iv
How to use this book — vi
Exam skills — xi

AS Level

Chapter 1   Kinematics — 1
Chapter 2   Accelerated motion — 8
Chapter 3   Dynamics: explaining motion — 18
Exam practice 1 — 24
Chapter 4   Forces — 28
Chapter 5   Work, energy and power — 35
Chapter 6   Momentum — 42
Chapter 7   Matter and materials — 50
Exam practice 2 — 56
Chapter 8   Electric current, potential difference and resistance — 60
Chapter 9   Kirchhoff's laws — 67
Chapter 10   Resistance and resistivity — 75
Chapter 11   Practical circuits — 81
Exam practice 3 — 87
Chapter 12   Waves — 93
Chapter 13   Superposition of waves — 102
Chapter 14   Stationary waves — 110
Chapter 15   Atomic structure and particle physics — 116
Exam practice 4 — 126
Practical skills for AS Level — 131

Contents

A Level

Chapter 16	Circular motion	141
Chapter 17	Gravitational fields	147
Chapter 18	Oscillations	154
Chapter 19	Thermal physics	166

Exam practice 5 — 173

Chapter 20	Ideal gases	178
Chapter 21	Uniform electric fields	186
Chapter 22	Coulomb's law	192
Chapter 23	Capacitance	200

Exam practice 6 — 210

Chapter 24	Magnetic fields and electromagnetism	215
Chapter 25	Motion of charged particles	223
Chapter 26	Electromagnetic induction	230
Chapter 27	Alternating currents	238

Exam practice 7 — 244

Chapter 28	Quantum physics	250
Chapter 29	Nuclear physics	261
Chapter 30	Medical imaging	271
Chapter 31	Astronomy and cosmology	279

Exam practice 8 — 286

Practical skills for A Level — 292

Acknowledgements — 298

There are extra digital questions for this title found online on Cambridge GO.
For more information on how to access and use your digital resource, please see inside the front cover.

CAMBRIDGE INTERNATIONAL AS & A LEVEL PHYSICS: EXAM PREPARATION AND PRACTICE

> How to use this series

This suite of resources supports students and teachers following the Cambridge International AS & A Level Physics syllabus (9702). All of the components in the series are designed to work together and help students develop the necessary knowledge and skills for this subject. With clear language and style, they are designed for international students.

The coursebook provides comprehensive support for the full Cambridge International Physics syllabus (9702). It includes exercises that develop problem-solving skills, practical activities to help students develop investigative skills, and real world examples of scientific principles. With clear language and style, the coursebook is designed for international students.

The teacher's resource supports and enhances the projects, questions and practical activities in the coursebook. This resource includes detailed lesson ideas, as well as answers and exemplar data for all questions and activities in the coursebook and workbook. The practical teachers guide, included with this resource, provides support for the practical activities and experiments in the practical workbook.

How to use this series

The workbook contains over 100 extra activities that help students build on what they have learned in the coursebook. Students can practise their experimentation, analysis and evaluation skills through exercises testing problem solving and data handling, while activities also support students' planning and investigative skills.

Hands-on investigations provide opportunities to develop key scientific skills including planning investigations, identifying equipment, creating hypotheses, recording results, and analysing and evaluating data.

The Exam Preparation and Practice resource provides dedicated support for students in preparing for their final assessments. Hundreds of questions in the book and accompanying digital resource will help students to check that they understand, and can recall, syllabus concepts. To help students to show what they know in an exam context, a specially developed framework of exam skills with corresponding questions, and past paper question practice, is also included. Self-assessment and reflection features support students to identify any areas that need further practice. This resource should be used alongside the coursebook, throughout the course of study, so students can most effectively increase their confidence and readiness for their exams.

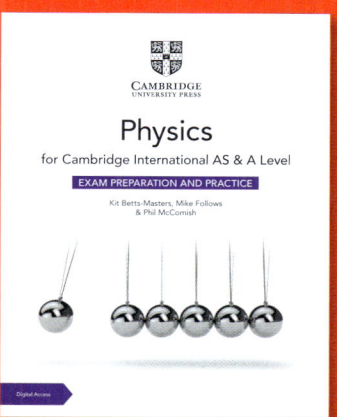

v

CAMBRIDGE INTERNATIONAL AS & A LEVEL PHYSICS: EXAM PREPARATION AND PRACTICE

> How to use this book

This book will help you to check that you **know** the content of the syllabus and practise how to **show** this understanding in an exam. It will also help you be cognitively prepared and in the **flow**, ready for your exam. Research has shown that it is important that you do all three of these things, so we have designed the Know, Show, Flow approach to help you prepare effectively for exams.

Know — You will need to consolidate and then recall a lot of syllabus content.

Show — You should demonstrate your knowledge in the context of a Cambridge exam.

Flow — You should be cognitively engaged and ready to learn. This means reducing test anxiety.

Exam skills checklist

Category	Exam skill
Understanding the question	Recognise different question types
	Understand command words
	Mark scheme awareness
Providing an appropriate response	Understand connections between concepts
	Keep to time
	Know what a good answer looks like
Developing supportive behaviours	Reflect on progress
	Manage test anxiety

This **Exam skills checklist** helps you to develop the awareness, behaviours and habits that will support you when revising and preparing for your exams. For more exam skills advice, including understanding command words and managing your time effectively, please go to the **Exam skills chapter**.

Know

The full syllabus content of your AS & A Level Physics course is covered in your Cambridge coursebook. This book will provide you with different types of questions to support you as you prepare for your exams. You will answer **Knowledge recall questions** that are designed to make sure you understand a topic, and **Recall and connect questions** to help you recall past learning and connect different concepts.

> ### KNOWLEDGE FOCUS
> Knowledge focus boxes summarise the topics that you will answer questions on in each chapter of this book. You can refer back to your Cambridge coursebook to remind yourself of the full detail of the syllabus content.

Knowledge recall questions

Testing yourself is a good way to check that your understanding is secure. These questions will help you to recall the core knowledge you have acquired during your course, and highlight any areas where you may need more practice. They are indicated with a blue bar with a gap, at the side of the page. We recommend that you answer the Knowledge recall questions just after you have covered the relevant topic in class, and then return to them at a later point to check you have properly understood the content.

> ### « RECALL AND CONNECT «
> To consolidate your learning, you need to test your memory frequently. These questions will test that you remember what you learned in previous chapters, in addition to what you are practising in the current chapter.

> ### UNDERSTAND THESE TERMS
> These list the important vocabulary that you should understand for each chapter. Definitions are provided in the glossary of your Cambridge coursebook.

Show

Exam questions test specific knowledge, skills and understanding. You need to be prepared so that you have the best opportunity to show what you know in the time you have during the exam. In addition to practising recall of the syllabus content, it is important to build your exam skills throughout the year.

> ### EXAM SKILLS FOCUS
>
> This feature outlines the exam skills you will practise in each chapter, alongside the Knowledge focus. They are drawn from the core set of eight exam skills, listed in the exam skills checklist. You will practise specific exam skills, such as understanding command words, within each chapter. More general exam skills, such as managing test anxiety, are covered in the Exam skills chapter.

Exam skills questions

These questions will help you to develop your exam skills and demonstrate your understanding. To help you become familiar with exam-style questioning, many of these questions follow the style and use the language of real exam questions, and have allocated marks. They are indicated with a solid red bar at the side of the page.

Looking at sample answers to past paper questions helps you to understand what to aim for.

The **Exam practice** sections in this resource contain example student responses and examiner-style commentary showing how the answer could be improved (both written by the authors).

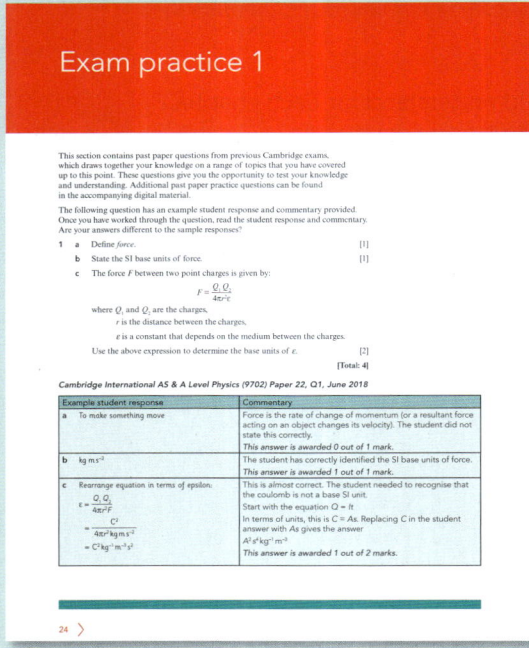

Flow

Preparing for exams can be stressful. One of the approaches recommended by educational psychologists to help with this stress is to improve behaviours around exam preparation. This involves testing yourself in manageable chunks, accompanied by self-evaluation. You should avoid cramming and build in more preparation time. This book is structured to help you do this.

Increasing your ability to recognise the signs of exam-related stress and working through some techniques for how to cope with it will help to make your exam preparation manageable.

> ### REFLECTION
>
> This feature asks you to think about the approach that you take to your exam preparation, and how you might improve this in the future. Reflecting on how you plan, monitor and evaluate your revision and preparation will help you to do your best in your exams.

> ### SELF-ASSESSMENT CHECKLIST
>
> These checklists return to the Learning intentions from your coursebook, as well as the Exam skills focus boxes from each chapter. Checking in on how confident you feel in each of these areas will help you to focus your exam preparation. The 'Show it' prompts will allow you to test your rating. You should revisit any areas that you rate 'Needs more work' or 'Almost there'.
>
> | Now I can: | Show it | Needs more work | Almost there | Confident to move on |
> |---|---|---|---|---|
> | | | | | |

Increasing your ability to recognise the signs of exam-related stress and working through some techniques for how to cope with it will help to make your exam preparation manageable. The **Exam skills chapter** will support you with this.

CAMBRIDGE INTERNATIONAL AS & A LEVEL PHYSICS: EXAM PREPARATION AND PRACTICE

Digital support

Extra self-assessment questions for all chapters can be found online at Cambridge GO. For more information on how to access and use your digital resource, please see inside the front cover.

You will find **Answers** for all of the questions in the book on the 'supporting resources' area of the Cambridge GO platform.

Multiple choice questions

These ask you to select the correct answer to a question from four options. These are auto-marked and feedback is provided.

Flip card questions

These present a question on one screen, and suggested answers on the reverse.

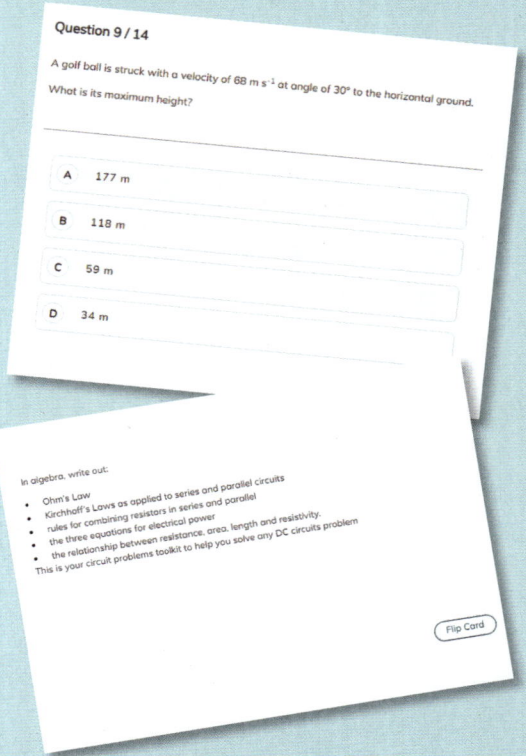

Syllabus Assessment Objectives for AS & A Level Physics

You should be familiar with the Assessment Objectives from the syllabus, as the examiner will be looking for evidence of these requirements in your responses and allocating marks accordingly.

The Assessment Objectives for this syllabus are:

Assessment Objective	AS Level weighting	A Level weighting
AO1: Knowledge and Understanding	30%	25%
AO2: Application	30%	25%
AO3: Analysis	20%	25%
AO4: Evaluation	20%	25%

Exam skills
by Lucy Parsons

What's the point of this book?

Most students make one really basic mistake when they're preparing for exams. What is it? It's focusing far too much on learning 'stuff' – that's facts, figures, ideas, information – and not nearly enough time practising exam skills.

The students who work really, really hard but are disappointed with their results are nearly always students who focus on memorising stuff. They think to themselves, 'I'll do practice papers once I've revised everything.' The trouble is, they start doing practice papers too late to really develop and improve how they communicate what they know.

What could they do differently?

When your final exam script is assessed, it should contain specific language, information and thinking skills in your answers. If you read a question in an exam and you have no idea what you need to do to give a good answer, the likelihood is that your answer won't be as brilliant as it could be. That means your grade won't reflect the hard work you've put into revising for the exam.

There are different types of questions used in exams to assess different skills. You need to know how to recognise these question types and understand what you need to show in your answers.

So, how do you understand what to do in each question type?

That's what this book is all about. But first a little background.

Meet Benjamin Bloom

The psychologist Benjamin Bloom developed a way of classifying and valuing different skills we use when we learn, such as analysis and recalling information. We call these thinking skills. It's known as Bloom's Taxonomy and it's what most exam questions are based around.

If you understand Bloom's Taxonomy, you can understand what any type of question requires you to do. So, what does it look like?

Bloom's Taxonomy of thinking skills

- Evaluation → **Passing judgement** on something
- Synthesis → **Putting together knowledge**, understanding, application and analysis **to create something new**
- Analysis → **Taking apart** information or data in order to **discover relationships**, motives, causes, patterns and connections
- Application → **Using knowledge** and understanding in **new and different circumstances**
- Understanding → **Distinguishing between two similar ideas** or things by using knowledge to **recognise the difference**
- Knowledge → **Recalling, memorising and knowing**

(Increasing difficulty from bottom to top)

The key things to take away from this diagram are:

- Knowledge and understanding are known as lower-level thinking skills. They are less difficult than the other thinking skills. Exam questions that just test you on what you know are usually worth the lowest number of marks.

- All the other thinking skills are worth higher numbers of marks in exam questions. These questions need you to have some foundational knowledge and understanding but are far more about how you think than what you know. They involve:

    - Taking what you know and using it in unfamiliar situations (application).
    - Going deeper into information to discover relationships, motives, causes, patterns and connections (analysis).
    - Using what you know and think to create something new – whether that's an essay, long-answer exam question, a solution to a maths problem, or a piece of art (synthesis).
    - Assessing the value of something, e.g. the reliability of the results of a scientific experiment (evaluation).

In this introductory chapter, you'll be shown how to develop the skills that enable you to communicate what you know and how you think. This will help you achieve to the best of your abilities. In the rest of the book, you'll have a chance to practise these exam skills by understanding how questions work and understanding what you need to show in your answers.

Every time you pick up this book and do a few questions, you're getting closer to achieving your dream results. So, let's get started!

Exam preparation and revision skills

What is revision?

If you think about it, the word 'revision' has two parts to it:

- re – which means 'again'
- vision – which is about seeing.

So, revision is literally about 'seeing again'. This means you're looking at something that you've already learned.

Typically, a teacher will teach you something in class. You may then do some questions on it, write about it in some way, or even do a presentation. You might then have an end-of-topic test sometime later. To prepare for this test, you need to 'look again' or revise what you were originally taught.

Step 1: Making knowledge stick

Every time you come back to something you've learned or revised you're improving your understanding and memory of that particular piece of knowledge. This is called **spaced retrieval**. This is how human memory works. If you don't use a piece of knowledge by recalling it, you lose it.

Everything we learn has to be physically stored in our brains by creating neural connections – joining brain cells together. The more often we 'retrieve' or recall a particular piece of knowledge, the stronger the neural connection gets. It's like lifting weights – the more often you lift, the stronger you get.

However, if you don't use a piece of knowledge for a long time, your brain wants to recycle the brain cells and use them for another purpose. The neural connections get weaker until they finally break, and the memory has gone. This is why it's really important to return often to things that you've learned in the past.

Great ways of doing this in your revision include:

- Testing yourself using flip cards – use the ones available in the digital resources for this book.
- Testing yourself (or getting someone else to test you) using questions you've created about the topic.
- Checking your recall of previous topics by answering the Recall and connect questions in this book.
- Blurting – writing everything you can remember about a topic on a piece of paper in one colour. Then, checking what you missed out and filling it in with another colour. You can do this over and over again until you feel confident that you remember everything.
- Answering practice questions – use the ones in this book.
- Getting a good night's sleep to help consolidate your learning.

> **The importance of sleep and creating long-term memory**
>
> When you go to sleep at night, your brain goes through an important process of taking information from your short-term memory and storing it in your long-term memory.
>
> This means that getting a good night's sleep is a very important part of revision. If you don't get enough good quality sleep, you'll actually be making your revision much, much harder.

Step 2: Developing your exam skills

We've already talked about the importance of exam skills, and how many students neglect them because they're worried about covering all the knowledge.

What actually works best is developing your exam skills at the same time as learning the knowledge.

What does this look like in your studies?

- Learning something at school and your teacher setting you questions from this book or from past papers. This tests your recall as well as developing your exam skills.
- Choosing a topic to revise, learning the content and then choosing some questions from this book to test yourself at the same time as developing your exam skills.

The reason why practising your exam skills is so important is that it helps you to get good at communicating what you know and what you think. The more often you do that, the more fluent you'll become in showing what you know in your answers.

Step 3: Getting feedback

The final step is to get feedback on your work.

If you're testing yourself, the feedback is what you got wrong or what you forgot. This means you then need to go back to those things to remind yourself or improve your understanding. Then, you can test yourself again and get more feedback. You can also congratulate yourself for the things you got right – it's important to celebrate any success, big or small.

If you're doing past paper questions or the practice questions in this book, you will need to mark your work. Marking your work is one of the most important things you can do to improve. It's possible to make significant improvements in your marks in a very short space of time when you start marking your work.

Why is marking your own work so powerful? It's because it teaches you to identify the strengths and weaknesses of your own work. When you look at the mark scheme and see how it's structured, you will understand what is needed in your answers to get the results you want.

This doesn't just apply to the knowledge you demonstrate in your answers. It also applies to the language you use and whether it's appropriately subject-specific, the structure of your answer, how you present it on the page and many other factors. Understanding, practising and improving on these things are transformative for your results.

The most important thing about revision

The most important way to make your revision successful is to make it active.

Sometimes, students say they're revising when they sit staring at their textbook or notes for hours at a time. However, this is a really ineffective way to revise because it's passive. In order to make knowledge and skills stick, you need to be doing something like the suggestions in the following diagram. That's why testing yourself and pushing yourself to answer questions that test higher-level thinking skills are so effective. At times, you might actually be able to feel the physical changes happening in your brain as you develop this new knowledge and these new skills. That doesn't come about without effort.

The important thing to remember is that while active revision feels much more like hard work than passive revision, you don't actually need to do nearly as much of it. That's because you remember knowledge and skills when you use active revision. When you use passive revision, it is much, much harder for the knowledge and skills to stick in your memory.

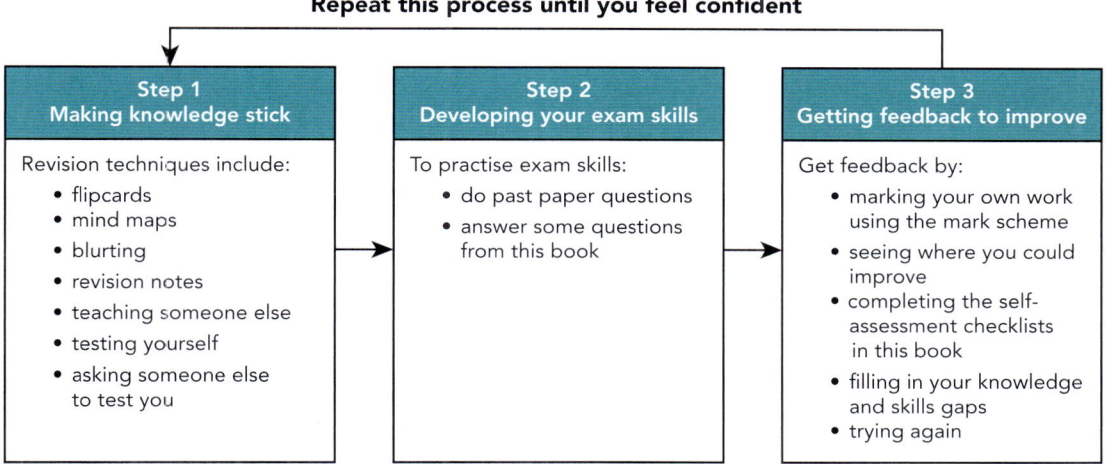

How to improve your exam skills

This book helps you to improve in eight different areas of exam skills, which are divided across three categories. These skills are highlighted in this book in the Exam skills focus at the start of each chapter and developed throughout the book using targeted questions, advice and reflections.

1. **Understand the questions: what are you being asked to do?**
   - Know your question types.
   - Understand command words.
   - Work with mark scheme awareness.

2. **How to answer questions brilliantly**
   - Understand connections between concepts.
   - Keep to time.
   - Know what a good answer looks like.

3. **Give yourself the best chance of success**
   - Reflect on progress.
   - Know how to manage test anxiety.

> CAMBRIDGE INTERNATIONAL AS & A LEVEL PHYSICS: EXAM PREPARATION AND PRACTICE

Understand the questions: what are you being asked to do?

Know your question types

In any exam, there will be a range of different question types. These different question types will test different types of thinking skills from Bloom's Taxonomy.

It is very important that you learn to recognise different question types. If you do lots of past papers, over time you will begin to recognise the structure of the paper for each of your subjects. You will know which types of questions may come first and which ones are more likely to come at the end of the paper. You can also complete past paper questions in the Exam practice sections in this book for additional practice.

You will also recognise the differences between questions worth a lower number of marks and questions worth more marks. The key differences are:

- how much you will need to write in your answer
- how sophisticated your answer needs to be in terms of the detail you give and the depth of thinking you show.

Types of questions

1   Multiple choice questions

Multiple choice questions are generally worth smaller numbers of marks. You will be given several possible answers to the question, and you will have to work out which one is correct using your knowledge and skills.

There is a chance of you getting the right answer with multiple choice questions even if you don't know the answer. This is why you must **always give an answer to multiple choice questions** as it means there is a chance you will earn the mark.

Multiple choice questions are often harder than they appear. The possible answers can be very similar to each other. This means you must be confident in how you work out answers or have a high level of understanding to tell the difference between the possible answers.

Being confident in your subject knowledge and doing lots of practice multiple choice questions will set you up for success. Use the resources in this book and the accompanying online resources to build your confidence.

This example of a multiple choice question is worth one mark. You can see that all the answers have one part in common with at least one other answer. For example, palisade cells is included in three of the possible answers. That's why you have to really know the detail of your content knowledge to do well with multiple choice questions.

Which two types of cells are found in plant leaves?

    A   Palisade mesophyll and stomata

    B   Palisade mesophyll and root hair

    C   Stomata and chloroplast

    D   Chloroplast and palisade mesophyll

2 Questions requiring longer-form answers

Questions requiring longer-form answers need you to write out your answer yourself.

With these questions, take careful note of how many marks are available and how much space you've been given for your answer. These two things will give you a good idea about how much you should say and how much time you should spend on the question.

A rough rule to follow is to write one sentence, or make one point, for each mark that is available. You will get better and better at these longer-form questions the more you practise them.

In this example of a history question, you can see it is worth four marks. It is not asking for an explanation, just for you to list Lloyd George's aims. Therefore, you need to make four correct points in order to get full marks.

What were Lloyd George's aims during negotiations leading to the
Treaty of Versailles? [4]

3 Essay questions

Essay questions are the longest questions you will be asked to answer in an exam. They examine the higher-order thinking skills from Bloom's Taxonomy such as analysis, synthesis and evaluation.

To do well in essay questions, you need to talk about what you know, giving your opinion, comparing one concept or example to another, and evaluating your own ideas or the ones you're discussing in your answer.

You also need to have a strong structure and logical argument that guides the reader through your thought process. This usually means having an introduction, some main body paragraphs that discuss one point at a time, and a conclusion.

Essay questions are usually level-marked. This means that you don't get one mark per point you make. Instead, you're given marks for the quality of the ideas you're sharing as well as how well you present those ideas through the subject-specific language you use and the structure of your essay.

Practising essays and becoming familiar with the mark scheme is the only way to get really good at them.

Understand command words
What are command words?

Command words are the most important words in every exam question. This is because command words tell you what you need to do in your answer. Do you remember Bloom's Taxonomy? Command words tell you which thinking skill you need to demonstrate in the answer to each question.

Two very common command words are **describe** and **explain**.

When you see the command word 'describe' in a question, you're being asked to show lower-order thinking skills like knowledge and understanding. The question will either be worth fewer marks, or you will need to make more points if it is worth more marks.

The command word 'explain' is asking you to show higher-order thinking skills. When you see the command word 'explain', you need to be able to say how or why something happens.

You need to understand all of the relevant command words for the subjects you are taking. Ask your teacher where to find them if you are not sure. It's best not to try to memorise the list of command words, but to become familiar with what command words are asking for by doing lots of practice questions and marking your own work.

How to work with command words

When you first see an exam question, read it through once. Then, read it through again and identify the command word(s). Underline the command word(s) to make it clear to yourself which they are every time you refer back to the question.

You may also want to identify the **content** words in the question and underline them with a different colour. Content words tell you which area of knowledge you need to draw on to answer the question.

In this example, command words are shown in red and content words in blue:

1   a   Explain **four** reasons why governments might support business start-ups.   [8]

> *Adapted from Cambridge IGCSE Business Studies (0450) Q1a Paper 21 June 2022*

Marking your own work using the mark scheme will help you get even better at understanding command words and knowing how to give good answers for each.

Work with mark scheme awareness

The most transformative thing that any student can do to improve their marks is to work with mark schemes. This means using mark schemes to mark your own work at every opportunity.

Many students are very nervous about marking their own work as they do not feel experienced or qualified enough. However, being brave enough to try to mark your own work and taking the time to get good at it will improve your marks hugely.

Why marking your own work makes such a big difference

Marking your own work can help you to improve your answers in the following ways:

1   **Answering the question**

   Having a deep and detailed understanding of what is required by the question enables you to answer the question more clearly and more accurately.

   It can also help you to give the required information using fewer words and in less time, as you can avoid including unrelated points or topics in your answer.

2   **Using subject-specific vocabulary**

   Every subject has subject-specific vocabulary. This includes technical terms for objects or concepts in a subject, such as mitosis and meiosis in biology. It also includes how you talk about the subject, using appropriate vocabulary that may differ from everyday language. For example, in any science subject you might be asked to describe the trend on a graph.

Your answer could say it 'goes up fast' or your answer could say it 'increases rapidly'. You would not get marks for saying 'it goes up fast', but you would for saying it 'increases rapidly'. This is the difference between everyday language and formal scientific language.

When you answer lots of practice questions, you become fluent in the language specific to your subject.

3 Knowing how much to write

It's very common for students to either write too much or too little to answer questions. Becoming familiar with the mark schemes for many different questions will help you to gain a better understanding of how much you need to write in order to get a good mark.

4 Structuring your answer

There are often clues in questions about how to structure your answer. However, mark schemes give you an even stronger idea of the structure you should use in your answers.

For example, if a question says:

'Describe and explain two reasons why...'

You can give a clear answer by:

- Describing reason 1
- Explaining reason 1
- Describing reason 2
- Explaining reason 2

Having a very clear structure will also make it easier to identify where you have earned marks. This means that you're more likely to be awarded the number of marks you deserve.

5 Keeping to time

Answering the question, using subject-specific vocabulary, knowing how much to write and giving a clear structure to your answer will all help you to keep to time in an exam. You will not waste time by writing too much for any answer. Therefore, you will have sufficient time to give a good answer to every question.

How to answer exam questions brilliantly

Understand connections between concepts

One of the higher-level thinking skills in Bloom's Taxonomy is **synthesis**. Synthesis means making connections between different areas of knowledge. You may have heard about synoptic links. Making synoptic links is the same as showing the thinking skill of synthesis.

Exam questions that ask you to show your synthesis skills are usually worth the highest number of marks on an exam paper. To write good answers to these questions, you need to spend time thinking about the links between the topics you've studied **before** you arrive in your exam. A great way of doing this is using mind maps.

How to create a mind map

To create a mind map:

1   Use a large piece of paper and several different coloured pens.

2   Write the name of your subject in the middle. Then, write the key topic areas evenly spaced around the edge, each with a different colour.

3   Then, around each topic area, start to write the detail of what you can remember. If you find something that is connected with something you studied in another topic, you can draw a line linking the two things together.

This is a good way of practising your retrieval of information as well as linking topics together.

Answering synoptic exam questions

You will recognise questions that require you to make links between concepts because they have a higher number of marks. You will have practised them using this book and the accompanying resources.

To answer a synoptic exam question:

1   **Identify the command and content words.** You are more likely to find command words like **discuss** and **explain** in these questions. They might also have phrases like 'the connection between'.

2   **Make a plan for your answer.** It is worth taking a short amount of time to think about what you're going to write in your answer. Think carefully about what information you're going to put in, the links between the different pieces of information and how you're going to structure your answer to make your ideas clear.

3   **Use linking words and phrases in your answer.** For example, 'therefore', 'because', 'due to', 'since' or 'this means that'.

Here is an example of an English Literature exam question that requires you to make synoptic links in your answer.

1   Discuss Carol Ann Duffy's exploration of childhood in her poetry.
    Refer to two poems in your answer. [25]

Content words are shown in blue; command words are shown in red.

This question is asking you to explore the theme of childhood in Duffy's poetry. You need to choose two of her poems to refer to in your answer. This means you need a good knowledge of her poetry, and to be familiar with her exploration of childhood, so that you can easily select two poems that will give you plenty to say in your answer.

Keep to time

Managing your time in exams is really important. Some students do not achieve to the best of their abilities because they run out of time to answer all the questions. However, if you manage your time well, you will be able to attempt every question on the exam paper.

Why is it important to attempt all the questions on an exam paper?

If you attempt every question on a paper, you have the best chance of achieving the highest mark you are capable of.

Students who manage their time poorly in exams will often spend far too long on some questions and not even attempt others. Most students are unlikely to get full marks on many questions, but you will get zero marks for the questions you don't answer. You can maximise your marks by giving an answer to every question.

Minutes per mark

The most important way to keep to time is knowing how many minutes you can spend on each mark.

For example, if your exam paper has 90 marks available and you have 90 minutes, you know there is 1 mark per minute.

Therefore, if you have a five-mark question, you should spend five minutes on it.

Sometimes, you can give a good answer in less time than you have budgeted using the minutes per mark technique. If this happens, you will have more time to spend on questions that use higher-order thinking skills, or more time on checking your work.

How to get faster at answering exam questions

The best way to get faster at answering exam questions is to do lots of practice. You should practise each question type that will be in your exam, marking your own work, so that you know precisely how that question works and what is required by the question. Use the questions in this book to get better and better at answering each question type.

Use the 'Slow, Slow, Quick' technique to get faster.

Take your time answering questions when you first start practising them. You may answer them with the support of the coursebook, your notes or the mark scheme. These things will support you with your content knowledge, the language you use in your answer and the structure of your answer.

Every time you practise this question type, you will get more confident and faster. You will become experienced with this question type, so that it is easy for you to recall the subject knowledge and write it down using the correct language and a good structure.

> **Calculating marks per minute**
>
> Use this calculation to work out how long you have for each mark:
>
> total time in the exam / number of marks available = minutes per mark
>
> Calculate how long you have for a question worth more than one mark like this:
>
> minutes per mark × marks available for this question = number of minutes for this question
>
> **What about time to check your work?**
>
> It is a very good idea to check your work at the end of an exam. You need to work out if this is feasible with the minutes per mark available to you. If you're always rushing to finish the questions, you shouldn't budget checking time. However, if you usually have time to spare, then you can budget checking time.
>
> To include checking time in your minutes per mark calculation:
>
> (total time in the exam − checking time) / number of marks available = minutes per mark

Know what a good answer looks like

It is much easier to give a good answer if you know what a good answer looks like.

Use these methods to know what a good answer looks like.

1. **Sample answers** – you can find sample answers in these places:
   - from your teacher
   - written by your friends or other members of your class
   - in this book.

2. **Look at mark schemes** – mark schemes are full of information about what you should include in your answers. Get familiar with mark schemes to gain a better understanding of the type of things a good answer would contain.

3. **Feedback from your teacher** – if you are finding it difficult to improve your exam skills for a particular type of question, ask your teacher for detailed feedback. You should also look at their comments on your work in detail.

Give yourself the best chance of success

Reflection on progress

As you prepare for your exam, it's important to reflect on your progress. Taking time to think about what you're doing well and what could be improved brings more focus to your revision. Reflecting on progress also helps you to continuously improve your knowledge and exam skills.

Exam skills

How do you reflect on progress?

Use the 'Reflection' feature in this book to help you reflect on your progress during your exam preparation. Then, at the end of each revision session, take a few minutes to think about the following:

	What went well? What would you do the same next time?	What didn't go well? What would you do differently next time?
Your subject knowledge		
How you revised your subject knowledge – did you use active retrieval techniques?		
Your use of subject-specific and academic language		
Understanding the question by identifying command words and content words		
Giving a clear structure to your answer		
Keeping to time		
Marking your own work		

Remember to check for silly mistakes – things like missing out the units after you carefully calculated your answer.

Use the mark scheme to mark your own work. Every time you mark your own work, you will be recognising the good and bad aspects of your work, so that you can progressively give better answers over time.

When do you need to come back to this topic or skill?

Earlier in this section of the book, we talked about revision skills and the importance of spaced retrieval. When you reflect on your progress, you need to think about how soon you need to return to the topic or skill you've just been focusing on.

For example, if you were really disappointed with your subject knowledge, it would be a good idea to do some more active retrieval and practice questions on this topic tomorrow. However, if you did really well you can feel confident you know this topic and come back to it again in three weeks' or a month's time.

The same goes for exam skills. If you were disappointed with how you answered the question, you should look at some sample answers and try this type of question again soon. However, if you did well, you can move on to other types of exam questions.

Improving your memory of subject knowledge

Sometimes students slip back into using passive revision techniques, such as only reading the coursebook or their notes, rather than also using active revision techniques, like testing themselves using flip cards or blurting.

You can avoid this mistake by observing how well your learning is working as you revise. You should be thinking to yourself, 'Am I remembering this? Am I understanding this? Is this revision working?'

If the answer to any of those questions is 'no', then you need to change what you're doing to revise this particular topic. For example, if you don't understand, you could look up your topic in a different textbook in the school library to see if a different explanation helps. Or you could see if you can find a video online that brings the idea to life.

You are in control

When you're studying for exams it's easy to think that your teachers are in charge. However, you have to remember that you are studying for your exams and the results you get will be yours and no one else's.

That means you have to take responsibility for all your exam preparation. You have the power to change how you're preparing if what you're doing isn't working. You also have control over what you revise and when: you can make sure you focus on your weaker topics and skills to improve your achievement in the subject.

This isn't always easy to do. Sometimes you have to find an inner ability that you have not used before. But, if you are determined enough to do well, you can find what it takes to focus, improve and keep going.

What is test anxiety?

Do you get worried or anxious about exams? Does your worry or anxiety impact how well you do in tests and exams?

Test anxiety is part of your natural stress response.

The stress response evolved in animals and humans many thousands of years ago to help keep them alive. Let's look at an example.

The stress response in the wild

Imagine an impala grazing in the grasslands of East Africa. It's happily and calmly eating grass in its herd in what we would call the parasympathetic state of rest and repair.

Then the impala sees a lion. The impala suddenly panics because its life is in danger. This state of panic is also known as the stressed or sympathetic state. The sympathetic state presents itself in three forms: flight, fight and freeze.

The impala starts to run away from the lion. Running away is known as the flight stress response.

The impala might not be fast enough to run away from the lion. The lion catches it but has a loose grip. The impala struggles to try to get away. This struggle is the fight stress response.

However, the lion gets an even stronger grip on the impala. Now the only chance of the impala surviving is playing dead. The impala goes limp, its heart rate and breathing slow. This is called the freeze stress response. The lion believes that it has killed the impala so it drops the impala to the ground. Now the impala can switch back into the flight response and run away.

The impala is now safe – the different stages of the stress response have saved its life.

What has the impala got to do with your exams?

When you feel test anxiety, you have the same physiological stress responses as an impala being hunted by a lion. Unfortunately, the human nervous system cannot tell the difference between a life-threatening situation, such as being chased by a lion, and the stress of taking an exam.

If you understand how the stress response works in the human nervous system, you will be able to learn techniques to reduce test anxiety.

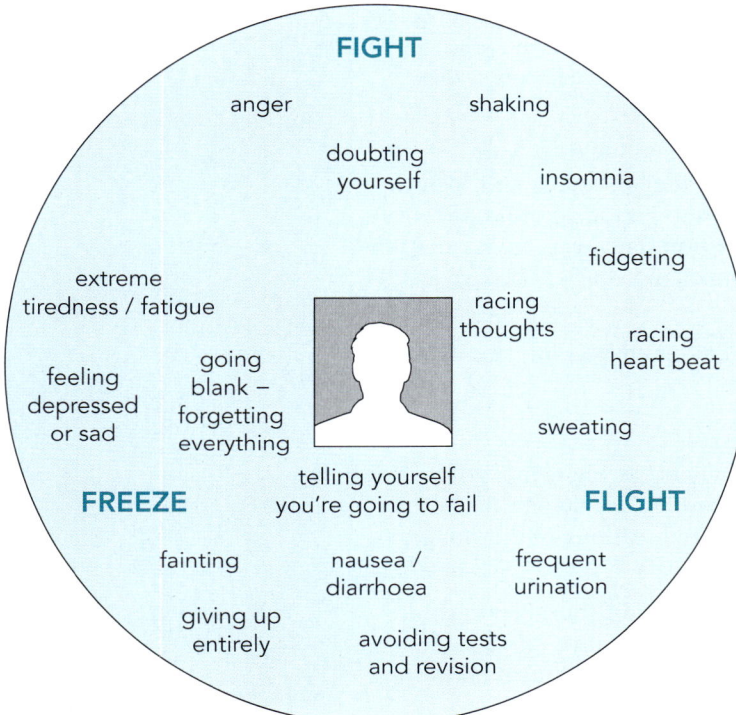

The role of the vagus nerve in test anxiety

The vagus nerve is the part of your nervous system that determines your stress response. Vagus means 'wandering' in Latin, so the vagus nerve is also known as the 'wandering nerve'. The vagus nerve wanders from your brain, down each side of your body, to nearly all your organs, including your lungs, heart, kidneys, liver, digestive system and bladder.

If you are in a stressful situation, like an exam, your vagus nerve sends a message to all these different organs to activate their stress response. Here are some common examples:

- **Heart** beats faster.
- **Kidneys** produce more adrenaline so that you can run, making you fidgety and distracted.
- **Digestive system** and **bladder** want to eliminate all waste products so that energy can be used for fight or flight.

If you want to feel calmer about your revision and exams, you need to do two things to help you move into the parasympathetic, or rest and repair, state:

1   Work with your vagus nerve to send messages of safety through your body.
2   Change your perception of the test so that you see it as safe and not dangerous.

How to cope with test anxiety

1   Be well prepared

Good preparation is the most important part of managing test anxiety. The better your preparation, the more confident you will be. If you are confident, you will not perceive the test or exam as dangerous, so the sympathetic nervous system responses of fight, flight and freeze are less likely to happen.

This book is all about helping you to be well prepared and building your confidence in your knowledge and ability to answer exam questions well. Working through the knowledge recall questions will help you to become more confident in your knowledge of the subject. The practice questions and exam skills questions will help you to become more confident in communicating your knowledge in an exam.

To be well prepared, look at the advice in the rest of this chapter and use it as you work through the questions in this book.

2   Work with your vagus nerve

The easiest way to work with your vagus nerve to tell it that you're in a safe situation is through your breathing. This means breathing deeply into the bottom of your lungs, so that your stomach expands, and then breathing out for longer than you breathed in. You can do this with counting.

Breathe in deeply, expanding your abdomen, for the count of four; breathe out, drawing your navel back towards your spine, for the count of five, six or seven. Repeat this at least three times. However, you can do it for as long as it takes for you to feel calm.

The important thing is that you breathe out for longer than you breathe in. This is because when you breathe in, your heart rate increases slightly, and when you breathe out, your heart rate decreases slightly. If you're spending more time breathing out overall, you will be decreasing your heart rate over time.

3   Feel it

Anxiety is an uncomfortable, difficult thing to feel. That means that many people try to run away from anxious feelings. However, this means the stress just gets stored in your body for you to feel later.

When you feel anxious, follow these four steps:

1   Pause.
2   Place one hand on your heart and one hand on your stomach.
3   Notice what you're feeling.
4   Stay with your feelings.

What you will find is that if you are willing to experience what you feel for a minute or two, the feeling of anxiety will usually pass very quickly.

Exam skills

4   **Write or talk it out**

   If your thoughts are moving very quickly, it is often better to get them out of your mind and on to paper.

   You could take a few minutes to write down everything that comes through your mind, then rip up your paper and throw it away. If you don't like writing, you can speak aloud alone or to someone you trust.

Other ways to break the stress cycle

Exercise and movement	Being friendly	Laughter
• Run or walk. • Dance. • Lift weights. • Yoga. Anything that involves moving your body is helpful.	• Chat to someone in your study break. • Talk to the cashier when you buy your lunch.	• Watch or listen to a funny show on TV or online. • Talk with someone who makes you laugh. • Look at photos of fun times.
Have a hug	**Releasing emotions**	**Creativity**
• Hug a friend or relative. • Cuddle a pet e.g. a cat. Hug for 20 seconds or until you feel calm and relaxed.	It is healthy to release negative or sad emotions. Crying is often a quick way to get rid of these difficult feelings so if you feel like you need to cry, allow it.	• Paint, draw or sketch. • Sew, knit or crochet. • Cook, build something.

If you have long-term symptoms of anxiety, it is important to tell someone you trust and ask for help.

CAMBRIDGE INTERNATIONAL AS & A LEVEL PHYSICS: EXAM PREPARATION AND PRACTICE

Your perfect revision session

1 Intention

What do you want to achieve in this revision session?
- Choose an area of knowledge or an exam skill that you want to focus on.
- Choose some questions from this book that focus on this knowledge area or skill.
- Gather any other resources you will need e.g. pen, paper, flashcards, coursebook.

2 Focus

Set your focus for the session
- Remove distractions from your study area e.g. leave your phone in another room.
- Write down on a piece of paper or sticky note the knowledge area or skill you're intending to focus on.
- Close your eyes and take three deep breaths, with the exhale longer than the inhale.

3 Revision

Revise your knowledge and understanding
- To improve your knowledge and understanding of the topic, use your coursebook, notes or flashcards, including active learning techniques.
- To improve your exam skills, look at previous answers, teacher feedback, mark schemes, sample answers or examiners' reports.

4 Practice

Answer practice questions
- Use the questions in this book, or in the additional online resources, to practise your exam skills.
- If the exam is soon, do this in timed conditions without the support of the coursebook or your notes.
- If the exam is a long time away, you can use your notes and resources to help you.

5 Feedback

Mark your answers
- Use mark schemes to mark your work.
- Reflect on what you've done well and what you could do to improve next time.

6 Next steps

What have you learned about your progress from this revision session? What do you need to do next?
- What did you do well? Feel good about these things, and know it's safe to set these things aside for a while.
- What do you need to work on? How are you going to improve? Make a plan to get better at the things you didn't do well or didn't know.

7 Rest

Take a break
- Do something completely different to rest: get up, move or do something creative or practical.
- Remember that rest is an important part of studying, as it gives your brain a chance to integrate your learning.

1 Kinematics

KNOWLEDGE FOCUS

In this chapter you will answer questions on:
- speed
- distance and displacement, scalars and vectors
- speed and velocity
- displacement–time graphs
- combining displacements
- combining velocities
- subtracting vectors
- other examples of scalar and vector quantities.

EXAM SKILLS FOCUS

In this chapter you will:
- consider the differences between short-answer and multiple choice questions.

You might think that short-answer and multiple choice questions can be answered in a similar way. But you need to consider the differences between them. A multiple choice question has the answer given but will also contain a number of distractors. These are answers that may seem correct if you do not think about them properly. Short-answer questions do not give you the correct answer, but there is nothing to distract you away from the correct answer.

So, multiple choice questions need to be approached using a different strategy. Once you find the distractors in a multiple choice question, working out the correct answer will be less difficult. There are some multiple choice questions in this chapter for you to practise – can you spot the distractors?

1.1 Speed

1. Arrange these speeds in order, from slowest to fastest, by converting them all to m s^{-1}.

   (use 1 mile = 1600 metres)

15 m s^{-1}	0.0125 km s^{-1}	40 km h^{-1}	20 mph

2. A football is kicked between three players, A, B, and C, as shown in Figure 1.1.

   The time between the ball being kicked by player A and received by player B is 0.6 s.

   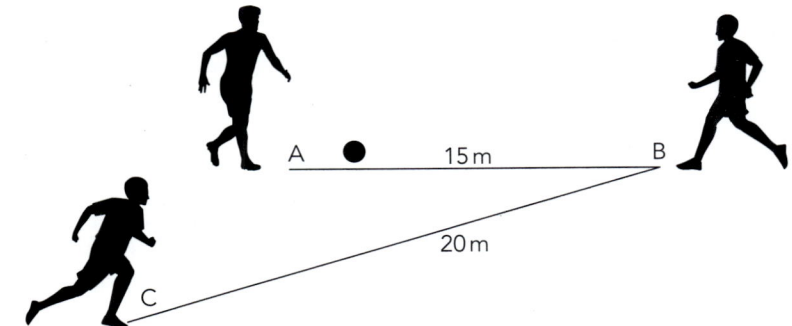

   Figure 1.1

   a Calculate the average speed of the ball between players A and B. [2]
   b Player B then kicks the ball to C with the same average speed.
      Calculate the time taken for the ball to get to player C from B. [2]
   c Suggest a reason why the ball may change speed during its journey. [1]

   [Total: 5]

   UNDERSTAND THIS TERM
   - speed

1.2 Distance and displacement, scalar and vector

1. Which of these quantities are scalars, and which ones are vectors?

   speed   force
   velocity   time
   displacement   pressure
   distance   mass
   acceleration   weight

2 In the Olympics 1500 m race, an athlete runs around the 400 m track 3.75 times.

She completes the first 400 m lap (A) in 55 s, the second 400 m lap (B) in 65 s, the third 400 m lap (C) in 66 s, and the final 300 m lap (D) in 45 s.

- **a** Calculate which part of the race (A to D) had the fastest average speed.
- **b** What is the distance she ran?
- **c** How does the distance that she ran differ from the displacement?
- **d** Calculate her average speed for the whole race.

> **UNDERSTAND THIS TERM**
> - displacement

1.3 Speed and velocity

1 A geostationary satellite is in orbit around the Earth.

The orbit is circular, has a radius of 42 km, and takes 24 hours to complete.

- **a** What is the instantaneous speed of the satellite in:
  - **i** km h^{-1}
  - **ii** m s^{-1}?
- **b** Another satellite is measured to be moving at 5.2 m s^{-1}.
  What is the radius of its orbit?

> **UNDERSTAND THIS TERM**
> - instantaneous speed

2 At the particle accelerator called CERN in Switzerland, there is a circular proton accelerator with a circumference of 628 m.

- **a** During their acceleration, the protons travel approximately 80 000 km in the accelerator.
  The average speed of the protons during the acceleration is 3.0×10^7 m s^{-1}.
  Calculate the time taken for this acceleration. [2]
- **b** Calculate how many times the protons travel around the accelerator during this acceleration. [2]
- **c** After the acceleration, the protons travel at constant speed around the accelerator.
  Explain how the protons can be moving at constant speed and yet still undergoing acceleration. [2]

[Total: 6]

3   Figure 1.2 shows the path of a train that travels between three cities X, Y and Z.

Figure 1.2

A train starts at X and takes 20 minutes to reach Y.

The train stops at Y for 5 minutes.

The train then travels to Z, taking a further 15 minutes.

What is the average speed of the train between X and Z?

A $0.042 \, \text{m s}^{-1}$
B $1.25 \, \text{m s}^{-1}$
C $1.25 \, \text{m h}^{-1}$
D $20.8 \, \text{m s}^{-1}$

[Total: 1]

REFLECTION

How did you find the multiple choice question (MCQ), question **3** with Figure 1.2? Did you spot the units in the distractors? Can you think of a strategy you could apply to MCQs to help you to identify the distractors?

1.4 Displacement–time graphs and
1.5 Combining displacements

1   Copy and complete these sentences.

On a displacement–time graph, a diagonal straight line represents an object moving with ………………. ………………. .

The gradient of the graph is equal to the ……………… of the object.

The steeper the gradient, the ……………… the velocity.

If the slope is increasing in steepness, then the ……………… is increasing.

If the slope is decreasing in steepness, then the ……………… is ……………… .

A horizontal flat line represents an object that is ……………… .

UNDERSTAND THIS TERM

- resultant vector

2   Review the 1500 m Olympic athlete information in question 1.2.2.
Use the information given to plot the distance–time graph for the motion.

« RECALL AND CONNECT 1 «

You will have studied springs and forces during your IGCSE studies.
Write down Hooke's law; include the point at which the law no longer applies.

3   Starting at point X and moving in two consecutive displacements of 5 m and then 12 m, which one of the following finishing displacements from X is **not** possible?

   A   3 m   B   7 m   C   13 m   D   17 m   [Total: 1]

4   A boat travels 320 m due East. The boat stops and drops an anchor into the seafloor to stop the boat moving position during the night.

   Overnight the anchor comes loose and the boat drifts 240 m due North.

   Calculate the final displacement of the boat.   [Total: 3]

1.6 Combining velocities

1   A canoeist is about to paddle across a river that has a current of $0.8\,\mathrm{m\,s^{-1}}$, as shown in Figure 1.3.

   The canoeist wants to end up at point B, directly across the river from her starting point, A.

   She can paddle at $2.3\,\mathrm{m\,s^{-1}}$ in still water.

   At what angle, θ, should she aim up river?

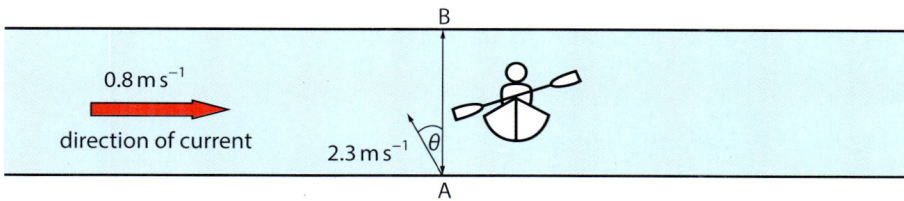

Figure 1.3 Canoeist paddling across a river with a current

2   A swimmer is swimming due South at $1.5\,\mathrm{m\,s^{-1}}$, and the current flows due West at $1.0\,\mathrm{m\,s^{-1}}$.

   By scale diagram, or otherwise, calculate:

   a   the magnitude of the resultant velocity of the swimmer   [2]
   b   the angle the velocity makes to due South.   [2]
   [Total: 4]

3   A boat is moving at constant velocity.
   a   Draw a displacement–time graph to show this motion.   [2]
   b   The boat is moving due West at a speed of $5.2\,\mathrm{m\,s^{-1}}$ relative to the water, and the water is moving due South at $2.6\,\mathrm{m\,s^{-1}}$.

   By considering the components of these velocities, calculate the resultant velocity of the boat.   [3]
   [Total: 5]

4   Figure 1.4 shows a golfer and a flag, which is 212 m away from the golfer.

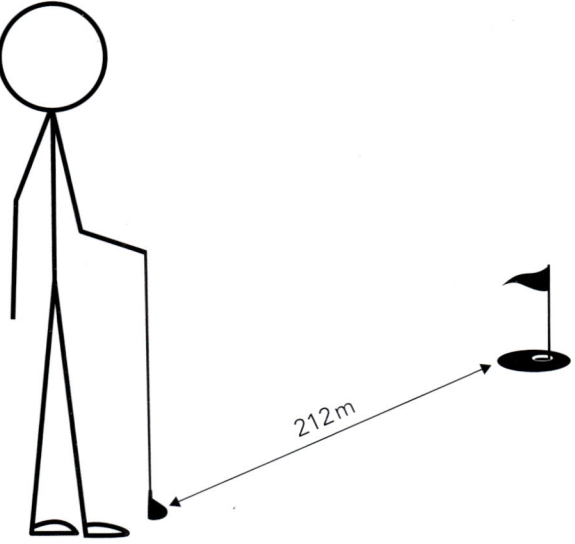

Figure 1.4

The wind is blowing at a constant $10\,\text{m s}^{-1}$ in a direction that is 90° to the line between the golfer and the flag.

The golfer aims at the flag and hits the ball straight towards the flag at $50\,\text{m s}^{-1}$.

a   By considering the components of these velocities, calculate the resultant velocity of the ball. Include the angle that the path of the ball makes with the direction in which it was hit. [3]

b   The ball is in the air for a total of 4.3 s. Calculate the displacement of the ball. [1]

[Total: 4]

1.7 Subtracting vectors and
1.8 Other examples of vector and scalar quantities

1   Vector A is $3.0\,\text{m s}^{-1}$ North.
    Vector B is $4.0\,\text{m s}^{-1}$ East.
    Vector C is $5.0\,\text{m s}^{-1}$ West.
    By diagram or otherwise, calculate the following:
    a   A + B
    b   B + C
    c   B − C
    d   A − C

2   a   Give **one** similarity and **one** difference between a scalar and a vector quantity.
    b   List **four** scalar quantities and **four** vector quantities.

1   Kinematics

> ## REFLECTION
>
> This chapter introduces mathematical techniques that will be important in the next few chapters when vectors are involved – such as Pythagoras' theorem and the trigonometry functions of sin, cos and tan. Are you confident adding two vectors? How will you remember that a vector needs a direction and, therefore, the angle should be calculated also?

SELF-ASSESSMENT CHECKLIST

Let's revisit the Knowledge focus and Exam skills focus for this chapter.

Decide how confident you are with each statement.

Now I can:	Show it	Needs more work	Almost there	Confident to move on
define and use displacement, speed and velocity	Create flashcards with definitions of displacement, speed and velocity.			
draw and interpret displacement–time graphs	Sketch a displacement–time graph whenever you go on a journey, such as walking to school, or travelling to a holiday destination.			
describe laboratory methods for determining the speed	Write down two sets of instructions: one for someone to use light gates and interrupt cards and one for someone to use sonar to work out speed in experiments.			
understand the differences between scalar and vector quantities and give examples of each	Practise writing out lists of vectors and scalars. Use the fact that scalars are magnitude only, whereas vectors have magnitude and direction.			
use vector addition to add and subtract vectors that are in the same plane	Try constructing scale diagrams or using Pythagoras' theorem and trigonometry to work out the sums of vectors at right angles.			
understand the differences between short-answer and multiple choice questions	Write from memory the differences between the two types of questions.			

2 Accelerated motion

KNOWLEDGE FOCUS

In this chapter you will answer questions on:
- the meaning of acceleration
- calculating acceleration
- units of acceleration
- deducing acceleration
- deducing displacement
- measuring velocity and acceleration
- determining velocity and acceleration in the laboratory
- the equations of motion
- deriving the equations of motion
- uniform and non-uniform acceleration
- acceleration caused by gravity
- determining g
- motion in two dimensions: projectiles
- understanding projectiles.

EXAM SKILLS FOCUS

In this chapter you will:
- show that you understand the 'calculate' command word and can answer 'calculate' questions.

You will come across questions using the 'calculate' command word in this topic and in many chapters in the book. Calculating different values is a key skill that you will need to demonstrate in many different topics. The definition of this command word is given below.

| Calculate | work out from given facts, figures or information |

You must remember to show all the steps in your working when answering 'calculate' questions. This is because you may receive marks for using the correct method, even if you have used the wrong values in your answer. You should also include the correct units in your answer: remember not to confuse milliseconds with minutes.

2 Accelerated motion

Practise showing all your working as you answer the 'calculate' questions in this chapter.

A good answer for 'calculate' questions includes:
- showing the mathematical steps you took leading to the answer
- using appropriate units
- using an appropriate number of significant figures asked for in the question.

When substituting values, check that you are using the correct units and the correct powers of ten. Is your answer in the expected range? If you are not sure of the right answer, does it make physical sense? For example, a speed that exceeds the speed of light will be wrong!

2.1 The meaning of acceleration

1. How can a body accelerate without changing speed?

> ≪ RECALL AND CONNECT 1 ≪
>
> Think back to Chapter 1. What is the difference between average speed and instantaneous speed?

UNDERSTAND THIS TERM
- acceleration

2.2 Calculating acceleration

1. Work out the missing values **A–D** in the table below.

Initial speed / $m\,s^{-1}$	Final speed / $m\,s^{-1}$	Time / s	Acceleration / $m\,s^{-2}$
2	7	2	A
13.4	33.5	60	B
33.5	13.4	60	C
3	D	4	2.25

2. The acceleration of a new transport system is to be limited to about $5\,m\,s^{-2}$. If it has a top speed of $1220\,km\,h^{-1}$, how long will it take to reach that speed?

3. A car is moving along a road at a steady speed. It reduces speed from $30\,m\,s^{-1}$ to $15\,m\,s^{-1}$ in $10\,s$. Calculate the acceleration. **[Total: 2]**

4. A bus is travelling along a road at $13\,m\,s^{-1}$. The driver sees a cat jump into the road and applies the brakes after a reaction time of $0.3\,s$. The bus comes to a complete stop $2\,s$ later.
   a. Calculate the acceleration of the car in the $2\,s$ that the brakes are active. [2]
   b. Calculate the total distance covered from the moment the driver sees the cat. [1]

   [Total: 3]

2.3 Units of acceleration

1   What is the standard SI unit of acceleration?

> **« RECALL AND CONNECT 2 «**
>
> What is the difference between a vector and a scalar?

2.4 Deducing acceleration and
2.5 Deducing displacement

1   Work out the average acceleration in the following examples. Express your answers in metres per second squared ($m\,s^{-2}$).

   a   A car moves from rest to $10\,m\,s^{-1}$ in 4 seconds.
   b   A bus moves from rest to $13\,m\,s^{-1}$ in 13 seconds.
   c   A rocket moves from rest to $21.6\,m\,s^{-1}$ in 9.26 seconds.
   d   A car changes speed from $30\,m\,s^{-1}$ to $13\,m\,s^{-1}$ in 5 seconds.
   e   A freight train changes speed from $6\,m\,s^{-1}$ to $33\,m\,s^{-1}$ in one and a half minutes.

2   Draw a velocity–time graph for each of the following situations:

   a   Velocity is constant.
   b   From an initial velocity, a body accelerates uniformly.
   c   A vehicle comes to a stop with uniform acceleration.

3   For all parts of question 1, draw the velocity–time graph for the motion described and use it to work out the distance travelled from the area under the curve.

2.6 Measuring velocity and acceleration and
2.7 Determining velocity and acceleration in the laboratory

1   Write down the two main ways of measuring speed in a laboratory.
2   Describe how the acceleration of a body can be measured by:
   a   one light gate and a U-shaped interrupt card [4]
   b   a ticker timer. [4]

[Total: 8]

3   A ticker timer was used to work out the acceleration of a trolley moving down an inclined plane. The data collected are presented in the following table.

   a   Calculate the acceleration of the trolley. [2]
   b   Calculate the missing values, **X** and **Y**, in the table. [2]

   [Total: 4]

Section of tape	Time at start / s	Time interval / s	Length of section / cm	Velocity / m s^{-1}
1	0.0	0.1	3.10	0.31
2	0.1	0.1	5.43	0.54
3	0.2	0.1	X	Y
4	0.3	0.1	10.09	1.01

4   An interrupt card is used to work out the acceleration of a car on an air track.

The interrupt card is shaped like the capital letter U.

The vertical sections are called interrupts.

The width of each interrupt used in this experiment is 2 cm.

A computer records the time that each of the four edges passes through a light gate, and these data are shown in this table:

Interrupt card	Times / s
card 1 (leading edge)	0.00
card 1 (trailing edge)	0.04
card 2 (leading edge)	0.20
card 2 (trailing edge)	0.28

Use the data to calculate:

   a   the velocity measured by interrupt card 1 [1]
   b   the velocity measured by interrupt card 2 [1]
   c   the acceleration of the car. [2]

   [Total: 4]

≪ RECALL AND CONNECT 3 ≪

How do you find velocity, acceleration and displacement on a velocity–time graph?

2.8 The equations of motion

1. The equations of motion can only be used when two conditions are met. What are the conditions?

2.9 Deriving the equations of motion and
2.10 Uniform and non-uniform acceleration

1. Outline how you derive the equations of motion.
2. Velocity–time graphs can tell us about the acceleration of an object.
   a. When looking at a velocity–time graph, how can you tell whether the acceleration is uniform or non-uniform?
   b. How would you work out the acceleration in both cases?

> **UNDERSTAND THIS TERM**
> - uniform acceleration

2.11 Acceleration caused by gravity and
2.12 Determining g

1. Astronauts arrive on a distant planet, and one of them drops a rock from the top of a cliff 20 m tall. The rock takes 5.0 s to reach the ground.
   Calculate the gravitational field strength of the planet. [Total: 2]

2. Describe how you would measure the gravitational field strength g (sometimes called the acceleration of free fall) using the motion of a falling body. [Total: 5]

3. Students conduct an experiment to find the gravitational field strength g. They measured the average time it took a ball bearing to drop from different heights. Their results are recorded in the table below.

   What graph should the students plot, and how can they use the graph to find the value of g?

Displacement / m	0.0	0.2	0.4	0.6	0.8	1.0
Time / s	0.00	0.20	0.29	0.35	0.40	0.45

> **UNDERSTAND THIS TERM**
> - free fall

2 Accelerated motion

4 The organisers of a fireworks display wish to calculate the maximum height reached by a particular firework. The firework is launched at time 0.0 s vertically upward from ground level beside a tall building.

At time 4.0 s the firework passes the roof of the building.

At time 17.0 s the firework passes the roof of the building again on the way down, as shown in Figure 2.1.

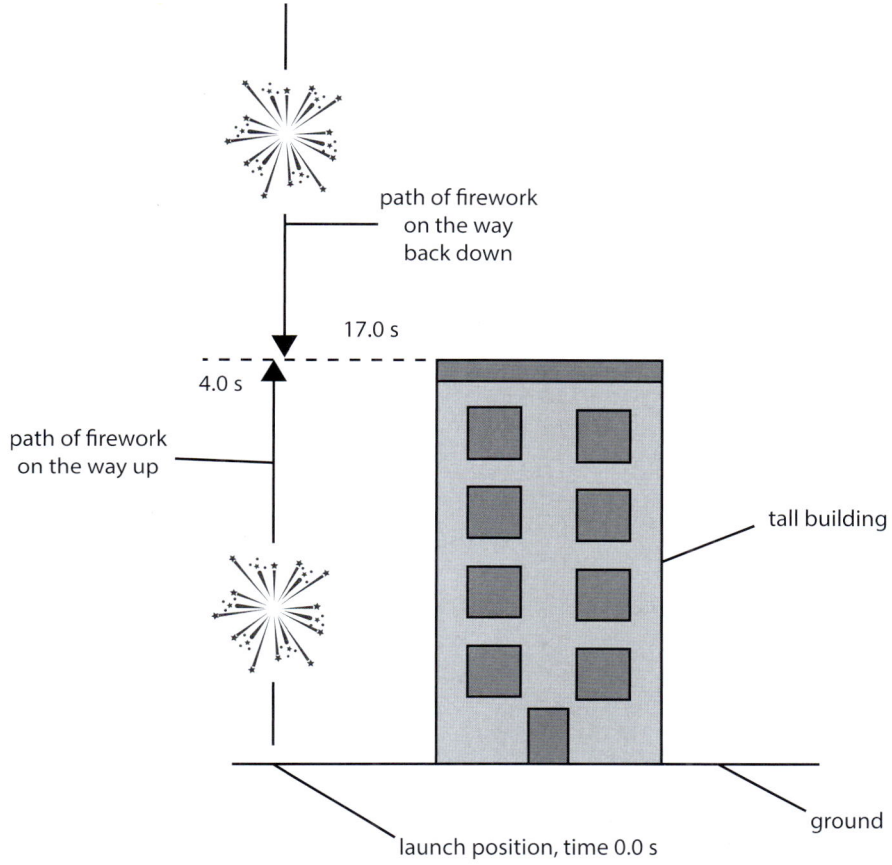

Figure 2.1

Calculate the maximum height reached by the firework.
Assume that air resistance is negligible.

[Total: 3]

REFLECTION

When asked to describe how they would measure g, some students visualise assembling the equipment, writing down and rearranging the equations, and so on. Have you developed a good technique for remembering the steps required in an experiment? What other problem-solving strategies could you apply to the different 'calculate' questions in this chapter?

2.13 Motion in two dimensions: projectiles

1 Copy and complete the table by finding the horizontal and vertical components of the following vectors. It may help to make a sketch for each example.

	Vector	Direction	Horizontal component	Vertical component
a	30 N	30° above the horizontal to the right		
b	33 N	80° below the horizontal to the left		
c	500 m s^{-1}	23° below the horizon to the right		

2 A boat is crossing from the South side to the North side of a river.
   The water flows from West to East (left to right) with a speed of 3 m s^{-1}.
   The boat moves with an average speed of 5 m s^{-1}.

   a Calculate the northwards component of its speed. [2]
   b Calculate the angle that the boat needs to be steered so that it arrives on the North side of the river exactly North of where it started. [2]

   [Total: 4]

2.14 Understanding projectiles

1 In this question, you are going to compare the trajectory of a ball when it falls from the top of a cliff to when it is launched horizontally from the top of a cliff.

   a Copy and complete the table below by working out the missing values. You can use a spreadsheet to do the calculations if you wish.

Time of flight / s	Horizontal speed = 0 m s^{-1}		Horizontal speed = 10 m s^{-1}		Horizontal speed = 40 m s^{-1}	
	Horizontal distance / m	Vertical distance / m	Horizontal distance / m	Vertical distance / m	Horizontal distance / m	Vertical distance / m
0						
1						
2						
3						

   b Plot the trajectories on the same axes (that is, vertical displacement against horizontal displacement).
   c What do you notice about the vertical distance for the different horizontal speeds?

2 **A projectile is fired at a speed of 200 m s⁻¹.**

a Copy and complete the table below. For each angle listed, work out the horizontal and vertical components of its speed, the highest point it reaches, its flight time, and its range.

Angle / °	Horizontal component / m	Vertical component / m	Zenith (highest point) / m	Flight time / s	Range / m
0					
15					
30					
45					
60					
75					
90					

b Plot a graph of range against angle. Add a curve of best fit.

3 A golfer hit a golf ball with an initial speed of 68 m s⁻¹ at an angle of 45° to the horizontal.

a Calculate how long the ball was airborne. [2]
b Calculate the height that the ball reached. [2]

[Total: 4]

4 A powerful tennis ball-serving machine is used to launch a tennis ball over a wall.

The distance from the machine to the wall is 30 m.

The ball reaches its maximum height of 12 m as it passes directly above the wall. The maximum height and distance from the wall are measured from the position of launch of the ball, as shown in Figure 2.2.

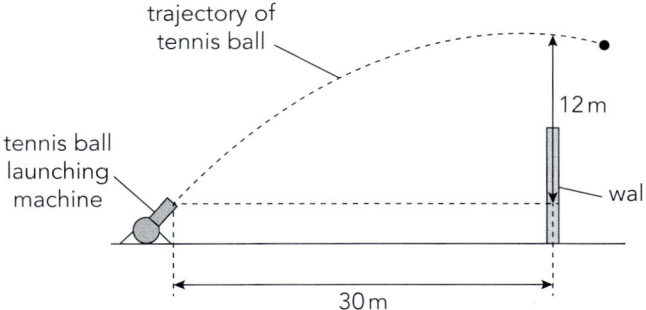

Figure 2.2

Assume that air resistance is negligible.

- a Calculate the magnitude and direction of the initial velocity of the ball. [6]
- b State the velocity of the ball at the highest point of its trajectory. [1]
- c The machine is moved to a new distance of 40 m from the wall.
     The ball is launched at the same angle and at the same speed as before.
     Now, the ball only just clears the top of the wall.
     Calculate the height of the top of the wall above the machine. [3]

[Total: 10]

REFLECTION

How did you find the 'calculate' questions in this chapter? Did you know which calculation to use? The questions used different units – did you identify these and apply them to your answer? How can you make sure you remember to include the correct units when answering 'calculate' questions?

SELF-ASSESSMENT CHECKLIST

Let's revisit the Knowledge focus and Exam skills focus for this chapter.

Decide how confident you are with each statement.

Now I can:	Show it	Needs more work	Almost there	Confident to move on
define acceleration	Make a flashcard with acceleration on one side and the definition on the other.			
draw and interpret graphs of speed, velocity and acceleration	Sketch graphs from the information given in a question or from examples on the internet.			
calculate displacement from the area under a velocity–time graph	As well as solving problems algebraically, use the information given in a question to sketch velocity–time graphs to work out the displacement from the area under the curve.			

CONTINUED

Now I can:	Show it	Needs more work	Almost there	Confident to move on
calculate velocity and acceleration using gradients of a displacement–time graph and a velocity–time graph	As well as solving problems algebraically, use the information given in a question to sketch velocity–time graphs to work out the acceleration from the gradient.			
derive and use the equations of uniformly accelerated motion	Practise doing this every few weeks, starting with a sketch of a velocity–time graph.			
describe an experiment to measure the acceleration of free fall, g	Write down the steps and ask a friend to check that there would be enough detail to allow them to do the experiment or check your answer using a textbook.			
use perpendicular components to represent a vector	Find perpendicular components to a vector and then use these components to get back to the resultant vector.			
explain projectile motion in terms of uniform velocity and uniform acceleration	Explain how to solve projectile problems to friends and then attempt practice questions.			
show that I understand the 'calculate' command word and can answer 'calculate' questions	Compare your answers for the 'calculate' questions in this chapter with those provided online and make a list of any information that you missed.			

3 Dynamics: explaining motion

KNOWLEDGE FOCUS

In this chapter you will answer questions on:

- force, mass and acceleration
- identifying forces
- weight, friction and gravity
- mass and inertia
- moving through fluids
- Newton's third law of motion
- understanding SI units.

EXAM SKILLS FOCUS

In this chapter you will:

- show that you understand the 'identify' command word and can answer 'identify' questions.

'Identify' questions will often ask you to name or recognise information from a diagram or a graph. You might be asked to draw a label line or a cross on a diagram. You may also be asked to select the correct choice from a selection of possible answers, or to interpret trends from a graph. Answers to 'identify' questions are often short responses, similar to the answers for 'state' or 'give' questions.

| Identify | name/select/recognise |

3 Dynamics: explaining motion

3.1 Force, mass and acceleration

1 Work out the missing values **A–E**. Note that 1 tonne = 10^3 kg.

Object	Mass	Acceleration / m s^{-2}	Force
car doing an emergency stop	1200 kg	−6.5	A
RMS Titanic	46328 tonnes	B	9.27 MN
Falcon Heavy rocket	C	119	7.6 MN
Usain Bolt	94 kg	9.5	D
flea (jumping)	0.7 mg	E	6.72 mN

2 Raindrops of mass 34 mg fall vertically at 10 m s^{-1}.

Mosquitoes have a mass of 5 mg. If a mosquito is hit by a raindrop while flying horizontally, its speed will increase by 2 m s^{-1} in 1 ms.

   a A raindrop is falling vertically. Calculate the acceleration of a mosquito when it is struck by the raindrop while it is flying horizontally. [2]

   b Calculate the average force on the flying mosquito when struck by the raindrop. [2]

   c A raindrop that lands on a hard surface will come to a stop in 2 ms.

   Calculate the force exerted by the raindrop when it lands on a hard surface. [2]

   [Total: 6]

3 A car of mass 1200 kg moves horizontally along a straight road and accelerates at 0.25 m s^{-2}.

There is a resistive force of 400 N.

Calculate the driving force provided by the engine of the car. **[Total: 2]**

> **« RECALL AND CONNECT 1 «**
>
> Think back to Chapter 2. How do you calculate acceleration when you have a change of speed and from a speed–time graph?

UNDERSTAND THESE TERMS
- mass
- Newton's second law of motion

3.2 Identifying forces and
3.3 Weight, friction and gravity

1 Write down a list of the different forces you have encountered in this chapter and summarise where they are encountered.

2 a Make a table to summarise the differences between mass and weight.

   b Write down the equation that links mass and weight.

UNDERSTAND THESE TERMS
- weight
- friction

19

3.4 Mass and inertia and
3.5 Moving through fluids

1. a Write down Newton's first law of motion.
   b What force acts to oppose motion so that objects usually need a force to keep them moving?
   c Why does the force you identified in part **b** make it difficult for some people to accept the validity of Newton's first law of motion?
   d What is inertia, and what property of an object gives it inertia?

> **UNDERSTAND THESE TERMS**
> - uniform motion
> - terminal velocity

> **« RECALL AND CONNECT 2 «**
>
> Think back to Chapter 2. Recall a strategy for solving problems about projectiles. What assumptions about projectiles make problems easier to solve?

> **REFLECTION**
>
> It is sometimes easier to remember a definition if you put it in your own words (provided it is still correct) or use an equation as a prompt. How do you remember Newton's equations of motion?

2. Assume that the objects have reached their maximum speed in a fluid where the drag force is given by the equation $F = kv^2$, where k is the constant for that object.

   a Work out the missing values in the table below.

Vehicle	Drag force / N	k	Velocity / m s^{-1}
A	2036	0.56	i
B	2225	ii	58
C	iii	0.46	65

   b Do you notice any correlation between k, the drag force experienced by the objects, and their velocity?

3. When a vehicle moves through air, it experiences a drag force $F = kv^2$, where k is a constant that depends on the shape and size of the vehicle as well as the density of the air it is moving through.

   a Determine the base SI units for the constant k. [2]
   b The engine of a car provides a maximum force of 1800 N.
      Calculate its top speed if $k = 0.3675$ units. [2]

   [Total: 4]

3 Dynamics: explaining motion

4 A skydiver experiences a drag force F described by the equation $F = kv^2$, where k is a constant.

   a The skydiver has a mass of 60 kg.

      Calculate her terminal velocity when k has the numerical value 0.214. [2]

   b Her velocity is reduced to 14 m s^{-1} after her parachute opens.

      Calculate the new k value. [2]

   c Sketch a velocity–time graph for the vertical motion of a skydiver from the moment she jumps from an aircraft ($t = 0$) to the moment just before she lands ($t = 100$ s).

      Identify on the graph:

- the two moments she starts falling at terminal velocity
- the moment she opens her parachute. [5]

[Total: 9]

> ### REFLECTION
>
> How did you find the 'identify' question in this section? How confident are you that you understand what is required from questions containing this command word?

5 The Artemis 1 rocket has a mass of 2.6 million kg.

   a Calculate the weight of the rocket. [1]

   b State the force required to achieve lift-off. [1]

   c Sketch the free-body diagram for each of the following situations, and label the forces acting on the rocket.

      i The rocket while sitting on the launchpad before the fuel is ignited. [2]

      ii The rocket when the booster is providing 1.55×10^7 N of thrust. [2]

      iii The rocket when it is providing 3×10^7 N of thrust. [2]

   d Calculate the acceleration of the rocket when its thrust is 3×10^7 N. [2]

[Total: 10]

> **UNDERSTAND THESE TERMS**
> - resistive force
> - drag
> - contact force
> - upthrust

3.6 Newton's third law of motion

1 Why might it be misleading to define Newton's third law of motion as 'for every action, there's an equal and opposite reaction'?

> **UNDERSTAND THIS TERM**
> - Newton's third law of motion

3.7 Understanding SI units

> **UNDERSTAND THESE TERMS**
> - base units
> - derived units

1   Express $13\,\text{g}\,\text{cm}^{-3}$ in $\text{kg}\,\text{m}^{-3}$

2   **a**   Explain what is meant by a homogenous equation. [1]

   b   Express each term in these equations in base SI units and hence show that they are homogenous:

      i   weight = mass × acceleration of free fall [1]

      ii   momentum = mass × velocity [1]

      iii   moment = force × perpendicular distance from the pivot [1]

      iv   gravitational potential energy = mass × acceleration of free fall × change in height. [1]

[Total: 5]

3   A brick has the dimensions $0.2032\,\text{m}$ by $9.21\,\text{cm}$ by $57.15\,\text{mm}$.

Determine its volume in:

   a mm^3 [1]

   b cm^3 [1]

   c m^3 [1]

[Total: 3]

3 Dynamics: explaining motion

SELF-ASSESSMENT CHECKLIST

Let's revisit the Knowledge focus and Exam skills focus for this chapter.

Decide how confident you are with each statement.

Now I can:	Show it	Needs more work	Almost there	Confident to move on
recognise that mass is a property of an object that resists change in motion	Ensure that you understand what inertia means – that it is more difficult to change the velocity of a more massive body – and look for examples in everyday life.			
identify the forces acting on a body in different situations	Make flashcards for the different forces that were introduced in this chapter. Observe and name them in action in your everyday life.			
describe how the motion of a body is affected by the forces acting on it	Sketch free-body diagrams to show the forces acting on an object. Draw them for questions to work out the resultant force.			
recall $F = ma$ and solve problems using it, understanding that acceleration and resultant force are always in the same direction	Practise solving problems that involve rearranging $F = ma$.			
state and apply Newton's first and third laws of motion	Record these on flashcards and revise every few weeks.			
recall that the weight of a body is equal to the product of its mass and the acceleration of free fall	Practise using and rearranging the equation $W = mg$.			
show that I understand the 'identify' command word and can answer 'identify' questions	Write down how you would explain the difference between 'identify' and 'state' questions to a friend.			

Exam practice 1

This section contains past paper questions from previous Cambridge exams, which draws together your knowledge on a range of topics that you have covered up to this point. These questions give you the opportunity to test your knowledge and understanding. Additional past paper practice questions can be found in the accompanying digital material.

The following question has an example student response and commentary provided. Once you have worked through the question, read the student response and commentary. Are your answers different to the sample responses?

1   a   Define *force*. [1]

   b   State the SI base units of force. [1]

   c   The force F between two point charges is given by:

$$F = \frac{Q_1 Q_2}{4\pi r^2 \varepsilon}$$

   where Q_1 and Q_2 are the charges,

   r is the distance between the charges,

   ε is a constant that depends on the medium between the charges.

   Use the above expression to determine the base units of ε. [2]

   [Total: 4]

Cambridge International AS & A Level Physics (9702) Paper 22, Q1, June 2018

Example student response	Commentary
a To make something move	Force is the rate of change of momentum (or a resultant force acting on an object changes its velocity). The student did not state this correctly. **This answer is awarded 0 out of 1 mark.**
b $kg\ m\ s^{-2}$	The student has correctly identified the SI base units of force. **This answer is awarded 1 out of 1 mark.**
c Rearrange equation in terms of epsilon: $\varepsilon = \dfrac{Q_1 Q_2}{4\pi r^2 F}$ $= \dfrac{C^2}{4\pi r^2\ kg\ m\ s^{-2}}$ $= C^2\ kg^{-1}\ m^{-3}\ s^2$	This is *almost* correct. The student needed to recognise that the coulomb is not a base SI unit. Start with the equation $Q = It$ In terms of units, this is $C = As$. Replacing C in the student answer with As gives the answer $A^2\ s^4\ kg^{-1}\ m^{-3}$ **This answer is awarded 1 out of 2 marks.**

Here is a similar past paper question which you should attempt.

2 a The ampere, metre and second are SI base units.
State **two** other SI base units. [2]

b The average drift speed v of electrons moving through a metal conductor is given by the equation:

$$v = \frac{\mu F}{e}$$

where e is the charge on an electron

F is a force acting on the electron

and μ is a constant.

Determine the SI base units of μ. [3]

[Total: 5]

Cambridge International AS & A Level Physics (9702) Paper 22, Q1, March 2019

The following question has an example student response and commentary provided. Once you have worked through the question, read the student response and commentary. Are your answers different to the sample responses?
What information does this give about your understanding of this topic as a whole?

3 a State Newton's second law of motion. [1]

b A delivery company suggests using a remote-controlled aircraft to drop a parcel into the garden of a customer. When the aircraft is vertically above point P on the ground, it releases the parcel with a velocity that is horizontal and of magnitude 5.4 m s⁻¹. The path of the parcel is shown in Fig. 3.1.

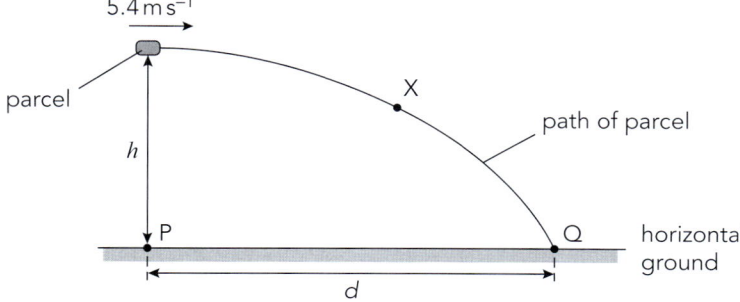

Fig. 3.1 (not to scale)

The parcel takes a time of 0.81 s after its release to reach point Q on the horizontal ground.

Assume air resistance is negligible.

i On Fig. 3.1, draw an arrow from point X to show the direction of the acceleration of the parcel when it is at that point. [1]

ii Determine the height h of the parcel above the ground when it is released. [2]

iii Calculate the horizontal distance d between points P and Q. [1]

c   Another parcel is accidentally released from rest by a different aircraft when it is hovering at a great height above the ground. Air resistance is now significant.

   i   On Fig. 3.2, draw arrows to show the directions of the forces acting on the parcel as it falls vertically downwards. Label each arrow with the name of the force.

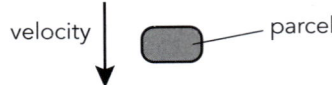

Fig. 3.2

[2]

   ii   By considering the forces acting on the parcel, state and explain the variation, if any, of the acceleration of the parcel as it moves downwards before it reaches constant (terminal) speed.   [3]

   iii   Describe the energy conversion that occurs when the parcel is falling through the air at constant (terminal) speed.   [1]

[Total: 11]

Cambridge International AS & A Level Physics (9702) Paper 21, Q 2, June 2020

Example student response	Commentary
a $F = ma$	The student identified the correct basic equation but did not explain it in words. This answer is awarded 0 out of 1 mark.
b i Arrow points vertically down from the point marked X.	This is correct. This answer is awarded 1 out of 1 mark.
ii $s = ut + \frac{1}{2}at^2$ $s = 0 \times 0.81 + \frac{1}{2} \times (-1) 9.81 \times 0.81^2$ $s = -3.21$ m	The student has correctly substituted into the equation, remembering that the acceleration of free fall is negative, and has given the correct final answer. This answer is awarded 2 out of 2 marks.
iii $s = vt$ $s = 5.4 \times 0.81$ $s = 4.37$ m	The student has correctly calculated the distance. This answer is awarded 1 out of 1 mark.
c i air resistance	This is correct, but there should also be an arrow labelled weight. This answer is awarded 1 out of 2 marks.

Exam practice 1

Example student response	Commentary
ii As it accelerates downwards, the air resistance acting on the parcel is less than the weight force. This means that the resultant force is downwards, causing the parcel to accelerate.	This is a good start. The student has identified one point correctly. The parcel will accelerate because – at first – weight exceeds drag. *This answer is awarded 1 out of 3 marks.*
iii Gravitational potential energy to kinetic energy.	The student response is incorrect. The speed (kinetic energy) is not increasing. *This answer is awarded 0 out of 1 mark.*

4   Now write an improved answer to the parts of question **3** where you did not score highly. You will need to carefully work back through each part of the question, ensuring that you include enough detail and clearly explain each point.
Use the commentary to guide you as you answer.

4 Forces

KNOWLEDGE FOCUS

In this chapter you will answer questions on:
- combining forces
- components of vectors
- centre of gravity
- the turning effect of a force
- the torque of a couple.

EXAM SKILLS FOCUS

In this chapter you will:
- show that you understand the 'explain' command word and can answer 'explain' questions.

The 'explain' command word is common in Physics questions. 'Explain' questions are usually worth between 2 and 6 marks, so make sure you plan your answer so it covers all the points needed for full marks.

Be careful not to write a description instead of an explanation in your answer.

When asked to provide an explanation, you must give reasons for the relationship, effect or trend you are provided with. Be sure to state as much evidence as you can to strengthen your response. This may include evidence from your own knowledge in addition to information from the question.

| Explain | set out purposes or reasons / make the relationships between things evident / provide why and/or how and support with relevant evidence |

4 Forces

4.1 Combining forces

UNDERSTAND THESE TERMS
- resultant force
- equilibrium

1. Calculate the size and direction of the resultant force caused by these sets of forces.
   a. 7 N force North and a 3 N force South
   b. 8 N force North and a 11 N force East
   c. 22 mN upwards, 14 mN to the right, 6 mN downwards

2. Use a scale diagram to calculate the resultant forces in these situations.
   a. 18 N upwards, 25 N to the left
   b. 9 µN left, 6 µN right, 4 µN down
   c. 5.0 kN to the right, 3.5 kN 30° down to the right from the horizontal

3. A Tyrolean traverse is a method used by mountain climbers to safely move across gaps.

   Figure 4.1 shows a simple diagram of this method.

   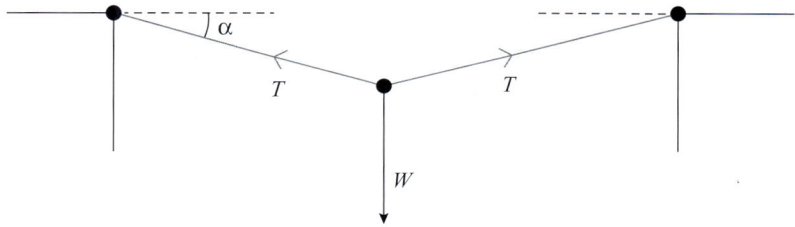

   Figure 4.1

   a. A climber wishes to evaluate whether there is less tension in the rope if they make their traverse with a large angle or a small angle to the horizontal. Determine which angle gives the lowest tension in the rope. [5]

b   During an abseiling manoeuvre, the forces on a climber are as shown in Figure 4.2.

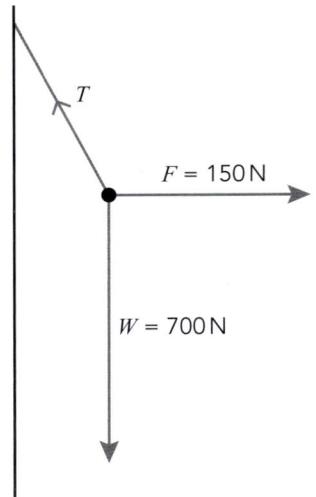

Figure 4.2

The force *F* is provided by the abseiler pushing on the wall with their feet.

Calculate the size of the tension force in the rope. [2]

[Total: 7]

> ### ⟪ RECALL AND CONNECT 1 ⟪
> In Chapter 2 you learned about calculating acceleration. What is meant by uniform acceleration? Write the three equations of uniform motion and what the terms mean.

4.2 Components of vectors

1   Use scale diagrams to resolve these vectors into their components in the x and y dimension.

   a   17 N, 30° to the horizontal
   b   22 mN, 12° to the horizontal
   c   140 kN, 8° to the vertical

2   Use trigonometry to resolve these vectors into their components in the x and y dimension.

   a   82 N, 45° to the horizontal
   b   3 N, 23° to the vertical
   c   42 kN, 12° to the vertical

3   A student investigates how the angle of a ramp affects the acceleration of a body.

They use a linear air track and sliders and change the angle, θ, as shown in Figure 4.3.

They measure distances with a ruler. They use light gates to accurately measure the speed at A and B and calculate the acceleration.

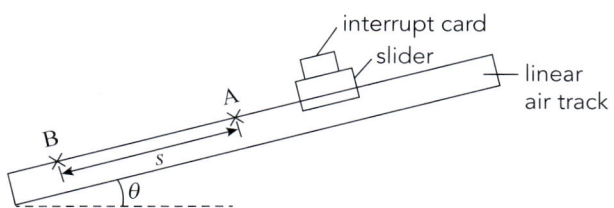

Figure 4.3

a   Draw a free-body diagram for the slider on the air track just as the slider is released.
    Include the angle θ on your free-body diagram. [2]

b   Use a calculation to predict the acceleration when the air track is at 15° to the horizontal. [2]

c   Predict the shape of a graph of angle against acceleration for the slider. [2]

d   Suggest how the shape of a graph of results will be different from the graph you predicted in part **c**. [3]

[Total: 9]

> **UNDERSTAND THESE TERMS**
> - components (of a vector)
> - vector triangle
> - free-body force diagram

4.3 Centre of gravity

1   How can the centre of gravity be found for a:

a   uniform shape
b   non-uniform shape?

> **UNDERSTAND THIS TERM**
> - centre of gravity

2   A tightrope walker can use a pole that helps the walker to balance.
    The ends of this poll are seen to hang beneath the rope.

Explain why this makes the tightrope walker more stable. **[Total: 3]**

4.4 The turning effect of a force

1 Calculate the force F in each of the situations in Figure 4.4. In each, the beam is in rotational equilibrium around point P.

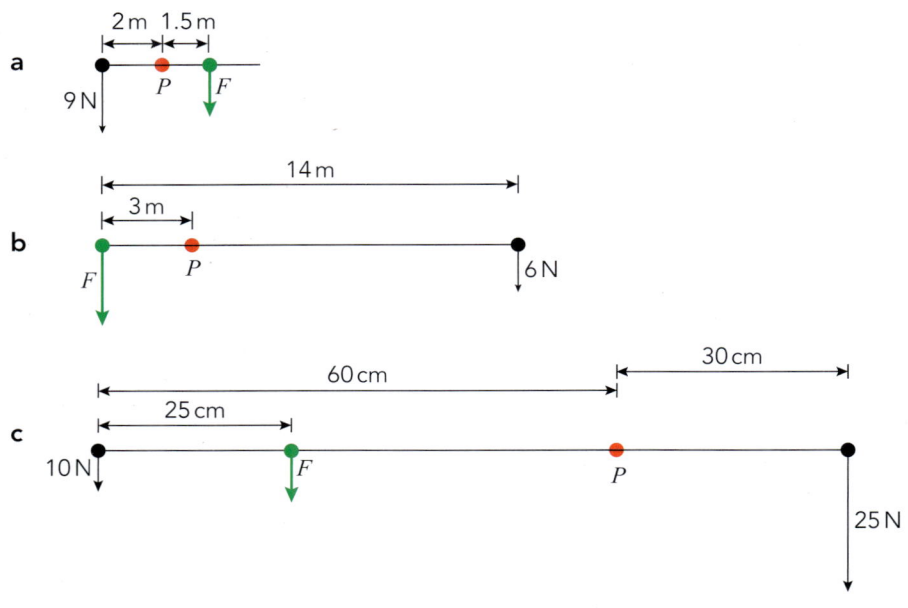

Figure 4.4

2 A simple beam bridge is shown in Figure 4.5.

The bridge spans between two supports, P and Q.

A lorry of mass 9000 kg drives from point P to point Q.

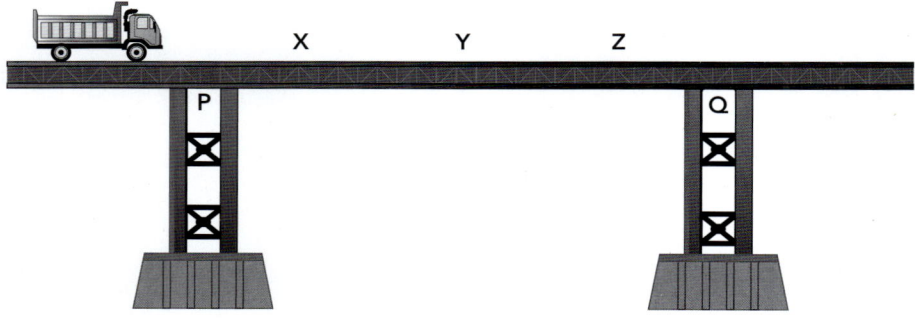

Figure 4.5

a Compare the force on the support at P when the lorry is in the two positions shown, X and Y.

Explain your answer. You do not need to include any calculations in your answer. [4]

b Treat the bridge as a beam of uniformly distributed mass 15 000 kg.
The distance between P and Q is 45 m.
Calculate the size of the reaction force upwards on the beam at point Q, when the lorry is at point Z, 15 m from support Q. [3]

[Total: 7]

UNDERSTAND THIS TERM
- moment of a force

4.5 The torque of a couple

1. Write an equation for the torque of a couple.
2. A driver exerts a force of 15 N vertically downward on one side of a steering wheel (Figure 4.6) that is mounted vertically. The steering wheel rotates about its centre, O. The distance from the centre of the steering wheel to the point at which the force is exerted is 24 cm.

UNDERSTAND THIS TERM
- resultant torque

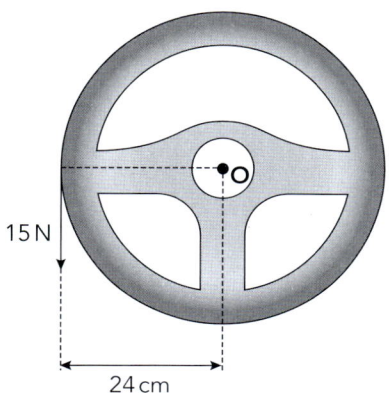

Figure 4.6

a Calculate the moment of this force. [1]
b The driver then exerts another force of 15 N upwards on the opposite side of the steering wheel. Explain why the forces now act as a couple. [2]

In modern vehicles, part of the effort required for rotating the steering wheel is provided by an electric motor. Older vehicles did not have these electric motors.

c Explain why heavier vehicles such as large trucks needed to have much larger steering wheels than small cars. [4]

[Total: 7]

UNDERSTAND THESE TERMS
- couple
- torque of a couple

SELF-ASSESSMENT CHECKLIST

Let's revisit the Knowledge focus and Exam skills focus for this chapter.
Decide how confident you are with each statement.

Now I can:	Show it	Needs more work	Almost there	Confident to move on
use a vector triangle to represent coplanar forces in equilibrium and add two or more coplanar forces	Practise drawing scale diagrams to calculate resultant forces.			
resolve a force into perpendicular components	Use both scale drawing and calculation to calculate the magnitude and directions of components of forces.			
represent the weight of a body as acting at a single point known as its centre of gravity	Draw accurate free-body diagrams with forces shown to be acting from a centre of mass.			
define and apply the moment of a force and the torque of a couple	Recognise situations where two forces of the same size are causing a turning motion around a pivot and practise using the equation for a torque of a couple.			
state and apply the principle of moments	Use good discipline in solving moments problems to sum clockwise and anticlockwise moments separately.			
use the idea that when there is no resultant force and no resultant torque, a system is in equilibrium	Apply the idea of dynamic and rotational equilibrium to solve problems.			
show that I understand the 'explain' command word and can answer 'explain' questions	Look through past papers and exam skills questions; answer some 'explain' questions, making sure you provide reasons why and/or how and support with relevant evidence when appropriate in your answers.			

5 Work, energy and power

KNOWLEDGE FOCUS

In this chapter you will answer questions on:
- doing work, transferring energy
- gravitational potential energy
- kinetic energy
- gravitational potential to kinetic energy transformations
- energy changes
- energy transfers
- power.

EXAM SKILLS FOCUS

In this chapter you will:
- show that you understand how to justify an answer in an exam.

When asked to justify something in an exam, you must give reasons (that is, evidence or a good argument) to support your answer or to support a given statement. In the exam skills questions on this topic, there are some questions that ask you to justify relationships using algebra or sketch the shape of a graph based on your knowledge. Graphs and relationships are how evidence is connected to theory in physics. It is important to get this right now so that the principle is secure when the relationships get more complex later on.

5.1 Doing work, transferring energy

1. A force used to hold an object in place can be said to do no work. Why is this?
2. What is the significance of the $\cos \theta$ in the equation for work done?
3. A student is investigating the energy transfers in an electric motor used to lift a series of masses.

   a. A student predicts that the energy supplied to the motor will be proportional to the mass lifted by the block as each mass is lifted through the same height.

      i. Sketch the graph that they would expect to see. [1]
      ii. Justify the student's hypothesis with algebra. [2]
      iii. Suggest an assumption that the student has made. [1]

   b. The motor and block are now rearranged so that the block is being pulled up a ramp with an angle of 30° to the horizontal.

      Calculate the work done in pulling a 600 g mass up a 1.2 m long ramp at this angle. [3]

   [Total: 7]

UNDERSTAND THESE TERMS
- energy
- work done

≪ RECALL AND CONNECT 1 ≪

Think back to Chapter 1. What is the difference between a scalar quantity and a vector quantity?

5.2 Gravitational potential energy

1. Copy and complete this table for gravitational potential energy calculations.

   Round all your answers to 3 significant figures.

Height / m	Mass / kg	Gravitational field strength / N kg^{-1}	Gravitational potential energy / J
7.60	4.20	9.81	
32.6		9.81	2.27
	0.320	1.62	435
260	1.38		0.0188

2. a. Derive the equation for gravitational potential energy. [3]
   b. Sketch the shape of a graph of height vs gravitational potential energy for a mass in a uniform gravitational field. [1]

   [Total: 4]

UNDERSTAND THESE TERMS
- gravitational potential energy, E_p
- uniform gravitation field

5.3 Kinetic energy

1. Derive the equation for kinetic energy from an equation of uniformly accelerated motion and the equation which defined work done.

2. Calculate the change in kinetic energy of these objects.
   a. A 1500 kg car accelerated from $12\,\text{m s}^{-1}$ to $18\,\text{m s}^{-1}$.
   b. A 56 g tennis ball hit against a wall at a speed of $25\,\text{m s}^{-1}$, rebounding from the wall at $13\,\text{m s}^{-1}$.
   c. A 3.2 kg mass accelerated from rest by a constant force of 22 N for 160 ms.

3. Tennis balls used in international competitions must have masses in the range 56.0–59.4 g.
   a. During an international game, the speed of a ball is measured at $30\,\text{m s}^{-1}$. Calculate the maximum kinetic energy of this ball. [3]
   b. When the same ball is served (hit first by the player starting the game) its speed is double that measured during the game. Explain why the kinetic energy of the ball is not also doubled. [1]
   c. At one time during the game, the kinetic energy of the ball is 34 J. Suggest reasons why the tennis player has to do less than 34 J of work to give the ball 34 J of kinetic energy. [2]

   [Total: 6]

5.4 Gravitational potential to kinetic energy transformations

1. Derive an equation from which you can calculate the speed of an object falling through small distances here on Earth if you are told only the height.

2. Copy and complete this table.

Height / m	Gravitational field strength / N kg^{-1}	Speed / m s^{-1}
3.50	9.81	
	9.81	6.83
6.47		18.3
160	5.24×10^{-5}	

3 A student suggests that they can measure gravitational field strength by varying height and measuring the speed of an object just as it reaches the ground.

   a Explain why the student does not need to measure the mass of the object that they drop. [2]

   b Justify why a graph of v^2 against $2\Delta h$ will give a gradient equal to gravitational field strength. Use ideas about the conservation of energy. [3]

   [Total: 5]

> **REFLECTION**
>
> How well did you answer question 5.4.3b? This is an example where your justification comes from comparing the equation in the question to an equation in the form $y = mx + c$. How could you use the formula sheet to practise this valuable skill? Just pick one quantity to be the gradient and rearrange it into the form $y = mx + c$. How will you remember this technique in an exam?

5.5 Energy changes when moving up and down

1 Calculate the maximum heights.

   a A 40 g ball launched vertically upwards with a kinetic energy of 90 J.
   b A ball launched vertically upwards with a speed of $14\,\text{m s}^{-1}$.
   c A ball launched at an angle of 35° to the horizontal at a speed of $9.0\,\text{m s}^{-1}$.

2 A rollercoaster carriage and passengers gain speed by rolling down a steep slope, called a downhill, on a track.

   a In one particular roller coaster, the carriage and passengers must arrive at the start of the first uphill part with a speed of $32\,\text{m s}^{-1}$.
      Calculate the minimum height that the downhill should be. [2]

   b The maximum energy wasted during the downhill part is 30%.
      Calculate the minimum height of the downhill based on this information. [2]

   c The predictions that you have made in parts **a** and **b** did **not** require you to know the mass of the carriage or its passengers.
      Explain why. [1]

   [Total: 5]

5 Work, energy and power

5.6 Energy transfers

1. Calculate these efficiencies.

   a A machine supplied with 1500 J of energy from the mains of electrical supply and does 430 J of work.

   b A 2 kW kettle raises the internal energy of a mass of water by 320 000 J in 3 minutes and 40 s.

   c An electric motor which raises a 500 g block up by 1.25 m.
   It is supplied with an average power of 6.0 W for a period of 8.4 s.

2. Use the principle of conservation of energy to explain why the statement 'you can't get something for nothing' is true in every situation in physics.

3. A student measures the speed of a block as they release it with a light gate and an interrupt card. They keep the surface area of the block the same, and they use the same surface to slide the block on. They record the distance that it travels as it slides across the surface. They want to test the idea that the friction between the block and the table is a constant value independent of speed.

   a The student varies the speed of the block and measures the distance the block travels before it comes to a stop.

   Use ideas about energy stores and transfers to predict what shape a graph of speed against stopping distance will form. [2]

   b i Use ideas about the conservation of energy and energy transfers to determine a graph the student could plot to verify that the frictional force was constant. [2]

   ii Suggest how the student use this graph to calculate a value for friction
   State any other quantities that they would need to measure to obtain a value for friction. [2]

   c A second student suggests that friction depends on mass.
   Suggest an alteration to the method that the student could make to test this idea. [2]

   [Total: 8]

> **UNDERSTAND THIS TERM**
>
> - principle of conservation of energy

5.7 Power

1. Copy and complete this table using the relationship between power, work done and time.

Power / W	Work done / J	Time / s
600		95
0.24	192	
20 × 10³		864 000
	9.7	0.54

39

2. The maximum power output of a 2022 Formula 1 race car engine was 746 kW. The highest recorded speed of one of these cars was 110 m s^{-1}.

    a   **i**   Derive the equation that links power, force and velocity. [2]

          ii Calculate the force provided by the engine. Assume that the engine is running at full power at this speed. [2]

    b   In 2008, Formula 1 cars had a power output of 596 kW and an overall efficiency of 29%. A race lasted 1 hour 30 minutes.

        Calculate the total energy input into the engine in a 2008 Formula 1 race. Assume that the power output of the engine is maximum for the whole race. [3]

[Total: 7]

> **UNDERSTAND THESE TERMS**
> - power
> - watt

SELF-ASSESSMENT CHECKLIST

Let's revisit the Knowledge focus and Exam skills focus for this chapter.

Decide how confident you are with each statement.

Now I can:	Show it	Needs more work	Almost there	Confident to move on
use the concept of work and energy	Discuss energy transfers and work done when a force acts to move a body over a certain distance.			
recall and apply the principle of conservation of energy	Practise identifying the starting and final energy stores in a given transfer, and use the equations for these stores to make calculations.			
recall and understand that the efficiency of a system is the ratio of useful energy output from the system to the total energy input	Discuss and compare the efficiency of systems in terms of their input and output energies.			
use the concept of efficiency to solve problems	Calculate the efficiency of systems and use efficiency to calculate input or output energies.			
define and use the equation for power using $P = W/t$ and derive $P = Fv$	Create flashcards to help memorise the definition of power and the derivation of the equation linking power force and speed.			

CONTINUED

Now I can:	Show it	Needs more work	Almost there	Confident to move on
derive and use the formulae for kinetic energy and gravitational potential energy.	Create flashcards to help memorise the derivations for kinetic energy and gravitational potential energy.			
understand how to justify an answer in an exam	Look through past papers and practise 'justify' type questions, remembering always to support your argument with evidence.			

6 Momentum

KNOWLEDGE FOCUS

In this chapter you will answer questions on:
- the idea of momentum
- modelling collisions
- understanding collisions
- explosions and crash-landings
- collisions in two dimensions
- momentum and Newton's laws
- understanding motion.

EXAM SKILLS FOCUS

In this chapter you will:
- practise carrying out two-step calculations
- show that you can give concise definitions in an exam.

You will see that this topic often requires you to do an initial calculation before going on to the second part of the question; for example, applying the conservation of momentum law after working out the initial conditions for each part of the collision.

Showing all of your working is very important in these two-step questions. You can practise showing your working as you answer the questions in this chapter.

Many exam questions require you to give precise and concise descriptions – or definitions – in your answer. Expressing definitions in your own words makes them more memorable, but it is worth checking that your meaning is clear and correct. Learning definitions may not be the most exciting part of science, but it deepens your understanding of physics so it is worth the time. And, of course, they are worth marks in an exam! This chapter has a lot of key terms which will be useful to memorise.

6.1 The idea of momentum

1 a In this topic, you will see two different units for momentum. Show that kg m s⁻¹ and N s are equivalent units.

b A 2 kg ball is thrown with a velocity of 10 m s⁻¹ at an angle of 30° to the horizontal, as shown in Figure 6.1. Air resistance has a negligible effect on the motion of the ball.

Look at Figure 6.1. What is the momentum of the 2 kg ball in:

i the vertical direction

ii the horizontal direction?

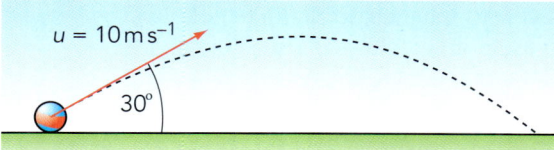

Figure 6.1

2 In a particle accelerator, protons move around a circular path at high speed.

a Calculate the momentum of one proton moving at 90% speed of light. Assume that the mass of the proton remains at its rest mass. [4]

b The protons are moved around the circular path in groups of 1.2×10^{11} protons. In one experiment, there are 3000 such groups moving at the same time. Calculate the total momentum of all the protons in this experiment. [2]

[Total: 6]

> ### « RECALL AND CONNECT 1 «
>
> In Chapter 1, you learned about SI units. By defining derived units in terms of the SI units, you will have to check for the homogeneity of an equation. Try it to show what the joule is equal to in terms of the base units.
> (Hint: use the equation work done = force × distance, and substitute in $F = ma$)

6.2 Modelling collisions

1 a Give **two** examples of resistive forces when an object is moving through a fluid.

b How do your two example forces change with speed?

2 Copy and complete this definition of conservation of momentum.

The .... momentum .... the collision is equal to the
.... momentum .... the collision; as long as there
are no .... acting.

3   A linear air track, as shown in Figure 6.2, is a piece of laboratory equipment that allows objects called gliders to move almost in the absence of friction.

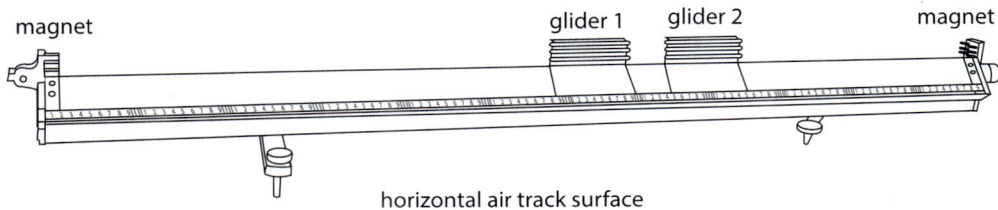

Figure 6.2

a   In an experiment, both gliders are fitted with magnets so that like poles will come together as the gliders approach each other. This will cause the gliders to repel without touching.

Each glider has a total mass of 180 g.

Each glider has an equal and opposite speed of $0.14\,\text{m}\,\text{s}^{-1}$ and they are moving towards each other.

   i   Calculate the total momentum of the gliders before the collision. [2]

   ii The magnets on the gliders repel and the gliders move away from each other.

       State the total momentum of the gliders after the collision. [1]

b   In a different experiment, the magnets are replaced by sticky tape so the gliders will join together on collision.

Glider 1 has a mass of 180 g and moves at $0.14\,\text{m}\,\text{s}^{-1}$ towards glider 2, also of mass 180 g, which is at rest.

The two join together and move as one object.

Calculate the speed of the two gliders after the collision. [2]

[Total: 5]

> **UNDERSTAND THIS TERM**
>
> - conservation of momentum

6.3 Understanding collisions

> **« RECALL AND CONNECT 2 «**
>
> Think back to Chapter 5. Can you remember the formula for kinetic energy? Can you also remember the formulae for: work done, power, gravitational potential energy, elastic potential energy and efficiency? Write them down and check back.

1   Work out which has more kinetic energy; a proton bunch (1.2×10^{11} protons) moving at 90% speed of light or a mosquito (mass of 5 mg) moving at $2\,\text{m}\,\text{s}^{-1}$.

2 Two snooker balls, one red and one white of the same mass are moving towards each other.

The initial speed of the white ball is 2.5 m s⁻¹

The initial speed of the red ball is 1.5 m s⁻¹ in the opposite direction.

They collide, and both move off in the original direction of the white ball.

The white ball is now moving at 0.25 m s⁻¹.

- a Define an elastic collision and describe why elastic collisions are less likely to happen than inelastic collisions. [2]
- b Calculate the velocity of the red ball after the collision. [3]
- c Explain how this is an inelastic collision. [3]

[Total: 8]

> **UNDERSTAND THESE TERMS**
> - elastic collision
> - inelastic collision

> **REFLECTION**
>
> This topic uses ideas of conservation of quantities in different situations. How confident do you feel when working out a two-step calculation? Are you breaking the question down into smaller chunks? For example, look back at the previous snooker ball question. Even if you cannot see where to start a question, try applying the conservation laws and remembering to use horizontal and vertical components.

6.4 Explosions and crash-landings

1 Copy and complete these sentences.

- a .... is conserved in all collisions as long as there are no .... forces acting on the system.
- b Kinetic energy is conserved in an .... collision.

2 An arrow of mass 20 g is fired from a gun bow of mass 5 kg. The arrow is fired at 75 m s⁻¹.

- a Define the conservation of momentum. [1]
- b State the total momentum of the system after the arrow is fired. [1]
- c Calculate the recoil velocity of the bow. [1]

[Total: 3]

3   A sealed metal cylinder, which is at rest, contains gas at high pressure.

    The cylinder explodes.

    Two small pieces of metal fly apart in opposite directions.
    The largest part of the cylinder remains at rest after the explosion.

    Copy and complete the table below.

    Assume that the momentum and kinetic energy of the gas are negligible.

Momentum before the explosion	Momentum after the explosion	Kinetic energy before	Kinetic energy conserved in this event?

    [Total: 2]

6.5 Collisions in two dimensions

1   Use 'conserved' or 'not conserved' to fill in this table for an inelastic collision.

Mass	Momentum	Kinetic energy	Total energy

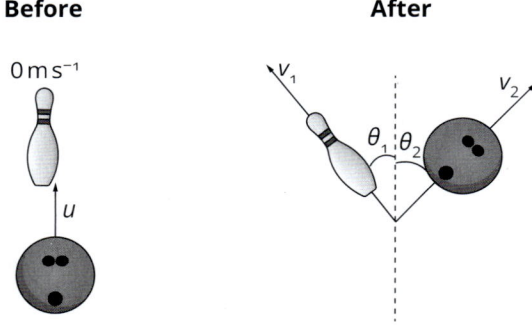

Figure 6.3

2   Look at Figure 6.3. What are the vertical and horizontal components of this vector?

3   A bowling ball hits the first pin at an angle (see Figure 6.4).

    Before   **After**

    0 m s⁻¹

    v_1 v_2

    θ_1 θ_2

    u

    Figure 6.4

    a   What is the initial momentum at 90° to the lane/ball direction
        (that is, across the lane)? [1]
    b   Give an expression for the momentum of the ball and pin along the
        lane (that is, front-to-back along the initial direction of the bowling ball)
        after the collision. [2]

    [Total: 3]

6.6 Momentum and Newton's laws

1. **a** Write down each of Newton's laws.

   b Show how Newton's second law can lead to the equation $F = ma$.

2. A rocket is launched. At the moment of lift-off, the mass of the rocket and fuel is 1.2×10^6 kg.

   There is a constant force produced by the thrusters of 2.1×10^7 N.

   a By considering the weight and upward forces acting, work out the resultant force on the rocket.

   b What is the initial acceleration of the rocket?

   c Why does this initial acceleration change as the rocket continues to rise?

> **UNDERSTAND THIS TERM**
>
> - resultant force

6.7 Understanding motion

1. **a** Use Newton's laws and conservation of momentum to explain why an astronaut on a spacewalk can push off the spaceship to move.

   Describe what happens to the motion of the spaceship.

   b How can you use Newton's second law to explain why a tennis ball moves faster off the tennis racket if the player follows through?

2. A car of mass 800 kg in a crash test hits a barrier at $20\,\text{m}\,\text{s}^{-1}$.

   It is brought to a stop in 0.02 s.

   a Calculate the force exerted on the car. [3]

   b Another car of the same mass is tested with an improved crumple zone. In this test, the car was brought to rest from $20\,\text{m}\,\text{s}^{-1}$ in 0.05 s.

   Why is there potentially less injury to the passengers in this case? [3]

   [Total: 6]

3. Water of density $1000\,\text{kg}\,\text{m}^{-3}$ leaves a hosepipe of cross-sectional area of $5.0 \times 10^{-2}\,\text{m}^2$ at $1.3 \times 10^{-3}\,\text{m}\,\text{s}^{-1}$.

   Calculate the momentum of the water leaving the hose per second. **[Total: 3]**

> **REFLECTION**
>
> How well did you answer the 'define' questions in this chapter? Were you accurate in your definition? Be sure to write out the complete definition, looking out for a phrase at the start of the definition. This may well be a mark on its own. For example, 'total momentum is conserved, **in a closed system**'; you need both parts for the marks. What techniques do you have to help you remember definitions?

SELF-ASSESSMENT CHECKLIST

Let's revisit the Knowledge focus and Exam skills focus for this chapter.

Decide how confident you are with each statement.

Now I can:	Show it	Needs more work	Almost there	Confident to move on
define and use linear momentum	Make flashcards with key terms and definitions; practise writing out the definition and correctly use the formula.			
state and apply the principle of conservation of momentum to collisions in one and two dimensions	Correctly define the conservation of momentum and use it in a collision question.			
relate force to the rate of change of momentum and state Newton's second law of motion	Apply Newton's second law equation to real life situations such as a crumple zone, car airbag or soft flooring in a playground, where increasing the time to stop will decrease the force.			
recall that, for a perfectly elastic collision, the relative speed of approach is equal to the relative speed of separation	Successfully use the relative speed of approach is equal to the relative speed of separation in questions with calculations involving elastic collisions.			
discuss energy changes in perfectly elastic and inelastic collisions.	List the energy changes that occur due to a collision and back this up with a calculation to prove that kinetic energy is (or is not) conserved.			

CONTINUED

Now I can:	Show it	Needs more work	Almost there	Confident to move on
carry out 2-step calculations	Find a question where you had to work out the components of the momentum horizontally and then use those components in the conservation of momentum formula.			
give concise definitions in an exam	Practise writing out concise, accurate definitions. For example: 'In a closed system, total momentum is conserved in a collision.' Now go back through the chapter and ensure you can define all the terms in the 'Understand these terms' feature.			

7 Matter and materials

> **KNOWLEDGE FOCUS**
>
> In this chapter you will answer questions on:
> - density
> - pressure
> - Archimedes' principle
> - compressive and tensile forces
> - stretching materials
> - elastic potential energy.

> **EXAM SKILLS FOCUS**
>
> In this chapter you will:
> - show that you understand how to write equations in words to help write definitions.

As discussed in the previous chapter, 'define' questions require you to be precise and concise in your answer.

This chapter has a lot of key terms which will be useful to memorise. In this chapter, you need to be able to define properties such as stress, strain and the Young modulus. The equation for stress is $\sigma = \dfrac{F}{A}$ but is defined as, 'the force per unit cross-sectional area that acts at right angles to a surface.' The equation is not the definition! It may help to write down the equation as a reminder, but make sure you say what it means in words.

7 Matter and materials

7.1 Density and 7.2 Pressure

UNDERSTAND THESE TERMS
- density
- pressure

1. Imagine you are sitting in a room with dimensions 3 m by 2 m by 10 m.

    If the density of air is 1.3 kg m^{-3}, what is the mass of air in the room?

2. a Work out the approximate atmospheric pressure at sea level. Assume that our atmosphere is about 10 km deep and that air is about 1000 times less dense than water. (Density of water = 1000 kg m^{-3}.)

    b Calculate the air pressure on top of Mount Everest (8849 m).

3. There are two equations for pressure.

    a Show that the equation for hydrostatic pressure can be derived from the equation $p = \dfrac{F}{A}$, where pressure is the normal force per unit of cross-sectional area.

    b Show that they both have the same base SI units.

4. A brick has a mass of 2.3 kg and dimensions of 0.215 m by 10.25 cm by 65 mm.

    a Calculate its density. [2]

    b Calculate the pressure it exerts on the ground when it rests on the side with:

        i the biggest area [1]

        ii the smallest area. [1]

    [Total: 4]

5. Some underwater swimmers wear ear plugs to protect the delicate tympanic membrane in the ear from the pressure of the water. The area of the tympanic membrane in one ear is 90 mm². The density of water is 1000 kg m^{-3}.

    Calculate the force exerted by the water at a depth of 4.0 m on the tympanic membrane in one ear in a swimmer who is **not** wearing ear plugs. **[Total: 3]**

UNDERSTAND THIS TERM
- hydrostatic pressure

7.3 Archimedes' principle

1. The Plimsoll line painted on the sides of ships should still be visible even when the ship is fully laden. The captain of a ship has been asked how many more containers can be safely loaded on his ship.

    Each container has a mass of 2000 kg. The Plimsoll line is still 15 cm above the waterline, and the ship has a cross-sectional area at the waterline of about 450 m².

    The density of seawater is 1200 kg m^{-3}.

    Calculate how many more containers can be loaded.

2. Construction workers need to calculate the mass of a wooden pole.

   They decide to float the pole on a nearby pond when half of it is visible above the water surface.

   The pole is 9 m long and has a diameter of 25 cm.

   They assume that freshwater has a density of about 1000 kg m^{-3}.

   a. Calculate the mass of the pole. [2]
   b. Calculate the number of poles that can be carried in a truck if it has a maximum load of 44 tonnes.
   (1 tonne = 1000 kg) [1]

   [Total: 3]

   UNDERSTAND THIS TERM
   - Archimedes' principle

> **« RECALL AND CONNECT 1 «**
> You learned about vectors and scalars earlier in this course. Is pressure a scalar or a vector quantity? Use your answer to explain the origin of upthrust.

7.4 Compressive and tensile forces and 7.5 Stretching materials

UNDERSTAND THESE TERMS
- compression
- tensile
- extension
- load
- spring constant
- Hooke's law
- limit of proportionality

1. A student investigated Hooke's law by increasing the load on a spring. These are the results.

Force / N	0	9	15	23	30	40	46	53	61	70	77
Length / mm	113	131	144	160	174	195	207	222	246	291	340

   a. Plot a graph of the results that will allow you to determine the spring constant.
   b. Determine the spring constant.
   c. What is the load when the limit of proportionality is reached?

2. Use the equation for the Young modulus to find the missing values **A–E** in the table.

Material	Young modulus / GPa	Force	Cross-sectional area	Extension	Length / m
aluminium	68	20	2 mm²	2 × 10⁻⁴ m	A
brass	106	10	20 mm²	B	0.20
copper	110	1.5 kN	C	54 µm	3.00
lead	13	D	2 mm²	1.15 µm	0.15
steel	E	600	20 cm²	15 µm	10.00

   UNDERSTAND THESE TERMS
   - strain
   - stress
   - Young modulus

3   An experiment was done to find how the time period, T, of oscillations of a beam varied with the Young modulus, E, of the material in the beam.

Various beams of identical sizes were clamped at one end.

A mass, M, was attached to the other end, and this was made to oscillate vertically, as shown in Figure 7.1.

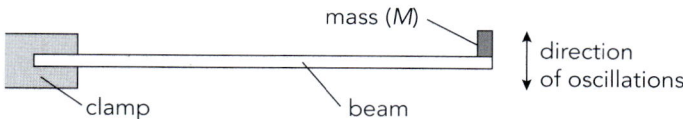

Figure 7.1

It was found that: $T \propto \sqrt{\dfrac{M}{E}}$

Explain what will happen to the value of T when the beam is changed to one with a 20% greater Young modulus. [Total: 2]

7.6 Elastic potential energy

1   How much energy is stored in spider silk if a mass of 20 mg attached to one end stretches it by 0.3 m? (Assume that the silk obeys Hooke's law.)

2   Students investigated how the length of four different specimens changed as the load on them was increased. The curves end when the specimens break.

They plotted their results on a graph, as shown in Figure 7.2.

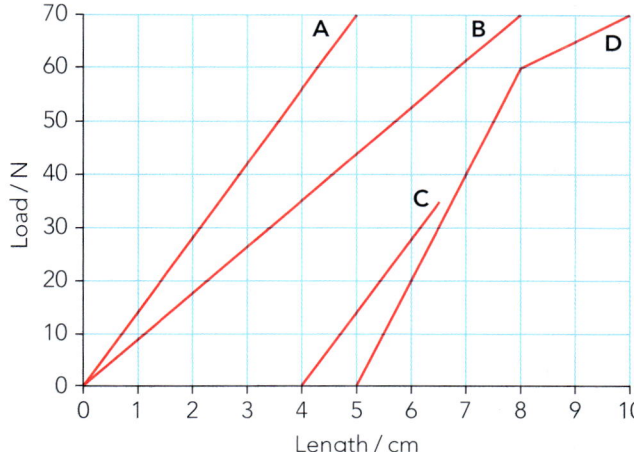

Figure 7.2

For each specimen, A–D, calculate:

a   the spring constant [4]
b   the energy stored. [4]

[Total: 8]

UNDERSTAND THESE TERMS

- elastic deformation
- plastic deformation
- elastic limit
- independent variable
- dependent variable

« RECALL AND CONNECT 2 «

Think back to your previous physics and maths studies when you learned about drawing graphs. On which axis is the independent variable usually plotted? What is the independent variable when investigating Hooke's law? Why do we sometimes break convention and plot the independent variable against the dependent variable?

SELF-ASSESSMENT CHECKLIST

Let's revisit the Knowledge focus and Exam skills focus for this chapter.

Decide how confident you are with each statement.

Now I can:	Show it	Needs more work	Almost there	Confident to move on
define and use density	Perform density calculations.			
define and use pressure and calculate the pressure in a fluid	Perform calculations using hydrostatic pressure.			
derive and use the equation $\Delta p = \rho g \Delta h$	Practise deriving this equation from $p = \frac{F}{A}$.			
use a difference in hydrostatic pressure to explain and calculate upthrust	Try calculating the upthrust on a cube by subtracting the pressure on the top surface from the pressure on the bottom surface. This should give the same answer as upthrust calculated as a result of the displaced fluid.			
explain how tensile and compressive forces cause deformation	Think about the direction of these forces when the shape of an object is changed.			
describe the behaviour of springs and use Hooke's law	Recall the different regions of a force–extension graph.			
distinguish between elastic and plastic deformation, limit of proportionality and the elastic limit	Recall the definitions and locate the points or regions on a graph.			

CONTINUED

Now I can:	Show it	Needs more work	Almost there	Confident to move on
define and use stress, strain and the Young modulus	Practise recalling the definitions and performing calculations that involve stress, strain and the Young modulus.			
describe an experiment to measure the Young modulus	Write a checklist of the steps and periodically check that you can remember the details of what measurements to make etc.			
calculate the energy stored in a deformed material	Perform these calculations frequently (every fortnight).			
write equations in words to help write definitions	Make flashcards of all the key terms throughout this chapter – and the rest of the book. Practise writing out equations in words to explain what they mean.			

Exam practice 2

This section contains past paper questions from previous Cambridge exams, which draws together your knowledge on a range of topics that you have covered up to this point. These questions give you the opportunity to test your knowledge and understanding. Additional past paper practice questions can be found in the accompanying digital material.

The following question has an example student response and commentary provided. Once you have worked through the question, read the student response and commentary. Are your answers different to the sample responses?

1   a   State what is meant by the centre of gravity of an object. [1]

   b   A uniform beam AB is attached by a frictionless hinge to a vertical wall at end A. The beam is held so that it is horizontal by a metal wire CD, as shown in Fig. 1.1.

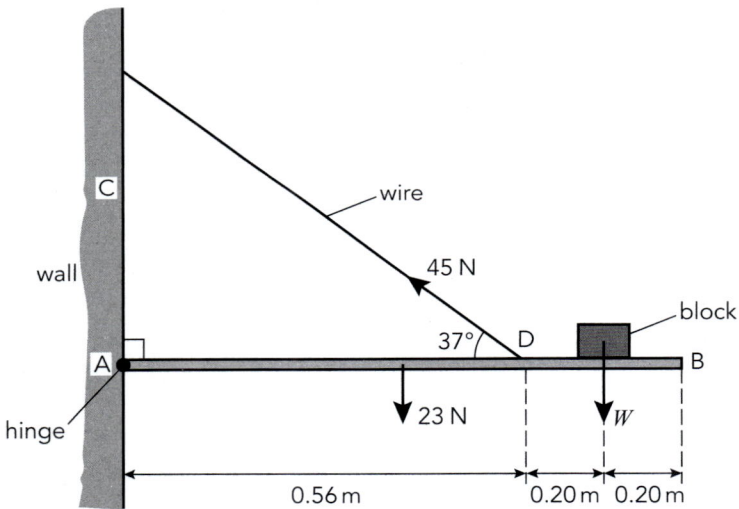

Fig. 1.1 (not to scale)

The beam is of length 0.96 m and weight 23 N. A block of weight W rests on the beam at a distance of 0.20 m from end B. The wire is attached to the beam at point D which is a distance of 0.40 m from end B. The wire exerts a force on the beam of 45 N at an angle of 37° to the horizontal. The beam is in equilibrium.

   i   Calculate the vertical component of the force exerted by the wire on the beam. [1]

   ii   By taking moments about A, calculate the weight W of the block. [3]

Exam practice 2

    iii   The hinge exerts a force on the beam at end A.

           Calculate the horizontal component of this force. [1]

    iv   The block is now placed closer to point D on the beam.

           State whether this change will increase, decrease or have no effect on the tension in the wire. [1]

    v   The stress in the wire is 5.3×10^7 Pa. The wire is now replaced by a second wire that has a radius which is three times greater than that of the original wire. The tension in the wire is unchanged.

           Calculate the stress in the second wire. [2]

[Total: 9]

Cambridge International AS & A Level Physics (9702) Paper 22, Q3, November 2022

		Example student response	Commentary
a		Where all the mass acts, it's the average point which you can model the object as a point mass	The student makes the common error of mistaking the centre of mass for the centre of gravity.
			To get the mark, they need to substitute the word 'mass' for 'weight'.
			This answer is awarded 0 out of 1 mark.
b	i	45 sin 37 = 27.1 N	This answer indicates that the student has clearly practised resolving forces into components.
			It is useful to be able to do this quickly. A shortcut is to use 'swing the angle open, use sine, close the angle, use cosine'. This means you don't have to draw out a triangle each time.
			This answer is awarded 1 out of 1 mark.
	ii	23 × 0.48 + W × 0.76 = 45 × 0.56 W = 18.6 N	The student has used the tension rather than the vertical component they worked out in part **i**. They still get two marks for the two correct magnitudes of the moments they work out.
			It is worth remembering that any question that is split apart using the numerals i, ii, and so on are very closely linked together.
			This answer is awarded 2 out of 3 marks.
	iii	41.6 N	The student has taken a bit of a guess here that the upwards force must be equal to the two downward forces here at the hinge. They might have rushed this one because the question clearly says they're looking for a horizontal force.
			The only horizontal force can be provided by the horizontal component of the tension in the wire. And so, since this beam is in equilibrium, the hinge must do a horizontal force on the beam equal to the horizontal component of the tension. They should have done that to get the mark.
			This answer is awarded 0 out of 1 mark.

Example student response	Commentary
iv This will decrease the tension because it will decrease the clockwise moment.	The student has correctly qualitatively applied the principle of moments here. However, they didn't need to go on to explain why the tension decreases, as it is a 'state' command word question. *This answer is awarded 1 out of 1 mark.*
v $\sigma = \dfrac{F}{A} = \dfrac{45}{3r^2}$ $5.3 \times 10^7 \div 3 = 1.77 \times 10^7$ Pa	The student scores one mark for selecting the right equation. However, they substitute the factor into the equation incorrectly. To score the second mark, they need to recognise that's three times the radius, and so the factor is 9. *This answer is awarded 1 out of 2 marks.*

2 Now that you have read the sample answer and commentary for question **1**, think about a topic that could have similar questions asked about it. Write a similar exam question which asks students to apply the same understanding and skills to answer the questions. Also write a full mark scheme for your question.

The following question has an example student commentary and answer provided. Work through the question first, then compare your answer to the sample answer and commentary. How different were your answers to the example student answers? Are there any areas where you feel you need to improve your understanding of this topic?

3 **a** State the principle of conservation of momentum. [2]

   b Two balls, X and Y, move along a horizontal frictionless surface, as shown from above in Fig. 3.1.

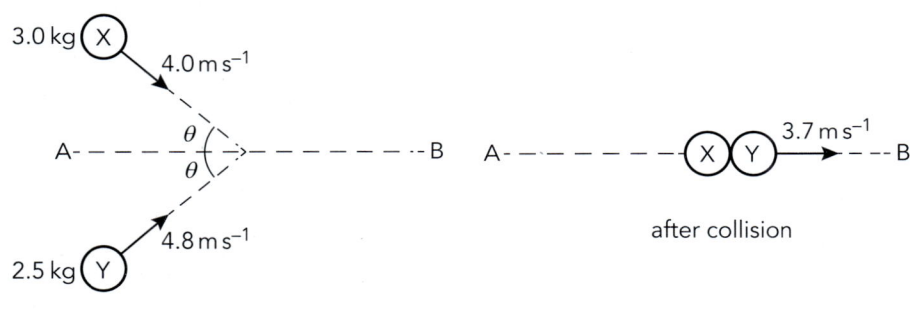

before collision

Fig. 3.1 (not to scale)   **Fig. 3.2** (not to scale)

Ball X has a mass of 3.0 kg and a velocity of 4.0 m s^{-1} in a direction at angle θ to a line AB. Ball Y has a mass of 2.5 kg and a velocity of 4.8 m s^{-1} in a direction at angle ϑ to the line AB.

The balls collide and stick together. After colliding, the balls have a velocity of 3.7 m s^{-1} along the line AB on the horizontal surface, as shown in Fig. 3.2.

   i By considering the components of the momenta along the line AB, calculate θ. [3]

Exam practice 2

ii By calculation of the kinetic energies, state and explain whether the collision of the balls is inelastic or perfectly elastic. [2]

[Total: 7]

Cambridge International AS & A Level Physics (9702) Paper 22, Q4, June 2022

Example student response			Commentary
a		The momentum before the collision is equal to the momentum after the collision, as long as there are no external forces acting.	The student scored 1 mark for stating 'as long as there are no external forces acting'. However, to achieve full marks, they need to use the word 'total' to describe both *before* and *after* momentum. *This answer is awarded 1 out of 2 marks.*
b	i	BEFORE (horizontally): X: momentum = mass × velocity = $3 \times 4 \sin\theta$ Y: momentum = mv = $2.5 \times 4.8 \sin\theta$ X + Y = $12\sin\theta + 12\sin\theta = 24\sin\theta$ AFTER (horizontally): XY: momentum = $(3 + 2.5) \times 3.7$ = 5.5×3.7 = 20.35 kg m s^{-1} momentum before = momentum after $24\sin\theta = 20.35$ $\sin\theta = \dfrac{20.35}{24}$ $\theta = 58°$	In the initial resolution of the vectors, the student has confused cos and sin, although the rest of the working is all correct. They have correctly used the total momentum horizontally before the collision is equal to the total momentum horizontally after the collision. *This answer is awarded 2 out of 3 marks.*
	ii	kinetic energy = $\frac{1}{2} \times 3.0 \times (4.0 \cos 32°)$ $+ \frac{1}{2} \times 2.5 \times (4.8 \cos 32°)$ = 38 J	The student did get one of the correct numerical answers, but that wasn't enough for a mark. The working is wrong as energy is a scalar quantity, and so the direction does not matter. This makes the resolution of the vector irrelevant. The correct answer needs to compare the total initial kinetic energy with the total final kinetic energy. The student needs to give both correct values and state that it is an inelastic collision: initial $E_K = \frac{1}{2} \times 3.0 \times 4.0^2 + \frac{1}{2} \times 2.5 \times 4.8^2$ $= 53$ J final $E_K = \frac{1}{2} \times 5.5 \times 3.7^2$ $= 38$ J *This answer is awarded 2 out of 2 marks.*

4 Now that you've gone through the commentary, have a go at writing a full mark scheme for question **3**. This will check that you've understood exactly why each mark has (or has not) been allocated.

8 Electric current, potential difference and resistance

> **KNOWLEDGE FOCUS**
>
> In this chapter you will answer questions on:
> - circuit symbols and diagrams
> - electric current
> - an equation for current
> - the meaning of voltage
> - electrical resistance
> - electrical power.

> **EXAM SKILLS FOCUS**
>
> In this chapter you will:
> - evaluate your prior learning and plan the next stage of your revision
> - know how to improve your answers.

One of the most important skills when preparing for exams is understanding how you learn and where you are on your revision journey. When revising electric current, for example, you should think about how well you managed learning about electricity topics at GCSE. This chapter underpins everything that you will revise in the next three chapters on electricity, and contains key knowledge which will help you with the difficult topics later on. It is important to get it right now.

The exam skills questions in this chapter are a good opportunity to evaluate your learning. Don't be satisfied with just checking your answer. Reflect on each answer as you complete a self-assessment and identify things you can do to improve your performance.

8 Electric current, potential difference and resistance

8.1 Circuit symbols and diagrams

> **« RECALL AND CONNECT 1 «**
>
> Think back to your work on electricity at IGCSE. What is meant by a series circuit? What is meant by a parallel circuit? What is the unit of current, and how can the current be measured? What is the unit of potential difference, and how can the potential difference be measured?

UNDERSTAND THESE TERMS
- current
- charge carriers
- potential difference

1.
    a. Draw a circuit containing a lamp and a resistor in series.
    b. Draw a circuit which could be used to measure the potential difference across and the current through a variable resistor.
    c. Draw a circuit with an alternating signal in parallel with both a capacitor and a diode.

8.2 Electric current

1. What is meant by the phrase 'the charge on charge carriers is quantised'?

2. Copy and complete the table.

Current / A	Charge / C	Time / s
1.5	800	
0.50		20
	1.8	300
0.74×10^{-9}	24×10^{-3}	

3. A current flowing through a metallic conductor is measured.

   The rate of flow of charge is 32×10^{-2} C every second.

    a. Calculate the number of electrons that pass a point in the metal every second. [1]
    b. The circuit is then connected to either side of an electrolysis cell. The current decreases by a factor of 4.

       In the electrolyte, there are ions with a charge of +2e.

       Calculate the number of positive charge carriers which arrive at the negative electrode in 2 minutes. [3]

       [Total: 4]

UNDERSTAND THESE TERMS
- quantised
- ampere
- coulomb

8.3 An equation for current

1. Write out the equation for electric current (transport equation) and define the terms.

2. Figure 8.1 shows a conductor, A with a square cross-section that makes an electrical connection to another conductor, B with circular cross-section.

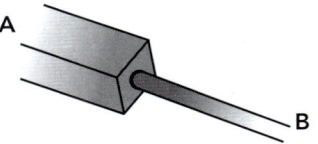

Figure 8.1

The width of A is 6.0 mm.

The diameter of B is 0.62 mm.

A is made from a material with a number density of charge carriers of 2.3×10^{13}.

B is made from a material with a number density of charge carriers of 8.5×10^{28}.

a Calculate the ratio

$$\frac{\text{mean drift velocity in rectangular conductor}}{\text{mean drift velocity in the wire}}$$ [4]

b Another material has a number density of charge carriers that depends on light intensity.

As light intensity increases, the number density of charge carriers also increases.

Explain the effect of increasing light intensity on the resistance of the wire. [1]

[Total: 5]

> **UNDERSTAND THIS TERM**
> - mean drift velocity

8.4 The meaning of voltage

1. Copy and complete the table.

Energy transferred / J	Charge / C	Potential difference / V
15 000		12
	80	24
27 000	900	
1.2		6

2. A student sets up a simple circuit to measure the potential difference and current through a 10.0 Ω resistor.

Before completing the circuit, the student measures the e.m.f. of the power supply as 3.20 V.

8 Electric current, potential difference and resistance

The circuit is then completed, and the current is measured by an ammeter in series with the resistor. The ammeter reads 0.26 A.

The circuit remains connected for 30 s while the student takes their readings.

a Calculate the energy transferred in driving the charge through the resistor. [3]

b Calculate the energy transferred in driving the charge through the complete loop. [1]

[Total: 4]

UNDERSTAND THIS TERM
• e.m.f.

8.5 Electrical resistance

1 Calculate the resistance in each case. Give your answer to 2 significant figures and use appropriate prefixes.

a potential difference = 9.0 V current = 0.53 A

b potential difference = 32 mV current = 1.8 A

c potential difference = 100 kV current = 20 μA

2 USB cables operate at a potential difference of 5.0 V.

a Explain what a manufacturer should change if they wish to draw a higher current from a USB charger. [2]

b Some USB chargers can use different modes depending on the device that they are charging. In one situation, a charger is drawing a 3.0 A current.

Calculate the effective resistance of the circuit, including the charger and the device being charged in this situation. [2]

c Two USB chargers are connected to the same mains power output.

A user notices that one of the chargers charges their phone in a quarter of the time.

They also notice that the phone and charger heat up more for this charger.

Explain why the faster charger heats up more. [4]

[Total: 8]

UNDERSTAND THESE TERMS
• resistance
• ohm

8.6 Electrical power

1 Calculate the electrical power in each of these situations. Give your answers to 2 significant figures.

a Potential difference = 24 V and current = 0.65 A

b Potential difference = 115 V and resistance = 47 Ω

c Current = 9.0 A and resistance = 22 Ω

63

> **CAMBRIDGE INTERNATIONAL AS & A LEVEL PHYSICS: EXAM PREPARATION AND PRACTICE**

2. A laptop computer can be used with two different power supplies, A and B. Both provide the same potential difference of 20 V.

   Power supply A has a rating of 135 W.

   Power supply B has a rating of 60 W.

   a. Compare the current provided to the laptop by each supply. [3]

   A Watt-hour, Wh is a non-SI unit used to express the energy capacity of a battery.

   The laptop computer has a battery capacity of 83 Wh.

   b. Compare the time taken to fully charge the battery with each power supply. Assume the battery starts with no charge in each case. [3]

   c. In practice, the battery takes longer than expected to fully charge. Suggest one reason for this. [1]

   [Total: 7]

REFLECTION

Electric current, potential difference and resistance are difficult topics. There are abstract quantities that you need to be able to define and apply in 'explain' questions and difficult electric circuit problems to solve.

Think back to your previous studies in electricity at IGCSE, and ask yourself: *how well do I understand this topic?* If you found it difficult at the IGCSE level, then it is worth spending time practising the basics until your confidence grows.

Keep all of your old assessments. These make the most valuable revision. Take yourself back through a question where you lost marks and explain the steps you should have taken. Now write an improved answer to the question. Do you think it is likely that you would make the same mistake again? What other self-explanation techniques could you use?

SELF-ASSESSMENT CHECKLIST

Let's revisit the Knowledge focus and Exam skills focus for this chapter.

Decide how confident you are with each statement.

Now I can:	Show it	Needs more work	Almost there	Confident to move on
understand the nature of electric current	Describe current as a rate of flow of charge, including the different charged particles and the charges on them.			

8 Electric current, potential difference and resistance

CONTINUED

Now I can:	Show it	Needs more work	Almost there	Confident to move on
understand the term charge and recognise its unit, the coulomb	Use charge in calculations and written questions, correctly and in its correct SI units.			
understand that charge is quantised	Use the elementary charge, e, in calculations, including being able to make calculations of numbers of charged particles.			
solve problems using the equation $Q = It$	Practise calculations including complex circuit diagram problems.			
solve problems using the formula $I = nAve$	Use good discipline to recognise quantities and make calculations using the transport equation.			
solve problems involving the mean drift velocity of charge carriers	Use higher order maths skills to make complex calculations including the use of ratios to solve problems.			
understand the terms potential difference, e.m.f. and the volt	Distinguish between closely related quantities using exacting definitions to ensure that you are responding to exactly what the questions are asking of you.			
use energy considerations to distinguish between p.d. and e.m.f.	Use a model of charge and energy to explain the difference between two closely related quantities.			
define resistance and recognise its unit, the ohm	give an exact definition of a quantity and its unit based upon an equation			
solve problems using the formula $V = IR$	Practise questions involving calculating p.d., current and resistance.			

CONTINUED

Now I can:	Show it	Needs more work	Almost there	Confident to move on
solve problems concerning energy and power in electric circuits	Practise using the equations for electrical power and the relationship between energy, power and time.			
evaluate my prior learning and plan the next stage of my revision	Briefly review your current understanding and skills in electricity, and check these against the learning objectives in this chapter to identify the new knowledge that you need to master.			
improve my answers	Review and rewrite your answers with the mark schemes provided to improve the accuracy and quality of your responses.			

9 Kirchhoff's laws

KNOWLEDGE FOCUS

In this chapter you will answer questions on:
- Kirchhoff's first law
- Kirchhoff's second law
- applying Kirchhoff's laws
- resistor combinations.

EXAM SKILLS FOCUS

In this chapter you will:
- show that you understand the 'describe' and 'explain' command words and can answer 'describe' and 'explain' questions
- show that you understand how to make comparisons.

'Describe' and 'explain' are two of the most common exam command words, but they are different. In short, the 'describe' command word asks you *what* something is like, whereas the 'explain' command word asks you *why* it is like it is. Sometimes, the two command words are combined, and you must describe and explain something.

Many questions also ask you to compare two or more things. In this chapter, for example, you are asked to compare the resistance of a diode when it has different potential differences across it. You don't need to do the calculation – you just need to know what would happen if the potential difference (p.d.) was different. Sometimes, you may be asked to justify or explain your comparison. In these cases, you may need to perform a calculation or show an understanding of formulae or laws.

Describe	state the points of a topic/give characteristics and main features
Explain	set out purposes or reasons/make the relationships between things evident/provide why and/or how and support with relevant evidence

9.1 Kirchhoff's first law

1. **a** Copy and complete this definition of Kirchhoff's first law.

   The .... of the currents entering is equal to the .... of the currents leaving any .... in a circuit.

   b Copy and complete this explanation of why Kirchhoff's first law is a consequence of conservation of charge.

   The total .... entering a point must exit the point.

   c What is the ammeter reading on the ammeter in the circuit with two resistors in parallel, shown in Figure 9.1?

   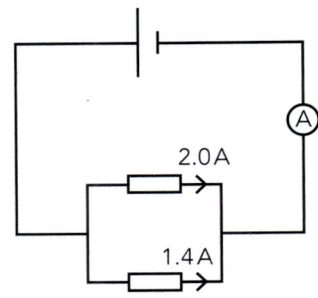

   Figure 9.1

2. A diagram of a parallel circuit is shown in Figure 9.2.

   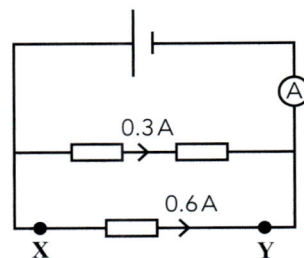

   Figure 9.2

   a Calculate the total current through the cell in this circuit. [1]

   b A student adds another parallel branch to the circuit above, and the ammeter reading changes to 2.6 A.

   Determine the current in the new branch. [1]

   c A student adds a wire of negligible resistance between points X and Y on the circuit above.

   Using Kirchhoff's first law, explain why the reading on the ammeter must change. [2]

   [Total: 4]

9 Kirchhoff's laws

> **REFLECTION**
>
> Kirchhoff's first law can be written as: $\Sigma I_{in} = \Sigma I_{out}$
>
> Kirchhoff's second law can be written as: $\Sigma E = \Sigma V$
>
> How confident are you that you can expand these formulae into worded definitions and apply them to the calculation or even explain questions? How could you increase your confidence?

UNDERSTAND THESE TERMS
- Kirchhoff's first law
- conservation of charge

9.2 Kirchhoff's second law

1
 a State Kirchhoff's second law.

 b Copy and complete this explanation of why Kirchhoff's second law is a consequence of the conservation of energy:

   The .... is energy per charge; energy is neither created nor destroyed.

   Therefore, all the energy .... to the loop must be transferred from the loop.

UNDERSTAND THESE TERMS
- Kirchhoff's second law
- conservation of energy

2 Determine the unknown potential differences (V) in the three circuits shown in Figure 9.3. **[Total: 3]**

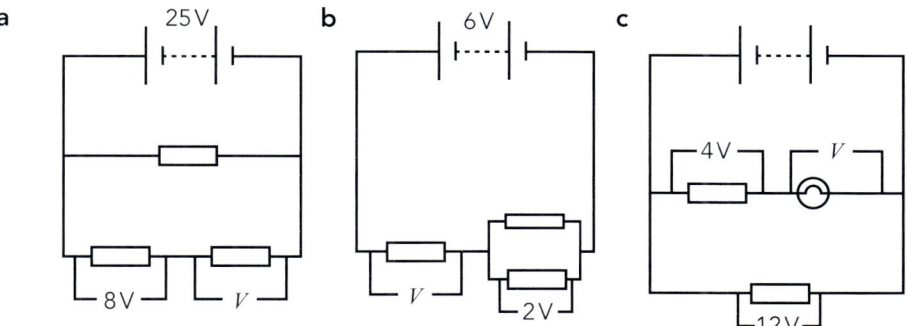

Figure 9.3

UNDERSTAND THESE TERMS
- parallel
- series

9.3 Applying Kirchhoff's laws

1
 a Why must a voltmeter have a high resistance?

 b Why must an ammeter have a low resistance?

2 Look at Figure 9.4.

a 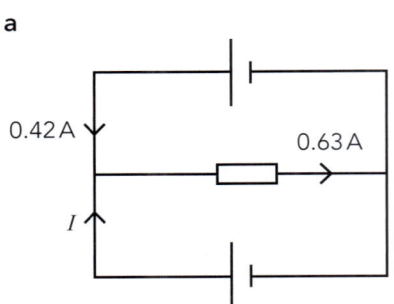 b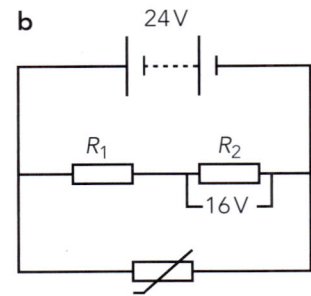

Figure 9.4

a   Determine the unknown current (I) in Figure 9.4a. [1]
b   Determine the p.d. across the resistor R_1 in Figure 9.4b. [1]
c   Describe and explain what would happen to the p.d. across resistor R_1 if the temperature of the thermistor increases. [2]

[Total: 4]

3 Figure 9.5 shows a 15 W resistor and a 20 W resistor in series.

Figure 9.5

Explain any difference in energy transferred when moving charge through these two resistors. [Total: 3]

4 A teacher demonstrates the electrolysis of copper sulfate solution. They explain that the copper ions each gain two electrons at the cathode and are deposited as a neutral copper atom. The teacher suggests that with an ammeter and a stopwatch, the students can calculate the number of copper atoms deposited at the cathode in 10 s.

Design a circuit that the students could use to calculate the number of copper atoms which are deposited in 10 s.

Explain the measurements that the students would need to take to calculate their answer and how they would make the calculation.

9.4 Resistor combinations

> **« RECALL AND CONNECT 1 «**
>
> Think back to Chapter 8. Write the three equations you know for electrical power and the equation that links resistance, voltage and current.

1. Using Kirchhoff's laws, together with the equation that links resistance, voltage and current, give the steps needed to derive a formula for the combined resistance of two or more resistors:

    a in series

    b in parallel.

2. You have been given four $10\,\Omega$ resistors. Draw diagrams to show how you would connect them to make an effective resistance of:

    a $40\,\Omega$

    b $25\,\Omega$

    c $13\,\Omega$.

3. A student has a set of DC circuit components, including four 1.5 V cells and four $1\,k\Omega$ resistors. The internal resistances of the cells can be presumed to be negligible compared with the resistances of the resistors.

    Using all of the components, draw diagrams to show how the components could be connected to give a current of:

    a 24 mA

    b 750 µA

    c 6 mA.

4. A student is investigating potential difference and current with some different resistor combinations.

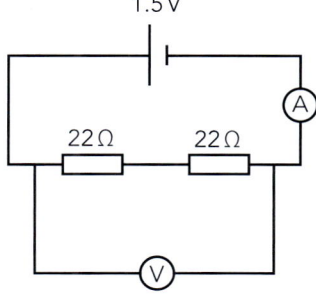

Figure 9.6

   a Calculate the combined resistance of the resistors in Figure 9.6. [1]

b A student draws the circuit in a computer simulation.
The simulation predicts a current through the cell of 34 mA.

The student then builds the circuit using real equipment with the same specifications. Cells have internal resistance.

Explain why the circuit produces a lower current than the student had calculated in the model circuit. [2]

c Explain how the values on the voltmeter and ammeter would change if the student adds a second cell in:

    i series [2]

    ii parallel. [2]

[Total: 7]

5 Silicon semiconductor diodes will melt if the current through them exceeds a given rating.

A student has access to a fixed 3 V battery and a set of 6 identical resistors. The student varies the p.d. across the diode. Here are their results.

p.d. / V	Current / A
0.5	0.01
1.0	0.05
1.5	0.11
2.0	0.17
2.5	0.23
3.0	0.29

a Explain how the student can use the resistors to obtain the results above. [2]

b Compare the resistance of the diode when it has a p.d. of 0.5 V across it to when it has a p.d. of 1.5 V. [2]

c The maximum forward current rating of their diode is 300 mA.

Calculate the current flowing through a pair of diodes in parallel connected to an e.m.f. of 1.5 V.

Comment whether the diodes will melt. [4]

d The student then places a third diode in series the opposite way around. Explain why the reading on the ammeter falls to near zero. [2]

[Total: 10]

≪ RECALL AND CONNECT 2 ≪

Which principles and laws are needed to derive a rule for combining resistors in series?

Which principles and laws are needed to derive a rule for combining resistors in parallel?

9 Kirchhoff's laws

> **REFLECTION**
>
> There were a number of 'describe' and 'explain' questions in this chapter, as well as questions that required a comparison. How confident are you that you understand what each of these command words means? Could you explain to a friend what is required in answers to exam questions containing them?

SELF-ASSESSMENT CHECKLIST

Let's revisit the Knowledge focus and Exam skills focus for this chapter.

Decide how confident you are with each statement.

Now I can:	Show it	Needs more work	Almost there	Confident to move on
recall and apply Kirchhoff's laws	Write Kirchhoff's first and second laws and check them against the definitions in your student book. Solve circuit problems involving summing currents into and out of a point and involving summing supplied e.m.f.s and transferred p.d.s around a circuit.			
use Kirchhoff's laws to derive the formulae for the combined resistance of two or more resistors in series and in parallel	Starting from Ohm's law and Kirchhoff's laws, derive a rule for combining resistors in series and in parallel. Apply these rules to solve circuit problems involving resistors in series, in parallel and in combinations of them.			
recognise that ammeters are connected in series within a circuit and, therefore, should have low resistance	Explain what would happen if an ammeter had a very high resistance and was connected in series.			
recognise that voltmeters are connected in parallel across a component, or components, and therefore should have high resistance.	Explain what would happen if a voltmeter had a very low resistance and was connected in parallel.			
show that I understand the 'describe' and 'explain' command words and can answer 'describe' and 'explain' questions	Write the differences between how you would answer 'describe' and 'explain' questions.			

CONTINUED

Now I can:	Show it	Needs more work	Almost there	Confident to move on
understand how to make comparisons	Work through all the questions that ask you to compare two things; look to see how many marks they are worth and check your answers against the mark scheme.			

10 Resistance and resistivity

KNOWLEDGE FOCUS

In this chapter you will answer questions on:
- the *I–V* characteristic for a metallic conductor
- Ohm's law
- resistance and temperature
- resistivity.

EXAM SKILLS FOCUS

In this chapter you will:
- show that you understand the 'sketch' command word and can answer 'sketch' questions.

The 'sketch' command word is often used for topics where information is shown graphically, or where simple diagrams can efficiently communicate important ideas. Various types of graphs, trends and circuit diagrams are examples of things you could be asked to sketch. Sketches are expected to be simple and show only the main features asked for by the question – remember to draw your diagrams clearly and accurately but keep them simple.

Sketch	make a simple freehand drawing showing the key features

10.1 The *I–V* characteristic for a metallic conductor and 10.2 Ohm's law

1   a   On an *I–V* characteristic, which variable is plotted on each axis?

    b   What shape is the *I–V* characteristic for a resistor whose temperature is constant?

    c   Imagine the *I–V* characteristics for three different resistors are drawn on the same axes.

    How could you tell which belonged to the resistor with the biggest resistance?

> **UNDERSTAND THIS TERM**
> - metallic conductor

> **« RECALL AND CONNECT 1 «**
> Think back to your previous physics studies. Can you remember Ohm's law and define resistance?

2   Voltage, current and resistance data are listed for five different ohmic components. Work out the missing values **A–O**.

Component	V	I	R	V	I	R
A	2.5 V	20 A	A	17.3 V	B	C
B	3675 V	2.5 A	D	E	50 A	F
C	230 V	2.5 mA	G	805 V	H	I
D	J	5 µA	2.3 MΩ	80.5 V	K	L
E	225 kV	5 mA	M	360 kV	N	O

> **UNDERSTAND THESE TERMS**
> - Ohm's law
> - ohmic

> **« RECALL AND CONNECT 2 «**
> Think back to your previous physics studies. Recall how a potential divider circuit works. Show how the supply voltage is shared between components in a series circuit. For example, what is the voltage across two resistors, 4 ohms and 6 ohms, when the supply voltage is 12 V?

10 Resistance and resistivity

10.3 Resistance and temperature

1. What **two** factors affect the resistance of a metal?

2. The circuit diagram (Figure 10.1A) shows a thermistor in series with a 3 kΩ resistor and a 12 V cell.

   The graph (Figure 10.1B) shows how the resistance of a thermistor varies with temperature.

   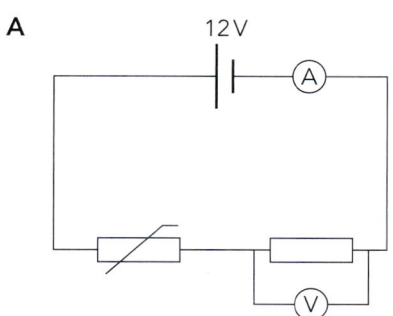
   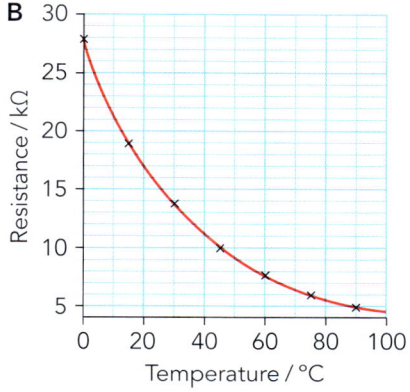

   Figure 10.1

   Make a copy of the table below and, for each temperature, use the graph to determine the resistance of the thermistor and therefore the current through the ammeter.

	Temperature / °C	Thermistor resistance / kΩ	Current / mA
a	10		
b	20		
c	30		
d	40		
e	50		

3. a Sketch the *I–V* characteristic for a tungsten filament lamp. [1]
   b Describe how the resistance changes as the voltage increases. [1]
   c Explain the shape of the characteristic. [4]

   [Total: 6]

   UNDERSTAND THESE TERMS
   - non-ohmic
   - NTC thermistor
   - threshold voltage
   - light-dependent resistor (LDR)

10.4 Resistivity

1. In the science laboratory, there are some reels of wire with missing labels. Your job is to find the resistivity of these samples and identify which metal they are by comparing them to known values.

   You record your measurements of the diameters, lengths and resistances of the unknown samples **a–e** in Table 10.1.
   Decide what metals the samples **a–e** are using the data in Table 10.2.

Unknown sample	Diameter / mm	Length / cm	Resistance / 10^{-3} Ω
a	1.130	10.20	1.71
b	0.912	15.82	314.83
c	3.660	4.60	0.24
d	0.610	12.2	201.20
e	5.640	3.20	0.63

   Table 10.1

Metal	Resistivity / Ω m
constantan	4.90×10^{-7}
copper	1.68×10^{-8}
manganin	4.82×10^{-7}
nichrome	1.30×10^{-8}
tungsten	5.60×10^{-8}

   Table 10.2

2. Explain the resistance of a length of wire in terms of different arrangements of resistors. **[Total: 2]**

3. The manufacturer of conductive putty states the following on its website: a cylinder 60 mm long and 20 mm in diameter has a resistance of about 20 Ω. Assume that its volume does not change when its shape changes.

   a. Show that the resistivity of the putty is 0.1047 Ω m. [2]
   b. Copy the table below and use the available information to calculate the resistance of the putty as its length increases.
   The first value has been found for you. [4]

Length / mm	Resistance / Ω
10	0.56
20	
50	
100	
150	

c Sketch a graph to show how the resistance of the putty changes with length. [1]

[Total: 7]

4 A short length of wire was used as a resistor to modify a circuit but it fell from the circuit board.

You can see where it needs to be soldered, but you did not keep your bench tidy. There are three pieces of wire, and you need to work out which one you need to use.

Copy the table then use the information to calculate the resistance of each wire.

Wire	Resistivity / $\Omega\,m$	Diameter / mm	Length / cm	Resistance / Ω
constantan	4.90×10^{-7}	0.812	2.2	
manganin	4.82×10^{-7}	0.559	1.7	
nichrome	1.00×10^{-6}	0.723	1.6	

> **UNDERSTAND THIS TERM**
> - resistivity

≪ RECALL AND CONNECT 3 ≪

Using knowledge from Chapter 3, show that the resistivity equation is homogeneous and express it in fundamental SI units.

REFLECTION

In question 10.4.2, you were asked to consider a wire as an arrangement of resistors. Would it be helpful to consider a wire as a network of roads? For example, increasing the number of roads connecting two places or the number of lanes on the road would be like increasing the cross-sectional area of the road and would reduce the 'resistance' to traffic flow. Could you extend this analogy to a single road and consider what would happen if this road was made longer? Do analogies like these make it easier to visualise what is going on or make it easier to remember the physics?

SELF-ASSESSMENT CHECKLIST

Let's revisit the Knowledge focus and Exam skills focus for this chapter.

Decide how confident you are with each statement.

Now I can:	Show it	Needs more work	Almost there	Confident to move on
state Ohm's law	Write the question 'What is the definition of resistance?' on the front of a flashcard (and its definition on the back of the card), so that Ohm's law is recalled frequently.			
sketch and explain the *I–V* characteristics for various components	Write the prompt '*I–V* characteristics?' onto the front of a flashcard with sketches on the back so that this knowledge is frequently reviewed.			
sketch the temperature characteristic for an NTC thermistor	Understand the behaviour of an NTC thermistor so that you can work out how to sketch the temperature characteristic without relying on memory.			
solve problems involving the resistivity of a material	Practise solving these calculations regularly (once a week) until they become routine.			
show that I understand the 'sketch' command word and can answer 'sketch' questions	Give the definition of the command word 'sketch' and attempt to answer a 'sketch' question from a past paper.			

11 Practical circuits

KNOWLEDGE FOCUS

In this chapter you will answer questions on:

- internal resistance
- potential dividers
- sensors
- potentiometer circuits.

EXAM SKILLS FOCUS

In this chapter you will:

- show that you understand the 'suggest' command word and can answer 'suggest' questions.

The 'suggest' command word can be used in two different ways: where there is not a conclusive answer to the question; or where you are required to apply knowledge to deal with an unfamiliar context. This type of question usually requires you to use higher order thinking skills such as analysis, critical thinking and problem solving. You will be able to practise answering this type of 'suggest' question in this chapter. You can prepare for challenging 'suggest' questions by working through past exam questions to enable you to understand unfamiliar physics and contexts.

11.1 Internal resistance

1. A student measures the e.m.f. of a cell with a voltmeter in parallel with it. They then make a simple series circuit with one resistor and the cell. They notice that the reading on their voltmeter changes. Describe and explain the change.

2. Derive an equation for e.m.f. including both the load and internal resistances.

3. A student finds that the e.m.f. of a power supply is given by the equation:

   $E = V + Ir$

   where, V is the terminal p.d. and r is the internal resistance of the power supply.

   a   The student varies the load resistance and records the potential difference, V, and the current, I, through the resistor. Show that a graph of V against I gives a gradient of $-r$. [2]

   b   Figure 11.1 shows a graph of the results.

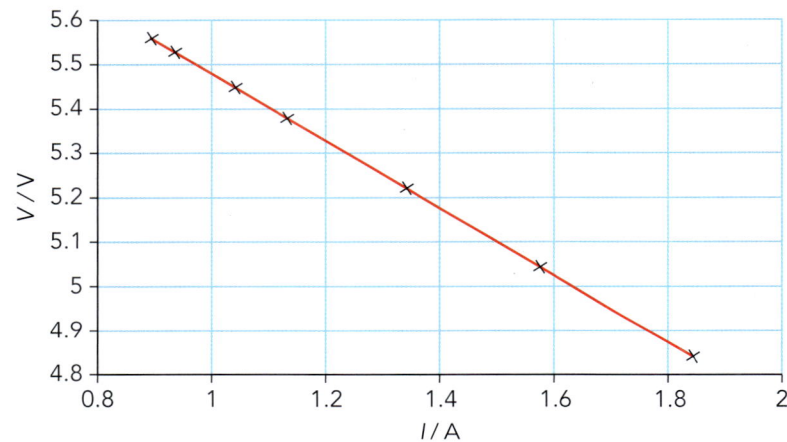

Figure 11.1

   i   Use the graph to calculate the internal resistance of the power supply. [2]

   ii Use the graph to determine the e.m.f. of the power supply. [2]

   c   Taking repeat readings is not the best practice in this practical.

   i   Suggest and explain a reason why. [2]

   ii Suggest another way to increase the precision of the line of best fit. [2]

   [Total: 10]

> **UNDERSTAND THESE TERMS**
> - internal resistance
> - terminal p.d.

> **« RECALL AND CONNECT 1 «**
>
> In Chapter 9, you learned Kirchhoff's laws. Write both laws in words and in algebra.

> **REFLECTION**
>
> How did you find the question containing both the 'suggest' and 'explain' command words? Did you find it easy to structure your response? Check your answer against the one provided – did you score well? How could you improve your answer so that both elements of the question are answered fully?

11.2 Potential dividers

1 For each of the circuits in Figure 11.2, calculate the unknown potential difference, V.

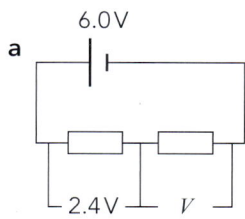

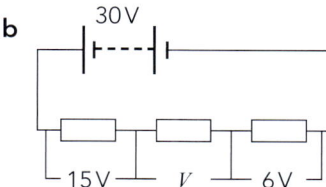

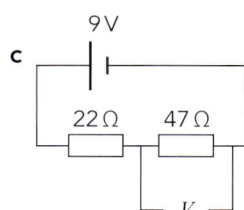

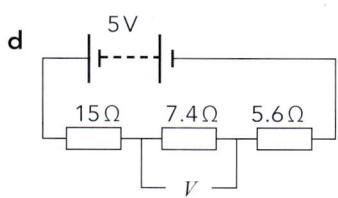

Figure 11.2

2 Variable resistors are lengths of wire of uniform cross-section that are coiled to make them compact. An e.m.f. is placed across the wire. There is a moveable connection to one side of an output circuit, and the other side of the output circuit is connected to a fixed connection on the wire.

   a The e.m.f. across the variable resistor is 12 V. The length of the variable resistor is 25 cm.

   Predict the distance between the moveable connection and the fixed connection when there is a 2.5 V p.d. across the output circuit. [2]

   b When using a variable resistor as a potential divider, a student notices that the output p.d. does not vary linearly with distance across the variable resistor.

   Suggest two reasons for this. [2]

   [Total: 4]

> **UNDERSTAND THIS TERM**
>
> - potential divider

11.3 Sensors

1   a Sketch a graph for temperature against resistance for a thermistor.

    b Sketch a graph for light intensity against resistance for an LDR.

2   LDRs can be used in potential divider circuits to turn on lights when the light falls below a certain level.

    a Sketch a simple potential divider circuit where the potential difference across an output would increase when the light intensity decreases. [2]

    b Figure 11.3 shows a graph showing resistance against temperature for a thermistor.

    The thermistor is placed in series with a fixed resistance. A p.d. of 110 V is placed across the pair of resistors. The output across the thermistor is measured.

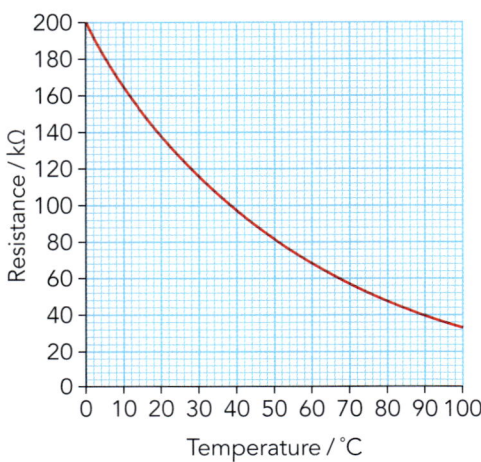

Figure 11.3

Determine a value for the fixed resistor which would give a p.d. output of 20 V at 45 °C. [4]

    c A student models a sensing circuit by setting up the circuit as in the diagram shown in Figure 11.4.

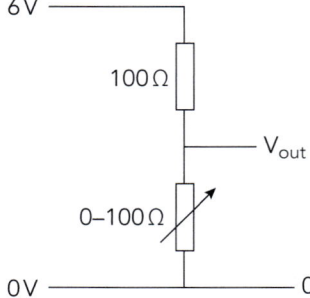

Figure 11.4

The student expects the bulb to light when the variable resistance is set to near its maximum resistance. However, the bulb does not light at any resistance setting. Suggest a reason for this. [3]

d Most thermistors are said to be NTC. Explain the difference between a PTC and an NTC thermistor. [2]

[Total: 11]

UNDERSTAND THESE TERMS
- sensor
- transducer

« RECALL AND CONNECT 2 «

Write down the transport equation from Chapter 8, and define all the terms.

11.4 Potentiometer circuits

1   Write an explanation of how a potentiometer circuit can be used to measure an unknown e.m.f.

2   Figure 11.5 shows a potentiometer circuit.

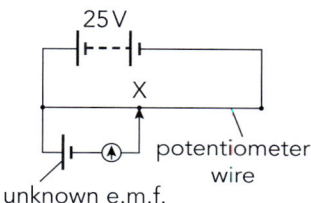

Figure 11.5

As the moveable connection is moved across the potentiometer wire, there is a point at which the galvanometer shows zero deflection. This point is called the balance point.

a Use Kirchhoff's second law to explain why the galvanometer shows zero deflection. [4]

b The balance point is marked X and is at 45 cm along an 80 cm potentiometer wire. Calculate the unknown e.m.f. [2]

[Total: 6]

UNDERSTAND THESE TERMS
- potentiometer
- galvanometer
- null method

SELF-ASSESSMENT CHECKLIST

Let's revisit the Knowledge focus and Exam skills focus for this chapter.

Decide how confident you are with each statement.

Now I can:	Show it	Needs more work	Almost there	Confident to move on
explain the effects of internal resistance on terminal p.d. and power output of a source of e.m.f.	Derive the equation for e.m.f., p.d. and lost volts from first principles and explain how internal resistance can be determined experimentally.			
explain the use of potential divider circuits	List all of the uses of potential dividers for control or sensing circuits that you've come across in this chapter.			
solve problems involving the potentiometer as a means of comparing voltages	Practise sharing p.d. in ratios of resistances.			
understand the 'suggest' command word and answer 'suggest' questions	Go through a set of past papers and highlight questions that include the 'suggest' command word. Make notes on how you would answer these questions.			

Exam practice 3

This section contains past paper questions from previous Cambridge exams, which draws together your knowledge on a range of topics that you have covered up to this point. These questions give you the opportunity to test your knowledge and understanding. Additional past paper practice questions can be found in the accompanying digital material.

The following question has an example student response and commentary provided. Once you have worked through the question, read the student response and commentary. Are your answers different to the sample responses?

1   a   Define electric potential difference.   [1]

     b   A battery is connected to two resistors X and Y, as shown in Fig. 1.1.

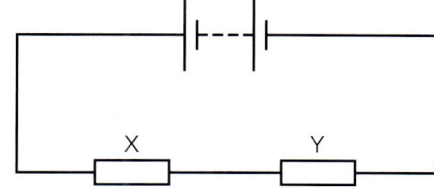

Fig. 1.1

The resistance of resistor X is greater than the resistance of resistor Y. State and explain which resistor dissipates more power.   [3]

c   A battery of electromotive force (e.m.f.) 9.0 V and internal resistance r is connected to two resistors P and Q, as shown in Fig. 1.2.

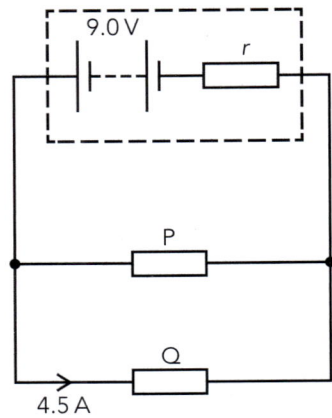

Fig. 1.2

A total charge of 650 C moves through resistor P in a time interval of 540 s. During this time resistor P dissipates 4800 J of energy. The current in resistor Q is 4.5A. Assume that the e.m.f. of the battery remains constant.

Calculate:

i   the current in resistor P [2]
ii the potential difference across resistor P [2]
iii the internal resistance r of the battery. [2]

[Total: 10]

Cambridge International AS & A Level Physics (9702) Paper 22, Q6, November 2022

Example student response	Commentary
a Energy per unit charge transferred in moving the charge between two points in a circuit.	This is a good definition of potential difference. The student has clearly learned exacting definitions of the electrical quantities in this unit. *This answer is awarded 1 out of 1 mark.*

Example student response	Commentary
b $P = I^2R$ So as the current is the same but the resistance of X is greater than Y, X must transfer more power.	The first mark is for recognising that the currents are the same. The second mark is for reference to the equation and the comparison of the resistances. The final mark is for the conclusion that X transfers more power. This is a good example of how to use an equation to make an explanation. They recognised that it was a series circuit and so the current was the common factor and, therefore, the only difference was the resistance. They then applied an equation for electrical power to solve the problem. The other way of solving this would be to use the idea of potential dividers to work out that the potential difference across acts must be greater. The current is the same and so power is greater in moving the charge through X. *This answer is awarded 3 out of 3 marks.*
c i $I = \dfrac{Q}{t} = \dfrac{650}{540} = 1.2$ A	The student has correctly identified the equation and the data they need to substitute into the equation. They then performed the calculation correctly. *This answer is awarded 2 out of 2 marks.*
ii 9 V because it is a parallel circuit	The student has presumed that because it is a parallel circuit, the p.d. across each branch is equal to the e.m.f. across the power supply. To get the marks, they need to recognise that the terminal p.d. is energy per charge supplied to the components in the branches. They can use the energy dissipated in P and the total charge move through P to calculate this. *This answer is awarded 0 out of 2 marks.*
iii $I_T = I_1 + I_2 = 5.7$ A $V = IR$ $9 = 5.7R$ $r = 1.58\ \Omega$	The student gets a mark for correctly calculating the current through the cell. However, they have then used 9 V divided by the current to give the resistance. To get the second mark, they need to work out the 'lost' volts, which is 9 V minus the 7.4 V, which was the answer for part **ii**, and use this and the current to calculate the internal resistance, r. *This answer is awarded 1 out of 2 marks.*

2   Question **1** is challenging. It combines an understanding of currents in series and parallel with an application of Ohm's law equation. To check that you understand how marks are allocated in these circuit problem questions, write your own similar question and mark scheme.

The following question has an example student commentary and answer provided. Work through the question first, using the information from the response and commentary to question 1 to guide you as you answer. After you have answered the question, compare your answers with the sample answer and commentary. How different were your answers to the example student responses? Are there any areas where you feel you need to improve your understanding?

3 a State Kirchhoff's first law. [1]

b A battery of electromotive force (e.m.f.) 12.0 V and internal resistance r is connected to a filament lamp and a resistor, as shown in Fig. 3.1.

The current in the battery is 3.6 A and the current in the resistor is 2.1 A. The I–V characteristic for the lamp is shown in Fig. 3.2.

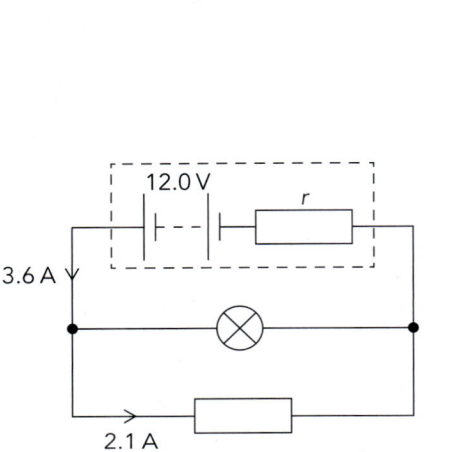

Fig. 3.1

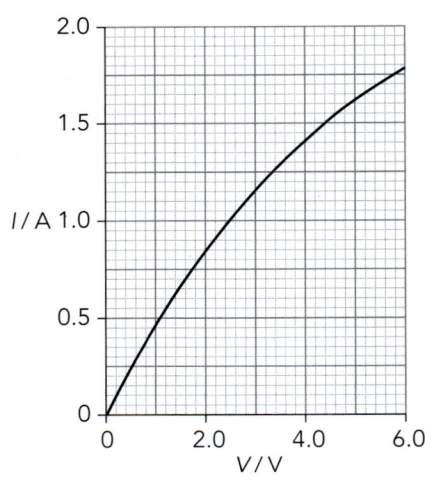

Fig. 3.2

i Determine the resistance of the lamp in Fig. 3.1. [3]

ii Determine the internal resistance r of the battery. [2]

iii The initial energy stored in the battery is 470 kJ. Assume that the e.m.f. and the current in the battery do not change with time.

Calculate the time taken for the energy stored in the battery to become 240 kJ. [2]

iv The filament wire of the lamp is connected in series with the adjacent copper connecting wire of the circuit, as illustrated in Fig. 3.3.

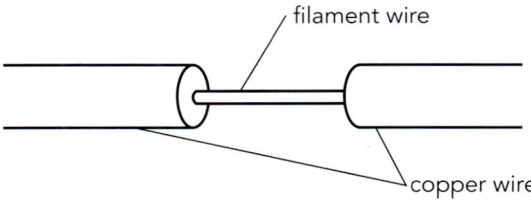

Fig. 3.3 (not to scale)

Some data for the filament wire and the adjacent copper connecting wire are given in Table 3.1.

	filament wire	copper wire
cross-sectional area	A	$360\,A$
number density of free electrons	n	$2.5\,n$

Table 3.1

Calculate the ratio:

$$\frac{\text{average drift speed of free electrons in filament wire}}{\text{average drift speed of free electrons in copper wire}} \quad [2]$$

[Total: 10]

Cambridge International AS & A Level Physics (9702) Paper 22, Q6, March 2021

Example student response			Commentary
a		sum of the currents into a point is equal to the sum of the currents out of that point	This is a detailed enough response for the mark. This student has clearly memorised their definitions in detail. *This answer is awarded 1 out of 1 mark.*
b	i	current through the lamp is 1.5 A. $R = \dfrac{V}{I} = \dfrac{12}{15} = 8\,\Omega$	The student gets one mark for correctly working out the current through the lamp. To get the second and third marks, they needed to recognise that the 12 volts marked on the power supply is the e.m.f. rather than the terminal potential difference. They should have used the current and read from the graph the terminal potential difference at 1.5 A. The student has gone on to complete part **ii** well here. If they had had the exam discipline to check their previous answers they would have realised the error they made. *This answer is awarded 1 out of 3 marks.*
	ii	$E = V + Ir$ $12 = 4.4 + 3.6r$ $r = \dfrac{12 - 44}{36} = 2.1\,\Omega$	The student has correctly recognised you can work out the terminal potential difference by using the I–V characteristic graph. They have then used the relationship between e.m.f. the terminal p.d. and the lost volts, and correctly use the current through the cell. *This answer is awarded 2 out of 2 marks.*

Example student response	Commentary
iii $E = Pt$ $P = IV$ $E = VIt$ $t = \dfrac{E}{VI}$ $= \dfrac{240 \times 10^3}{12 \times 3.6}$ $= 5555.6$ s $= 5600$ s	The student has done lots of things right, but still score no marks. They have correctly figured out which equations to use, made the derivation and rearranged correctly. They have also used chosen to use the e.m.f. of the cell and the current through the cell. However, they have simply misread the question, which asks them to calculate the time to reduce from 470 kJ to 240 kJ. They have simply used energy as 240 kJ. This means they cannot score either the compensatory mark which is for correct substitution, nor the accuracy mark which is for the final value of time, 5300 s. This is an example of where students should take their time to ensure they answer exactly what they're being asked. *This answer is awarded 0 out of 2 marks.*
iv $I = nAvq$ I constant, q constant $\dfrac{V_f}{V_c} = \dfrac{n_c A_c}{n_f A_f}$ $= \dfrac{360A \times 2.5n}{nA}$ $360 \times 2.5 = 900$	The student has done a good job of working with proportional reasoning and evaluating a final ratio. They decided which equation they were using and which values in that equation were constants. They've rearranged and input the values which do change into the ratio correctly. They then substitute in the values given in the question, cancel and finally calculate. A very good example of how to solve a tricky ratio question. *This answer is awarded 2 out of 2 marks.*

4   Write an exam question in the same context as question 3. Make the exam question ask for a detailed extended writing description of how a student could get similar results as those in the graph. Include a second part of the question that asks for evaluative detail about the practical, and/or a treatment of the expected uncertainties in the practical. Write a mark scheme for your question.

12 Waves

KNOWLEDGE FOCUS

In this chapter you will answer questions on:
- describing waves
- longitudinal and transverse waves
- wave energy
- wave speed
- the Doppler effect for sound waves
- electromagnetic waves
- electromagnetic radiation
- orders of magnitude
- the nature of electromagnetic waves
- polarisation.

EXAM SKILLS FOCUS

In this chapter you will:
- practise recognising high-quality responses.

When responding to questions, you will need to judge whether your answer needs to short, detailed, or structured, if you need to include calculations, or if you need to include specific units. Understanding what is a good answer is very important for questions on this topic, as there are lots of concepts you will need to understand. Any equations written need to be balanced and must completely fit the definition. This chapter will provide opportunities for you to practise answering questions on waves, including calculation questions. As you work through this chapter, compare your answers with the answers provided in the online Answers. Are you structuring your response in a logical sequence? Are you including all of the key points required? Are you able to use the structure and content of the question to help you make a high-quality response?

The Exam practice sections throughout this resource contain example answers to past paper questions with commentaries. These will help you to understand what a good response looks like.

12.1 Describing waves

> **« RECALL AND CONNECT 1 «**
>
> Can you recall from IGCSE the basic characteristics of waves? Can you explain what is meant by a peak and a trough? And what is meant by the equilibrium position?

1 a What is meant by a progressive wave?

   b Give an example of how you could show that a wave transferred energy rather than matter.

   c How could you calculate the frequency from a known time period?

2 Describe how we use an oscilloscope to accurately measure the frequency of a sound wave.

3 Figure 12.1 shows the display on a cathode ray oscilloscope (CRO).

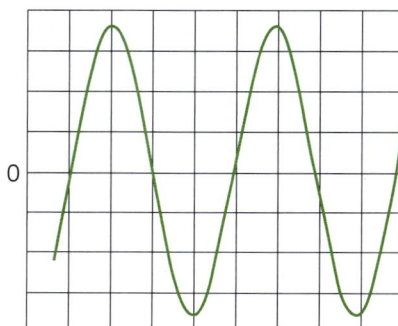

Figure 12.1

The time base is set to 200 μs. The y-gain is set to 50 mV per division.

a Calculate the frequency of the wave. [2]
b Calculate the amplitude of the wave. [2]

[Total: 4]

> **UNDERSTAND THESE TERMS**
> - wave motion
> - progressive wave
> - displacement
> - amplitude
> - wavelength
> - period
> - frequency

12.2 Longitudinal and transverse waves

1 What are the differences between longitudinal and transverse waves? Include information about energy transfer and examples of each type of wave. Use the words 'oscillations' and 'mechanical' in your explanation.

2. Complete the labels, **A–E**, in Figure 12.2a A longitudinal wave; and 12.2b A transverse wave.

> **UNDERSTAND THESE TERMS**
> - longitudinal wave
> - transverse wave
> - compression
> - rarefaction
> - phase difference

a
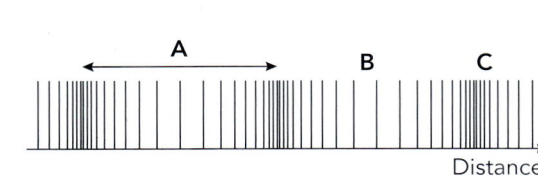

b
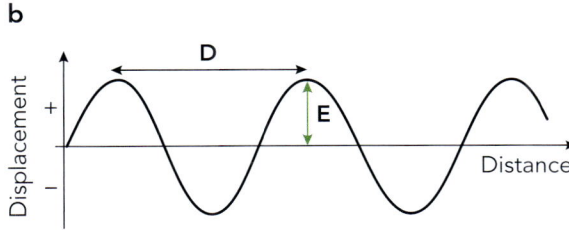

Figure 12.2

3. Copy and complete Tables 12.1 and 12.2 to practise calculating with phase angles.

Time period / s	Time / s	Phase angle / °
0.25	0.21	
	0.82	98
0.10		230

Table 12.1

Wavelength / m	Distance / m	Phase angle / radians
1500	750	
0.30		$\dfrac{5\pi}{6}$
	12	$\dfrac{3\pi}{2}$

Table 12.2

4   Figure 12.3 shows a displacement–time graph for a progressive wave.

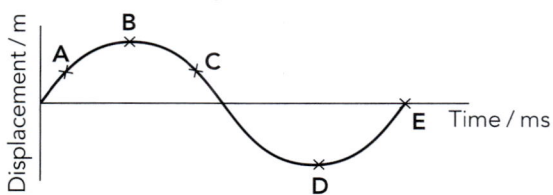

Figure 12.3

a   Identify **two** points on this wave that have a phase difference of π radians. [1]
b   Sketch a second wave on Figure 12.3, which has the same amplitude and a phase difference of $\frac{3\pi}{2}$ ahead of the wave. [2]
c   Give a letter where the displacement is equal to half the amplitude. [1]

[Total: 4]

12.3 Wave energy

1   Calculate these intensities. Give your answers in W m^{-2}.
    a   Power = 42 W; area = 0.20 m^2
    b   Power = 500 W; area = 40 cm^2
    c   Power = 900 kW; area = 3.4 mm^2
2   Write the relationship between intensity and amplitude.
3   The intensity of the Sun's radiation at noon on a cloudless day is approximately 1 kW m^{-2}.

    An array of six solar panels is arranged so that the sunlight is perpendicular to the surface.

    Each panel has an area of 1.9 m^2.
    Calculate the total energy on the solar panels in an hour.

    Give your answer in MJ. [Total: 4]

REFLECTION

Did you get all four marks for the previous exam skills question? Although it was quite a straightforward calculation, there were four marks because you had to demonstrate certain skills. How will you ensure that you show your working?

UNDERSTAND THIS TERM

- intensity

12.4 Wave speed

1   Copy and complete Table 12.3.

Frequency / Hz	Wavelength / m	Wave speed / m s⁻¹
200	0.20	
	0.058	330
3200		1500
2.8×10^{14}	7.8×10^{-7}	

Table 12.3

2   The visible portion of the electromagnetic spectrum has a wavelength range between 380 nm and 750 nm.

   a   Calculate the frequency range for light in the visible spectrum. [3]
   b   When electromagnetic waves travel across a boundary from air to water, their frequency is unchanged.
       The speed of electromagnetic waves in water is 2.26×10^{8} m s⁻¹.
       Calculate the wavelength of red light in water. [3]

[Total: 6]

12.5 The Doppler effect for sound waves

1   How does an observed sound differ from the sound emitted at the source if:

   a   A source of waves is coming towards an observer.
   b   A source of waves is moving away from an observer.
   c   A source of waves is distant but stationary relative to an observer.

2   Calculate the observed frequency of these sounds.
    Use the speed of sound in air as 340 m s⁻¹.

   a   A train approaching a station at 35 m s⁻¹ emitting a sound of 220 Hz.
   b   A race car moving away from a crowd at 90 m s⁻¹ emitting an engine sound of 250 Hz.

3   Sonar is a system used in ships.

   The sonar system emits a pulse of ultrasound into the water and measures the time taken for the pulse to be reflected back to the ship.

   Sonar is used to measure distances to objects in the water, such as rocks at the bottom of the sea.

The speed of ultrasound in water is 1500 m s⁻¹.

a The ultrasound frequency used by a particular sonar system is 150 kHz. Calculate the wavelength of this ultrasound in water. [2]

b The sonar system can make use of the Doppler effect to calculate the speed of a moving object in the water relative to the ship.

An object is moving directly towards a stationary ship with a constant speed of 26 m s⁻¹.

Calculate the ratio:

$$\frac{\text{emitted wavelength}}{\text{observed wavelength}}$$ [3]

[Total: 5]

> **UNDERSTAND THIS TERM**
> - Doppler effect

12.6 Electromagnetic waves and 12.7 Electromagnetic radiation

1 How are electromagnetic waves produced and detected?

2 Calculate the frequencies.

   a Visible light of wavelength 500 nm.
   b Ultraviolet light of wavelength 40 nm.
   c Radio waves of wavelength 2 km.

3 When light travels between boundaries, its speed can change.

   a When light travels from air into glass it slows down. Describe the effect that this has on:
      i the wavelength [1]
      ii the frequency. [1]

   b Red light, with wavelength 640 nm, enters a glass prism. The speed of light in glass, v, is 2.00×10^8 m s⁻¹.
      i Calculate the ratio $\frac{c}{v}$. [1]
      ii Calculate the wavelength of the light in glass. [2]

[Total: 5]

> **UNDERSTAND THESE TERMS**
> - electromagnetic spectrum
> - magnetic field
> - electromagnetic wave

12.8 Orders of magnitude

1 A student uses a prism to disperse the light from a filament lamp.

They project the spectrum that is produced onto a white screen.

   a They notice there is a continuous spectrum including all colours and that the yellow-orange portion of the spectrum is brighter than the other parts of the spectrum.

Suggest an explanation for these observations. [2]

b They expect there to be a further portion of the spectrum beyond the red end.
    i Explain why the student cannot see this portion of the spectrum. [2]
    ii Suggest how it could be detected. [1]

c Suggest how they could check if there were waves present from shorter wavelength portions of the electromagnetic spectrum. [1]

d The filament bulb is replaced with a 'daylight' temperature LED bulb. This is designed to give a similar, whiter spectrum to that of the Sun.

Predict how the visible spectrum will be different to the spectrum from the filament bulb. [2]

[Total: 8]

12.9 The nature of electromagnetic waves

1 Explain what is shown in Figure 12.4.

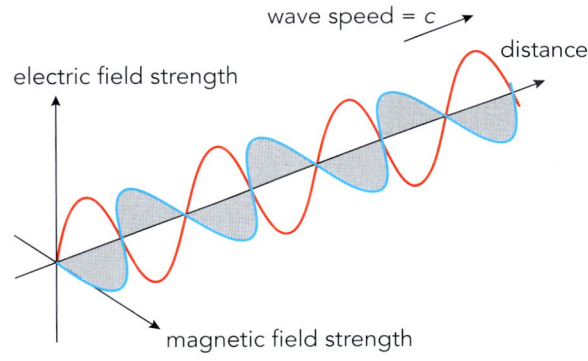

Figure 12.4

> **UNDERSTAND THESE TERMS**
> - electric field
> - plane polarised

2 What property of electromagnetic waves allows them to be plane polarised?

12.10 Polarisation

1 Plane polarised light with initial intensity 1.4 W m^{-2} is incident on a Polaroid at a 25° angle between the transmission axis of the Polaroid and the plane of polarisation of the light.

Calculate the transmitted intensity.

2 Explain why a light can be polarised but ultrasound **cannot** be polarised.

[Total: 3]

SELF-ASSESSMENT CHECKLIST

Let's revisit the Knowledge focus and Exam skills focus for this chapter.

Decide how confident you are with each statement.

Now I can:	Show it	Needs more work	Almost there	Confident to move on
describe a progressive wave	Write an accurate description of a progressive wave.			
describe the motion of transverse and longitudinal waves	Check that you can write accurate and complete definitions of longitudinal and transverse waves.			
describe waves in terms of their wavelength, amplitude, frequency, speed, phase difference and intensity	Ensure that you can label diagrams of waves and fluently use the terms to describe waves.			
use the time base and y-gain of a cathode ray oscilloscope (CRO) to determine frequency and amplitude	Practise determining frequencies and amplitudes from oscilloscope traces.			
use the wave equation $v = f\lambda$	Complete plenty of practice questions using the wave speed equation.			
use the equations intensity = $\frac{\text{power}}{\text{area}}$ and intensity $\propto$ amplitude^2	Work with equations for intensity to make calculations as well as to do proportional reasoning to determine quantitative answers.			
describe the Doppler effect for sound waves	Write a detailed set of notes describing the Doppler effect and situations in which you would expect to observe a perceived change in frequency or wavelength.			
use the equation $f_0 = \frac{f_s v}{(v \pm v_s)}$	Practise identifying and making calculations with quantities in the Doppler effect equation.			

CONTINUED

Now I can:	Show it	Needs more work	Almost there	Confident to move on
describe and understand electromagnetic waves	Explain how electromagnetic waves arise and memorise the orders of magnitude of the wavelengths of the portions of the electromagnetic spectrum.			
recall that wavelengths in the range 400–700 nm in free space are visible to the human eye	Memorise the properties of the visible part of the electromagnetic spectrum and how it can be detected.			
describe and understand polarisation	Explain that light can be polarised by a Polaroid as it is a transverse wave.			
use Malus's law to determine the intensity of transmitted light through a polarising filter	Practise making calculations using Malus's law equation.			
recognise high-quality responses	Compare your responses with the answers provided in the online Answers and identify areas you can improve. Practise more on similar types of questions to ensure that the level of your responses improve.			

13 Superposition of waves

KNOWLEDGE FOCUS

In this chapter you will answer questions on:
- the principle of superposition of waves
- diffraction of waves
- interference
- the Young double-slit experiment
- diffraction gratings.

EXAM SKILLS FOCUS

In this chapter you will:
- practise distinguishing command words in questions from other instructional text.

AS and A Level Physics questions can include additional information to show the context the questions are based on. This is often useful information that you may need to use within your answer. Sometimes it can be difficult to distinguish the command words from other instructional text.

In this chapter, you will come across questions using a variety of command words, and some will also contain other instructional text. It is important you are able to distinguish instructional text from command words, so pay attention to this as you work through the questions. More support and advice on recognising command words within questions is given in the Exam skills chapter.

13 Superposition of waves

13.1 The principle of superposition of waves

1 a What is the difference between a transverse and longitudinal wave in terms of the respective motion of their particles?

  b Give **one** example of a transverse wave and **one** example of a longitudinal wave.

> **UNDERSTAND THIS TERM**
> - principle of superposition

2 Two waves start their oscillations at the same time.

Their respective motions are shown in Figure 13.1.

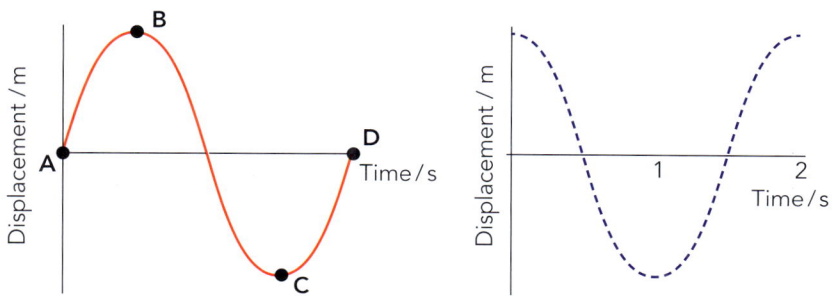

Figure 13.1

  a What is the phase difference between the particles of the two waves?
  b Look at the labels A, B, C and D.
   i Which particles are in phase?
   ii Which particles are completely out of phase?
   iii Which particles have a phase difference of 180°?

3 When an astronaut is on a spacewalk, signals are sent to the astronaut with electromagnetic waves at a frequency of 600 MHz.

  a i Explain why waves do not travel through space.
    ii State which part of the electromagnetic spectrum contains waves of a frequency of 600 MHz.
    iii Calculate the wavelength of these electromagnetic waves. [4]
  b The delay between an astronaut speaking and ground control receiving the sound is 1.4 ms.
    Calculate the distance between the astronaut and ground control. [3]

[Total: 7]

> ### « RECALL AND CONNECT 1 «
> Think back to Chapter 6 and the momentum topic. Can you define the conservation of momentum? What is the difference between an elastic and inelastic collision?

13.2 Diffraction of waves

1. Your friend is standing outside your room, and the door is open.

   When they shine a torch across the doorway, no light enters the room.

   However, when they ask if you can see the light, you can hear the sound in the room.

   Copy and complete the following:

   a   Diffraction occurs when a wave .... out as it passes through a .... or travels past the .... of an ....

   b   The greatest effect of the diffraction is when the .... of the wave and the size of the .... are roughly equal.

   c   The wavelength of light is measured in ....-metres. The doorway is roughly .... m wide. Therefore the .... and the .... size are very different, and no diffraction occurs.

   d   The wavelength of a .... wave is roughly equal to the size of a doorway, and so diffraction occurs; the .... wave can spread into the room.

> **UNDERSTAND THIS TERM**
> - diffraction

2. Figure 13.2 shows a water wave entering a harbour.

   There are two sea defence walls.

   Continue the pattern to include three wavefronts inside the inner harbour.

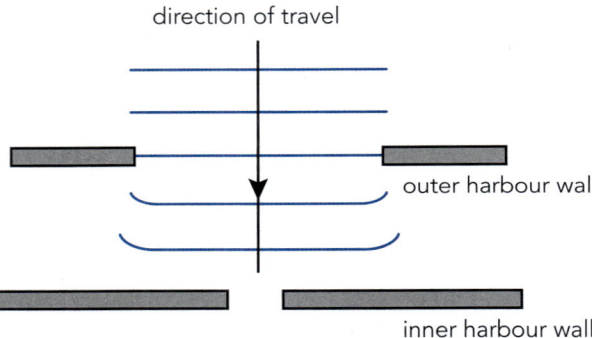

Figure 13.2

13 Superposition of waves

13.3 Interference

1 Look at Figure 13.3, two graphs showing the displacement of the same wave compared with (i) the time and (ii) position.

> **UNDERSTAND THIS TERM**
> - interference

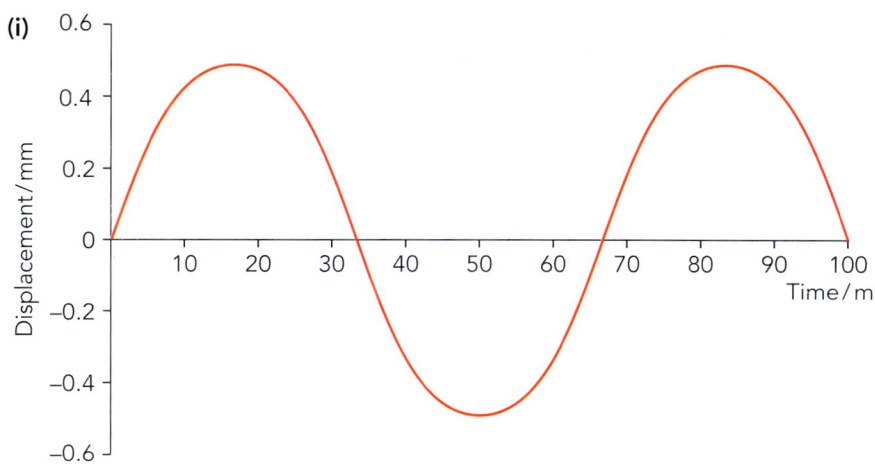

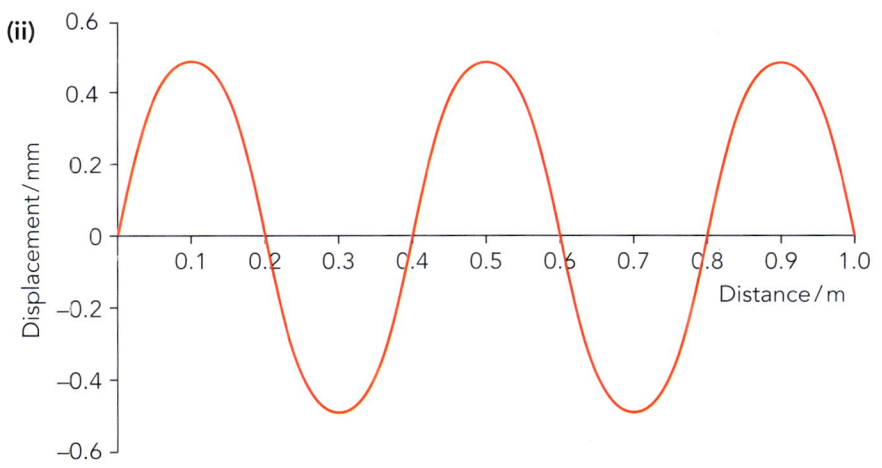

Figure 13.3

From these graphs, work out the:
- **a** amplitude of the wave
- **b** wavelength of the wave
- **c** frequency of the wave
- **d** speed of the wave.

2 Two waves that are in phase meet. Their wavelength is 0.50 m.

What kind of interference would take place if:
- **a** the waves have a path difference of 3.25 m
- **b** the waves have a path difference of 3λ?

> **UNDERSTAND THESE TERMS**
> - coherence
> - constructive and destructive interference

3   A microwave transmitter is set up as in Figure 13.4.

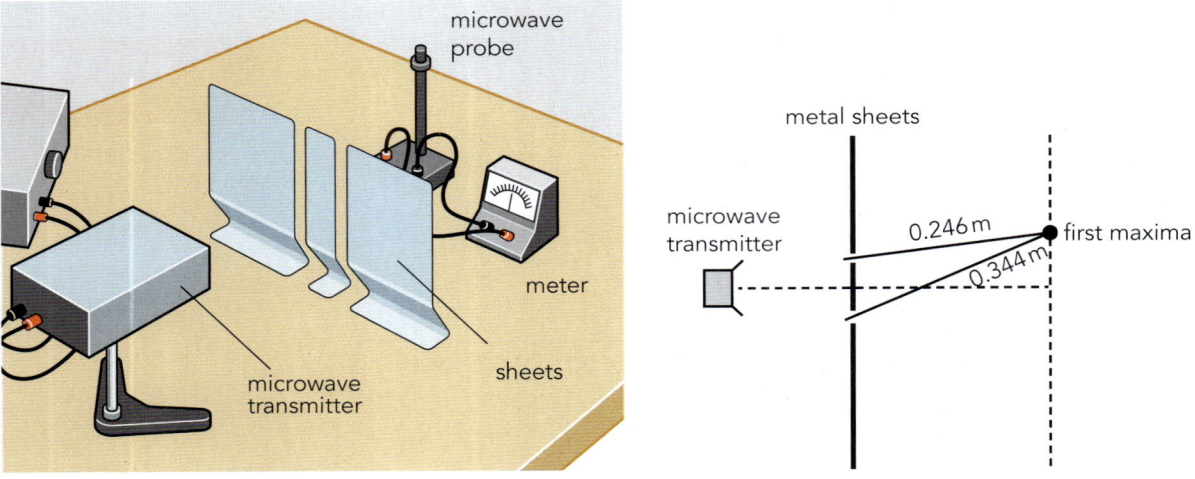

Figure 13.4

The receiver is moved along a horizontal line and picks up different intensities of microwave radiation. The distance from the receiver to each gap in the plates is measured and found to be 0.246 m and 0.344 m, respectively. At this point, the receiver shows the first maximum intensity.

a   Explain why there are areas of maximum and minimum intensity picked up by the receiver as it moves along. [3]
b   Calculate the frequency of the microwaves transmitted. [3]

[Total: 6]

> **UNDERSTAND THESE TERMS**
> - electromagnetic spectrum
> - magnetic field
> - electromagnetic wave

« RECALL AND CONNECT 2 «

In Chapter 10, you learnt about resistance. Can you explain why the resistance increases with temperature for a non-ohmic resistor, such as a filament in a lamp?

13.4 The Young double-slit experiment

1   The double-slit experiment is set up, and an interference pattern is seen on the screen.

The experiment uses red light of wavelength 450 nm, and is shone through slits which are 6.2 μm apart.

a   Give the double-slit equation. [1]
b   If the screen is 2.0 m from the slits, calculate the fringe separation on the screen. [2]

c Taking the conditions above as the norm, state how the fringe separation will change on the screen when:
  i the slit separation is halved [1]
  ii the wavelength is 150% of the original [1]
  iii the distance to the screen is three times further. [1]
d i Use this set-up to find the wavelength of the light source. Then copy and complete the following to show how to calculate the percentage error in wavelength.

  percentage error of wavelength =

  percentage error in .... + percentage error in .... + percentage error in .... [1]
  ii Describe what can be changed in the experiment to reduce the percentage error of the wavelength measured. [2]

[Total: 9]

> **« RECALL AND CONNECT 3 «**
>
> In Chapter 10, you learnt about semiconductors, such as thermistors. Can you explain how the resistance of a negative temperature coefficient thermistor **decreases** with temperature?

13.5 Diffraction gratings

1 a Consider a diffraction grating with light of wavelength λ, and slit separation 5λ.

  What is the angle of the second order maximum?

  b What is the difference of the observed fringes of the diffraction grating compared with the fringes seen in the double-slit experiment, assuming everything else stays the same?

2 a An argon-ion laser produces light of wavelength 488 nm.

  When fired at a diffraction grating, the first order maximum is found at 16.7°.

  Calculate:
   i the number of lines per metre on the diffraction grating [3]
   ii the maximum number of fringes seen on each side. [3]
  b When this grating is used with a different laser, the first order maximum is found at an angle of 21.9°.
  Calculate the wavelength of light produced by this laser. [2]

[Total: 8]

UNDERSTAND THIS TERM
- dispersion

> **REFLECTION**
>
> Were you able to distinguish command words from other instructional text in the exam skills questions in this chapter? What techniques could you apply in an exam to ensure that you identify the command word(s) in a question?

SELF-ASSESSMENT CHECKLIST

Let's revisit the Knowledge focus and Exam skills focus for this chapter.

Decide how confident you are with each statement.

Now I can:	Show it	Needs more work	Almost there	Confident to move on
explain and use the principle of superposition	Use the fact that when two or more waves meet at a point, the resultant displacement is the sum of the displacements of the individual waves.			
explain the meaning of diffraction, interference, path difference and coherence	Make flashcards with definitions of diffraction, interference, path difference and coherence.			
understand experiments that demonstrate diffraction	Write out methods for more than one experiment involving diffraction. Explain the expected results.			
understand experiments that demonstrate two-source interference	Look through any laboratory notes that you have to remind yourself of two-source interference experiments.			
understand the conditions required if two-source interference fringes are to be observed	Identify that the sources are coherent.			

CONTINUED

Now I can:	Show it	Needs more work	Almost there	Confident to move on
recall and use $\lambda = \frac{ax}{D}$ for double-slit interference using light	Write down and revise what each of the letters in the formula represents; practise rearranging the equation from the data given in a question and solve for each quantity in turn.			
recall and use $n\lambda = d\sin\theta$ for a diffraction grating	Recall and use the formula and be able to rearrange it to solve for each quantity. Predict how many fringes are possible by using $\theta = 90°$ in questions.			
use a diffraction grating to determine the wavelength of light	Be aware of the measurements to take from the diffraction grating experiment and then apply them in the formula to find λ.			
distinguish command words in questions from other instructional text	Highlight all the command words in a set of past paper questions. Highlight other instructional text in a different colour.			

14 Stationary waves

KNOWLEDGE FOCUS

In this chapter you will answer questions on:
- from moving to stationary
- nodes and antinodes
- formation of stationary waves
- determining the wavelength and speed of sound.

EXAM SKILLS FOCUS

In this chapter you will:
- practise recognising different question types.

In this chapter, you will be practising how to answer different question types, including questions that require a longer answer. To answer these questions successfully you need to draw on knowledge and the details of the topic or concept, so it is essential that you are able to show your understanding in an organised way. You will need to plan your answers for these questions.

Making a list of the key words and concepts for a long response question will help you to plan an answer that lists the necessary details in an organised manner. It is important to understand the difference between a short response question and a longer 5 or 6 mark question. This chapter has a variety of question types. Work out which ones you are best at and develop a strategy of which questions you will try to solve first. For example, if you are great with formulae, you can locate and solve those questions first and get some confidence to help in other parts of the paper.

14 Stationary waves

14.1 From moving to stationary

1. Use the wave equation to work out the wavelength of a microwave with a frequency of 30 GHz.

2. A string is fixed between points X and Y. The distance between X and Y is 50 cm. When the frequency of vibration is 40 Hz, the fundamental frequency (first harmonic) is set up.
   a. Calculate the wavelength of this wave. [2]
   b. Show that the speed of the progressive wave in the string is 40 m s^{-1}. [1]
   c. Calculate the speed of the wave for the second harmonic. [3]

   [Total: 6]

3. By using base units, show that the following formula is homogeneous:
$$f = \frac{1}{2l}\sqrt{\frac{T}{\mu}}$$
   where,

   l = length, f = frequency, T = tension and μ = mass per unit length of the string.

   (Hint: square both sides first.) [Total: 2]

> « RECALL AND CONNECT 1 «
>
> In Chapter 13, you learned about the principle of the superposition of waves. What happens to the resultant displacement of the wave when two waves meet at a point?

14.2 Nodes and antinodes

1. A stationary wave pattern is set up with three loops, as shown in Figure 14.1.

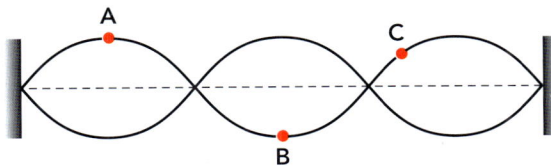

Figure 14.1

Which labelled point is:
   a. in phase with A
   b. out of phase with A?

UNDERSTAND THESE TERMS
- time period of a wave
- displacement of a particle in a wave
- node
- antinode

2. Calculate the minimum distance between two nodes in a stationary wave that is set up when two radio transmitters emit waves of a frequency of 2.2 MHz towards each other. [Total: 2]

14.3 Formation of stationary waves

UNDERSTAND THESE TERMS
- transverse wave
- longitudinal wave

1. In terms of λ, how far apart are adjacent nodes on a stationary wave?

2. A microwave oven plate is turned upside down to prevent rotation and is covered with chocolate buttons. The microwave is turned on for 15 seconds, and at the end of this time there are spots where the chocolate has melted. Two adjacent melted spots are measured to be 6 cm apart. The frequency of microwaves is 2450 MHz.

   The receiver is moved along a horizontal line and picks up different intensities of microwave radiation. The distance from the receiver to each gap in the plates is measured and found to be 0.246 m and 0.344 m, respectively. At this point, the receiver shows the first maximum intensity.

   a If the melted spots represent adjacent antinodes of the stationary wave, calculate the wavelength of the wave.

   b Use your answer to part **a** to show that the speed of the microwaves is approximately 3×10^8 m s^{-1}.

3. A guitar string is 60 cm long. The speed of the waves in the string is 380 m s^{-1}

   a Calculate the fundamental frequency of the guitar string. [2]

   b A second guitar string is required to make a fundamental frequency of a middle C note (262 Hz).

   Show that the guitar string must be about 0.80 m long if the speed of the wave is 420 m s^{-1}. [3]

   [Total: 5]

14.4 Determining the wavelength and speed of sound

1. Three different set-ups for a stationary wave are shown in Figure 14.2.

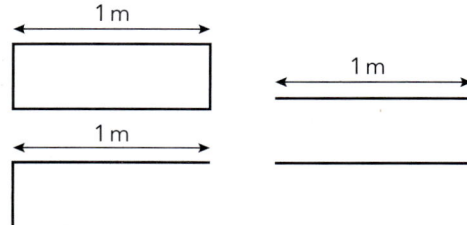

   Figure 14.2

   a Draw the fundamental stationary wave for each set-up.
   b Calculate the wavelength of the stationary wave in each case.

2   A tuning fork is vibrating at the top of a column of water, as shown in Figure 14.3.

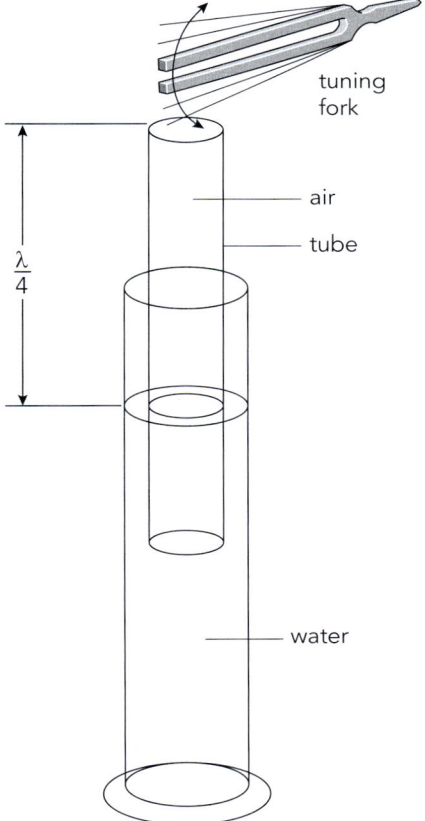

Figure 14.3

Resonance occurs when the distance from the water to the tuning fork is 20 cm.

a   Calculate the wavelength for this stationary wave. [1]
b   Determine the length of the air column when the next resonant sound is heard. [2]
c   If the frequency of the tuning fork is labelled 440 Hz, show that the speed of sound is approximately 340 m s^{-1}. [1]

[Total: 4]

3   Kundt's dust tube is set up to measure the speed of sound, as shown in Figure 14.4.

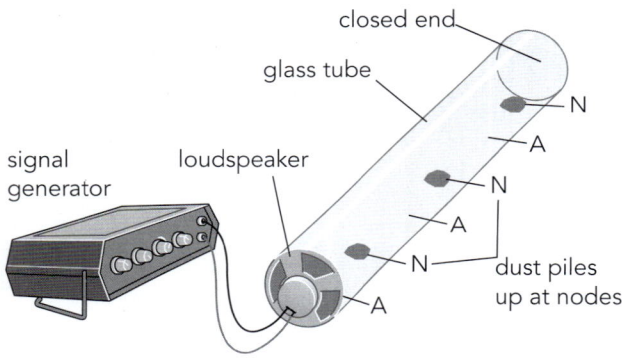

Figure 14.4

Describe the method.

Your answer should include the measurements taken and the calculations used.

[Total: 5]

> ### REFLECTION
> This topic uses a lot of diagrams to help to explain how the wave patterns are set up. How confident do you feel sketching the pattern produced in each example? Do you remember that a node is formed at a fixed point and an antinode at an open end? Are you able to work out the wavelength from the pattern and length?

4   A microwave detector is set up between a transmitter and a metal sheet.

As the detector moves towards the sheet of metal, it detects a region of minimum intensity.

The detector is moved 0.10 m closer and detects a region of maximum intensity.

a   Explain why there are areas of maximum and minimum intensity. [4]

The speed of the microwaves is 3.0×10^8 m s^{-1}.

b   By working out the wavelength from the stationary wave pattern set-up, show that the frequency of the microwaves is 7.5×10^8 m s^{-1}. [2]

[Total: 6]

> ### REFLECTION
> Did you think about the different question types as you worked through this chapter? Are there any you feel more confident answering? What strategy could you apply in an exam to ensure you gain some easy marks to start with to increase your confidence?

14 Stationary waves

SELF-ASSESSMENT CHECKLIST

Let's revisit the Knowledge focus and Exam skills focus for this chapter.

Decide how confident you are with each statement.

Now I can:	Show it	Needs more work	Almost there	Confident to move on
explain the formation of stationary waves using graphical methods	Practise drawing wave patterns to show how a stationary wave is formed. Label your graphs.			
understand experiments to demonstrate stationary waves using microwaves, stretched strings and air columns	Remind yourself of the different experiments, then try re-writing the methods from memory, including measurements taken and calculations used.			
identify nodes and antinodes	Write descriptions of progressive and stationary waves in terms of energy and wavelength.			
determine the wavelength of sound using stationary waves	Work out the pattern formed, and you can consider adjacent nodes or antinodes to work out the wavelength. You then can use this to work out the speed of sound using the wave equation ($v = f\lambda$).			
recognise different question types	Make a list of all the different question types you can think of and write a few notes on how best to approach each type.			

15 Atomic structure and particle physics

> ### KNOWLEDGE FOCUS
>
> In this chapter you will answer questions on:
> - looking inside the atom
> - alpha-particle scattering and the nucleus
> - a simple model of the atom
> - nucleons and electrons
> - forces in the nucleus
> - discovering radioactivity
> - radiation from radioactive substances
> - energies in α and β decay
> - equations of radioactive decay
> - fundamental particles
> - families of particles
> - another look at β decay
> - another nuclear force.

> ### EXAM SKILLS FOCUS
>
> In this chapter you will:
> - show that you understand the 'determine' command word and can answer 'determine' questions
> - think about problem-solving strategies to help in an exam.

When you are asked to 'determine', you are being asked to establish an answer using the information available, which might include graphs, tables, or diagrams (for example, nuclear decays may be represented on a graph as well as equations). You still need to recall facts or concepts, but the information provided will allow you to tackle a question in what might be an unfamiliar context.

Determine	establish an answer using the information available

Though they may look different, many questions on the same topic are testing the same material. Therefore, it is helpful to develop a strategy (or routine) for answering questions. Each of the nuclear decays in this chapter (alpha, beta-plus and beta-minus) changes the proton and nucleon numbers of the parent nucleus in a different way. However, charge and mass must be conserved, so it does not matter what nuclide you start with; you can work out any missing information in a nuclear reaction by following simple rules.

15 Atomic structure and particle physics

15.1 Looking inside the atom and
15.2 Alpha-particle scattering and the nucleus

1. Geiger and Marsden fired alpha particles at a thin foil of metal.
   a. Why was gold used?
   b. Why did they remove air from the apparatus?

2. State three findings of the α-particle scattering experiment.
   Use each one to explain the nuclear model of the atom. [Total: 6]

15.3 A simple model of the atom

1. Table 15.1 shows the density of various metals along with their molar masses (the mass that contains 6.02×10^{23} atoms).
   a. Copy and complete the table by calculating the radius of the atoms for each metal. Take care to use base SI units.
      It may help to calculate the molar volume and atomic volume as intermediate steps.
      Gold has been done for you. [2]
   b. State any assumption you make. [1]
   c. Comment on your results. [1]

> **UNDERSTAND THESE TERMS**
> - nuclear model of the atom
> - nucleus

Element	Density / kg m⁻³	Molar mass / g	Molar volume / $\times 10^{-6}$ m³	Volume of atom / $\times 10^{-29}$ m³	Atomic radius / $\times 10^{-10}$ m
gold	19 700	193.00	9.80	1.63	1.57
iron	7874	55.85			
lithium	534	6.94			
aluminium	2702	26.98			
uranium	19 100	238.03			

Table 15.1

[Total: 4]

15.4 Nucleons and electrons

1. a. State the particles that make up an atom and where they are located within the atom. [2]
   b. State the particles that determine the chemical properties of the atom. [1]
   c. State the particles that determine the physical properties of the atom. [1]

[Total: 4]

> **UNDERSTAND THESE TERMS**
> - proton number
> - nucleon number

2   Table 15.2 lists the relative abundance of the most common isotopes of lead.

    The proton number of lead is 82.

Isotopes of lead	Relative abundance / %
Pb-204	1.4
Pb-206	24.1
Pb-207	22.1
Pb-208	52.4

    Table 15.2

    Use this information to:

    a   determine the number of neutrons in each of the isotopes of lead
        in Table 15.2 [2]
    b   determine the relative atomic mass of lead (in other words,
        the 'average nucleon number'). [2]

    [Total: 4]

3   Eight different atoms are labelled A to H.

    Group them into isotopes and name them using the periodic table.

Atom	A	B	C	D	E	F	G	H
Proton number	90	82	90	82	11	8	82	8
Nucleon number	232	208	233	207	23	18	206	16

    UNDERSTAND THESE TERMS
    - protons
    - neutrons
    - orbital electrons

    REFLECTION

    How did you find the 'determine' questions in this section? Were you able to use the information provided to give the correct answers? Do you feel confident that you understand what is required from 'determine' questions?

15.5 Forces in the nucleus

1 Copy and complete Table 15.3.

a State the nucleon number and determine the number of neutrons for each element. [3]

Nuclide	A	Z	N
H-1		1	
B-11		5	
Ne-20		10	
Ca-40		20	
Zr-90		40	
Hg-202		80	

Table 15.3

> **UNDERSTAND THESE TERMS**
> - nucleon
> - nuclide

b Sketch a graph showing how the neutron number varies with the proton number. [2]

c You have sketched a Segrè chart. Comment on what it shows. [2]

[Total: 7]

15.6 Discovering radioactivity and
15.7 Radiation from radioactive substances

> **≪ RECALL AND CONNECT 1 ≪**
>
> Think back to Chapter 5. Write down the equation for kinetic energy and express it in terms of velocity.

1 Copy and complete Table 15.4 to summarise the symbol, composition, relative mass, relative charge and typical speed of alpha, beta and gamma radiation.

	Alpha	Beta-minus	Beta-plus	Gamma
Symbol				
Composition				
Relative mass				
Relative charge				
Typical speed				

Table 15.4

2. We can compare the speed of two different particles if they have the same kinetic energy but different masses.
   a. Show that an alpha particle is about 7000 times more massive than a beta particle. [2]
   b. Show how this leads to a beta particle travelling about 80 times faster than an alpha particle. [3]

   [Total: 5]

3. Compare the penetrating and ionising power of alpha, beta and gamma radiation and suggest why they differ. **[Total: 5]**

4. State how alpha, beta and gamma radiation was identified. **[Total: 2]**

> **« RECALL AND CONNECT 2 «**
> Think back to Chapter 3. Recall Fleming's left-hand rule.

15.8 Energies in α and β decay and
15.9 Equations of radioactive decay

> **UNDERSTAND THESE TERMS**
> - positron
> - β^- (beta-minus) decay
> - β^+ (beta-plus) decay
> - antimatter

1. In beta-minus decay, a neutron decays into a proton, an electron, and an antineutrino.
   a. Explain what happens in a radioactive nucleus during
      i. β^- decay [1]
      ii. β^+ decay. [1]
   b. Two identical radioactive nuclei emit β^- particles. Explain why the kinetic energy at which these particles are emitted may **not** be identical. [2]

   [Total: 4]

2. Sometimes, a nuclide is part of a decay chain.
   Three particles would need to be emitted for lead-208 ($^{208}_{82}\text{Pb}$) to decay into an isotope of lead.
   a. Write a decay equation as if all three particles were emitted at the same time.
   b. Use the decay equation to justify your answer.
   c. What is the nucleon number of lead at the end of this chain?

> **UNDERSTAND THESE TERMS**
> - electronvolt
> - electron neutrino
> - electron antineutrino

3. Copy and complete the following beta decays:
   a. $^{234}_{90}\text{Th} \rightarrow {}^{?}_{?}\text{Pa} + {}^{0}_{-1}\beta + \ldots\ldots$
   b. $^{131}_{53}\text{I} \rightarrow {}^{?}_{?}\text{Xe} + {}^{0}_{-1}\beta + \ldots\ldots$
   c. $^{?}_{?}\text{H} \rightarrow {}^{3}_{2}\text{He} + {}^{0}_{-1}\beta + \ldots\ldots$

4 a Figure 15.1 shows two decays:
   i   the decay of lead-210 ($^{210}_{82}$Pb) into an unidentified nuclide
   ii the decay of the unidentified nuclide into gold-206 ($^{206}_{79}$Au).

Use Figure 15.1 to determine the unknown nuclide and show the two decay equations. [3]

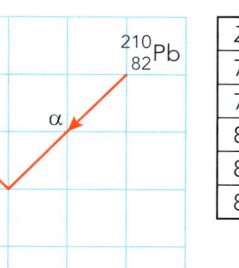

Figure 15.1

b Starting with lead-210 ($^{210}_{82}$Pb), show how it is possible to get gold-202 ($^{202}_{79}$Au) in three separate decays, starting with the heaviest particles. [3]

c Sketch these decays on a copy of the axes shown in Figure 15.2. [3]

[Total: 9]

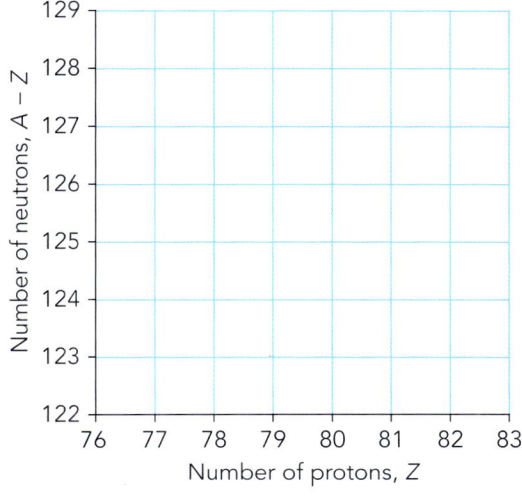

Figure 15.2

15.10 Fundamental particles and
15.11 Families of particles

1. Until the mid-1900s, scientists thought protons, neutrons and electrons were fundamental (i.e. could not be subdivided or broken down). How were new particles discovered?

2. What are the main differences between:
   a leptons and hadrons
   b mesons and baryons?

> **UNDERSTAND THESE TERMS**
> - quark
> - antiquark
> - hadron
> - baryon
> - meson

3. Copy and complete Table 15.5.

Particle		Baryon or meson?	Relative charge	Quark composition of antiparticle
Lambda, Λ°	uds			
Phi, Φ	s$\bar{s}$			
Sigma, Σ⁺	uus			
Upsilon, Y	b$\bar{b}$			
Sigma, Σ⁻	dds			
Xi, Ξ°	uss			
η$_c$	c$\bar{c}$			

Table 15.5

4. Table 15.6 lists some baryons. Alongside each baryon are its overall charge and two of its three quarks. Copy and complete the table by working out the charge of the third quark in each case.

Baryon	Overall charge	Two of three quarks	Charge of third quark
lambda	0	ud	
charmed lambda	+1	uc	
bottom lambda	0	db	
sigma-plus	+1	us	
sigma-minus	−1	ds	

Table 15.6

5   a   Pions (π) are mesons. Each of the three flavours has a different charge (i.e. π^-, π^0, π^+). They are composed of up and down quarks or their antiparticles. What is the quark combination for each pion?

   b   Kaons (K) are mesons. Each of the three flavours has a different charge (i.e. K^-, K^0, K^+). The charged kaons are composed of up and strange quarks or their antiparticles, and the neutral kaon is composed of down and strange quarks or their antiparticles. What is the quark combination for each kaon?

6   Copy and complete Table 15.7 for carbon-14 ($^{14}_{6}C$).

Particle	Number of up quarks	Number of down quarks	Number of leptons	Number of baryons	Number of mesons
carbon nucleus					
carbon atom					

Table 15.7

15.12 Another look at β decay and 15.13 Another nuclear force

1   Below is a beta-minus decay.

$$^{23}_{12}Mg \rightarrow \,^{23}_{13}Al + \,^{0}_{-1}\beta^-$$

   a   State the name and symbol for the missing particle. [1]
   b   Explain why this particle must have no charge and very little mass. [2]
   c   Identify the lepton and antilepton in the equation. [1]
   d   Re-write the equation at the nucleon level. [1]
   e   Re-write the equation at the quark level. [1]

   [Total: 6]

UNDERSTAND THESE TERMS
- leptons
- hadrons
- quarks
- baryon
- meson

2   Below is a beta-plus decay.

$$^{230}_{90}Mg \rightarrow \,^{230}_{89}Ac + \,^{0}_{+1}\beta^+$$

   a   State the name and symbol for the missing particle and use it to complete the equation. [2]
   b   Identify the lepton and antilepton in the equation. [1]
   c   Re-write the equation at the nucleon level. [1]
   d   Re-write the equation at the quark level. [1]

   [Total: 5]

UNDERSTAND THIS TERM
- strong nuclear force

3   List the differences between the strong nuclear force and the weak nuclear force.

> CAMBRIDGE INTERNATIONAL AS & A LEVEL PHYSICS: EXAM PREPARATION AND PRACTICE

REFLECTION

Do you often see questions as standalone problems, or do you recognise that they are sometimes old questions in disguise? Did you spot any such questions in this chapter? What problem-solving strategies could you use to ensure you spot such questions in the exam?

SELF-ASSESSMENT CHECKLIST

Let's revisit the Knowledge focus and Exam skills focus for this chapter.

Decide how confident you are with each statement.

Now I can:	Show it	Needs more work	Almost there	Confident to move on
describe the nuclear model of the atom and the evidence for it	Compare the nuclear model of the atom to the solar system. Describe and explain the results of Rutherford's alpha-scattering experiment.			
show an understanding of the nature and properties of α-, β- and γ-radiations	Write a table to summarise the symbol, composition, charge, speed, ionising power and penetrating power of alpha, beta-plus, beta-minus and gamma.			
understand that in α and β decay, a nuclide changes into a different nuclide	Nuclides X, Y and Z all have a nucleon number of 20 and proton numbers 8, 9 and 10, respectively. Write down the equations for alpha decay, beta-plus and beta-minus decay for each nuclide.			
recognise that there are two classes of sub-atomic particles – leptons and quarks	List all the fundamental particles.			
recognise that leptons are fundamental particles	What nuclear force do **all** fundamental particles interact with? What decay process is associated with that force?			

15 Atomic structure and particle physics

CONTINUED

Now I can:	Show it	Needs more work	Almost there	Confident to move on
appreciate that electrons and neutrinos are leptons	List the antileptons of the electron and the neutrino.			
recognise that hadrons are not fundamental particles	List the two classes of hadron and the combination of fundamental particles they are composed of.			
understand that hadrons are made up of particles called quarks.	List the quarks and their charges.			
show that I understand the 'determine' command word and can answer 'determine' questions	Explain to a partner what 'determine' means as a command word, and how it is different from, e.g., 'suggest'.			
think about problem-solving strategies to help in an exam	Look back at at least one of the Exam skills questions; write down anything you did not understand properly and state how you will improve your learning and avoid repeating your mistakes.			

Exam practice 4

This section contains past paper questions from previous Cambridge exams, which draws together your knowledge on a range of topics that you have covered up to this point. These questions give you the opportunity to test your knowledge and understanding. Additional past paper practice questions can be found in the accompanying digital material.

The following question has an example student response and commentary provided. Once you have worked through the question, read the student response and commentary. Are your answers different to the sample responses?

1   Light from a laser is used to produce an interference pattern on a screen, as shown in Fig. 1.1.

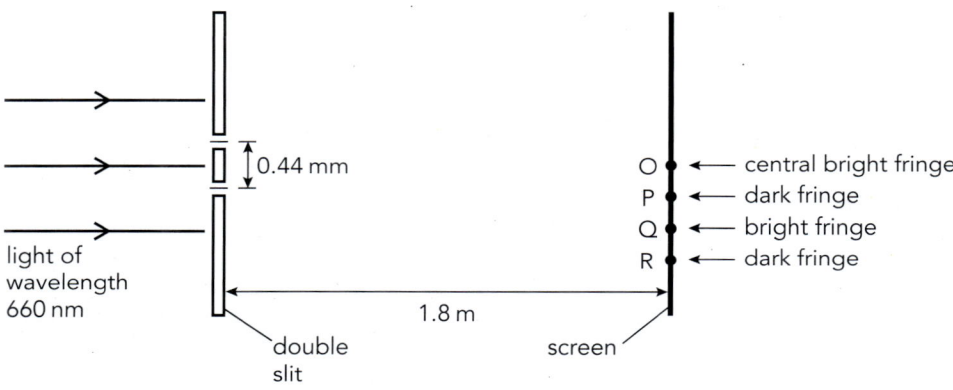

Fig. 1.1 (not to scale)

The light of wavelength 660 nm is incident normally on two slits that have a separation of 0.44 mm. The double slit is parallel to the screen.
The perpendicular distance between the double slit and the screen is 1.8 m.

The central bright fringe on the screen is formed at point O. The next dark fringe below point O is formed at point P. The next bright fringe and the next dark fringe below point P are formed at points Q and R, respectively.

a The light waves from the two slits are coherent.
State what is meant by coherent. [1]

b For the two light waves superposing at R, calculate:

   i the difference in their path lengths, in nm, from the slits [1]
   ii their phase difference. [1]

c Calculate the distance OQ. [3]

Exam practice 4

d The intensity of the light incident on the double slit is increased without changing the frequency.

Describe how the appearance of the fringes after this change is different from, and similar to, their appearance before the change. [3]

e The light of wavelength 660 nm is now replaced by blue light from a laser.

State and explain the change, if any, that must be made to the separation of the two slits so that the fringe separation on the screen is the same as it was for light of wavelength 660 nm. [2]

[Total: 11]

Cambridge International AS & A Level Physics (9702) Paper 22, Q5, June 2022

	Example student response	Commentary
a	The waves have the same frequency and constant phase relationship	Constant phase difference is the syllabus definition, but constant phase relationship would score the mark. *This answer is awarded 1 out of 1 mark.*
b i	path diff = $1.5 \times 660 \times 10^{-9} = 990 \times 10^{-9}$ m	The student got the calculations correct. *This answer is awarded 1 out of 1 mark.*
ii	phase diff = $1.5 \times 360° = 540°$	The student got the calculations correct. *This answer is awarded 1 out of 1 mark.*
c	$\lambda = \dfrac{ax}{D} \Rightarrow x = \dfrac{\lambda D}{a} = \dfrac{660 \times 10^{-9} \times 1.8}{0.44}$ $= 2.7 \times 10^{-6}$ m	The student receives the mark for stating the formula correctly. But the fringe spacing has not been converted to m. This one mistake costs 2 marks as neither the calculation nor the answer mark can be scored. *This answer is awarded 1 out of 3 marks.*
d	The bright fringes are still bright and they are the same distance apart	The student got one mark for correctly stating the fringe spacing. They also need a comparative i.e. the bright fringes are **brighter** and they need to describe the change to the dark fringes. *This answer is awarded 1 out of 3 marks.*
e	Blue light has a shorter wavelength, so need to increase the slit separation	The student has correctly identified the difference in the wavelength, but they got the relationship to the slit separation confused. *This answer is awarded 1 out of 2 marks.*

Here is a similar past paper question that you should attempt.

2 a By reference to two waves, state:

   i   the principle of superposition [2]

   ii what is meant by *coherence*. [1]

b The apparatus shown in Fig. 2.1 is used to produce an interference pattern on a screen.

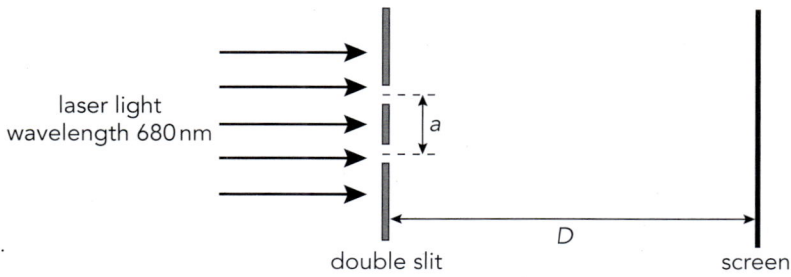

Fig. 2.1 (not to scale)

Light of wavelength 680 nm is incident on a double slit. The slit separation is a. The separation between adjacent fringes is x. Fringes are viewed on a screen at distance D from the double slit.

Distance D is varied from 2.0 m to 3.5 m. The variation with D of x is shown in Fig. 2.2.

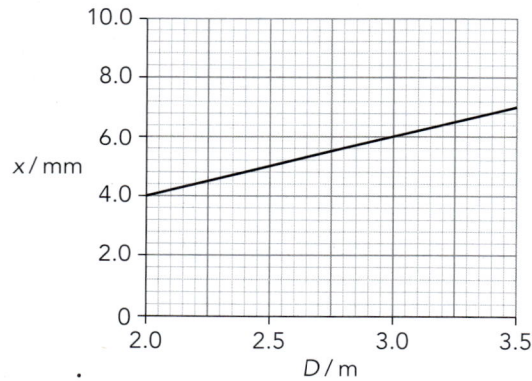

Fig. 2.2

   i   Use Fig. 2.2 to determine the slit separation a. [3]

   ii The laser is now replaced by another laser that emits light of a shorter wavelength.

   On Fig. 2.2, sketch a possible line to show the variation with D of x for the fringes that are now produced. [2]

[Total: 8]

Cambridge International AS & A Level Physics (9702) Paper 22, Q5a,c, March 2019

Exam practice 4

The following question has an example student response and commentary provided. Once you have worked through the question, read the student response and commentary. Compare your answer with the commentary and sample answer provided and identify how you could improve your answer. What information does this give about your understanding of this topic as a whole?

3 a A nucleus of caesium-137 ($^{137}_{55}Cs$) decays by emitting a β⁻ particle to produce a nucleus of an element X and an antineutrino. The decay is represented by:

$$^{137}_{55}Cs \rightarrow \, ^{Q}_{S}X + \, ^{P}_{R}\beta^- + \, ^{0}_{0}\bar{\nu}$$

   i State the number represented by each of the following letters. [2]

   P   Q   R   S

   ii State the name of the class (group) of particles that includes the β⁻ particle and the antineutrino. [1]

b A particle Y has a quark composition of ddd where d represents a down quark.

A particle Z has a quark composition of ūd where ū represents an up antiquark.

   i Show that the charges of particles Y and Z are equal. [2]

   ii State and explain which particle is a meson and which particle is a baryon. [2]

[Total: 7]

Cambridge International AS & A Level Physics (9702) Paper 22, Q7, June 2022

Example student response			Commentary
a	i	P = 0 Q = 137 R = −1 S = 56	The student has answered the question correctly. *This answer is awarded 2 out of 2 marks.*
	ii	neutrinos	The student got this wrong. The correct answer is leptons. *This answer is awarded 0 out of 1 mark.*
b	i	Charge of d = −1/3 so 3 × −1/3 = −1 Charge of u = +2/3 so ū = −2/3 Charge of ūd = −2/3 − 1/3 = −1	The whole answer is correct. *This answer is awarded 2 out of 2 marks.*
	ii	Meson: Z Baryon: Y	The student did not offer an explanation. There is a danger that the student could have scored zero for this part because they may have guessed the correct answer. Z is a meson because it is a quark–antiquark pair, and Y is a baryon because it is composed of three quarks (whose charge adds up to an integer value). *This answer is awarded 1 out of 2 marks.*

Now you have read the commentary to question **3**, here is a question on a similar topic that you should attempt. Use the information from the previous response and commentary to guide you as you answer.

4 **a** In the following list, underline all particles that are leptons.

　　antineutrino　　　positron　　　proton　　　quark　　　[1]

b A stationary nucleus of magnesium-27, $^{27}_{12}Mg$, decays by emitting a β⁻ particle and γ radiation.

An incomplete equation to represent this decay is:

$$^{27}_{12}Mg \rightarrow X + \beta^- + \gamma.$$

　i State the nucleon number and the proton number of nucleus X. [2]

　ii State the name of the interaction that gives rise to this decay. [1]

　iii State **two** possible reasons why the sum of the kinetic energy of the β⁻ particle and the energy of the γ radiation is less than the total energy released during the decay of the magnesium nucleus. [2]

[Total: 6]

Cambridge International AS & A Level Physics (9702) Paper 22, Q8, November 2018

Practical skills for AS Level

KNOWLEDGE FOCUS

In this chapter you will answer questions on:
- practical work in physics
- using apparatus and following instructions
- gathering evidence
- precision, accuracy, errors and uncertainties
- finding the value of an uncertainty
- percentage uncertainty
- recording results
- analysing results
- testing a relationship
- combining uncertainties
- identifying limitations in procedures and suggesting improvements.

EXAM SKILLS FOCUS

In this chapter you will:
- apply your knowledge of practical skills to varied and unfamiliar contexts.

Exam questions about practical work can often look difficult. But with practice, you will notice that they are structured in similar ways and require similar sets of skills – such as processing data and plotting graphs.

Practical skills questions may be based around experiments that you are familiar with, but they can also be about experiments you have not seen before. You need to apply your knowledge of practical skills even when you are not familiar with the theory behind the experiment.

P1.1 Practical work in physics

1. **a** Why do scientists conduct experiments?

   b When new evidence arises that disagrees with a model, what do scientists do?

> **« RECALL AND CONNECT 1 «**
>
> Think back to your science education before A Level. Can you explain what the three categories of variables are in the scientific model?

> **REFLECTION**
>
> How will you reinforce your skills in collecting and analysing data? You could try carrying out some simple experiments at home, such as *estimating the efficiency of a kettle* using some simple energy analysis or *calculating g by free fall* using video analysis. Can you think of any others?

P1.2 Using apparatus and following instructions

1. **a** How do you avoid parallax error when using an analogue scale, for example a ruler scale?

   b How do you use a micrometer screw gauge to measure to the nearest 0.01 mm?

P1.3 Gathering evidence

1. Look at the two sets of data in Figure P1.1.

   For each set of data, explain what improvements to the range of data the student should make to better identify their pattern or trend.

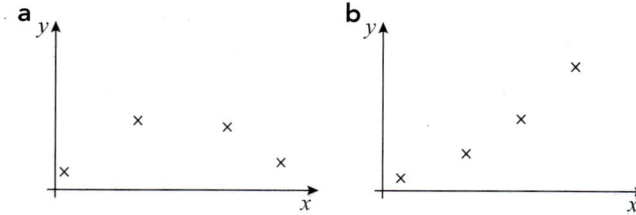

Figure P1.1

P1.4 Precision, accuracy, errors and uncertainties

1. Copy and complete this table indicating whether each statement discusses precision, accuracy or both.

Statement	Precision	Accuracy
Our final result has a 5% difference from the true value.		
Our repeats showed a very large spread around a mean.		
Our gradient was close to the value of the constant that we were measuring.		
The points showed very little scatter from the line of best fit.		
We used a measuring instrument with a resolution of 0.01, which was enough to see a difference between the results and the spread of repeats.		
We viewed the scale at right angles and with the object as close as possible to the scale.		

2. For each of these errors, decide whether the student is talking about a systematic, zero or random error.

Error	Random	Systematic	Zero
Our final value always comes out a little too high.			
It's hard to stop the timer exactly when the object passes the marker.			
Our readings show a large spread on either side of the mean value.			
When there is nothing on the balance, it reads 0.02 g.			

P1.5 Finding the value of an uncertainty

1 Give the uncertainty for each of these readings.

   a 4.3 V
   b 10.58 m
   c 0.92 mA

2 Calculate the mean value and uncertainties for these sets of readings.

   a 18.6, 19.2, 18.7, 18.9, 19.0 [1]
   b 2.13, 2.10, 2.09, 2.10, 2.11 [1]
   c 0.63, 0.65, 0.64, 0.66, 0.65 [1]

   [Total: 3]

> **UNDERSTAND THESE TERMS**
> - uncertainty
> - precision
> - precise
> - accuracy
> - accurate
> - systematic error
> - zero error
> - random errors

P1.6 Percentage uncertainty

1 Calculate the percentage uncertainties for these values:

   a 6.2 ± 0.4 A [1]   b 0.531 ± 0.002 s [1]   c 14.3 ± 0.1 mm [1]   [Total: 3]

P1.7 Recording results

1 What errors has this student made in their results table for this experiment?

Potential difference	Current
0.04	0.01
0.5	0.12
0.83	0.2
1.3	0.34
1.76	0.42
2.01	0.53
2.54	0.65

P1.8 Analysing results

1. A student is using a free fall method to measure gravitational acceleration.

   They know that $g = \dfrac{v^2}{2h}$.

   They drop a piece of dowel of known length through a piece of the curtain rail. It falls directly through a light gate. Figure P1.2 shows their experimental set-up.

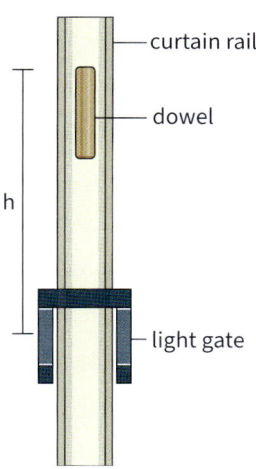

   Figure P1.2

   a Explain how the speed of the dowel can be determined as it falls through the light gate. [2]

   b The student varies the height from which the dowel is dropped. Their results are shown below.

   Process their results by completing the table, and plot a suitable graph. [7]

h / m	v / m s⁻¹		
0.10	1.43		
0.20	2.06		
0.30	2.42		
0.40	2.83		
0.50	3.11		
0.60	3.40		
0.70	3.72		
0.80	3.97		

   c Use your graph to determine the experimental value of gravitational acceleration. [2]

   [Total: 11]

> **« RECALL AND CONNECT 2 «**
>
> In maths IGCSE, you learned about the equations for straight-line graphs. What is the gradient and y-axis intercept for this line?
>
> $$y = 12x + 0.4$$

P1.9 Testing a relationship

1. A student uses a graphical method to verify Ohm's law.

   They use a simple series circuit with a fixed resistor and a variable power supply. They measure the current with an ammeter in series with the resistor and a voltmeter in parallel with the resistor.

   Figure P1.3 shows the graph of their results.

   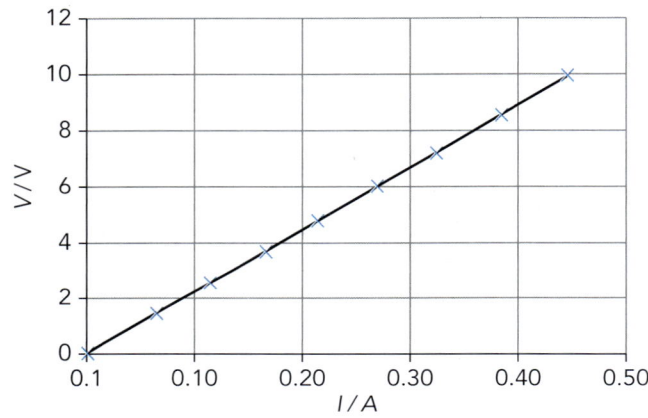

   Figure P1.3

   The manufacturer's stated value of the resistor is 22 Ω.

   a   Use the graph to calculate the resistance of the resistor. [2]

   b   Calculate a percentage difference between the student's result and the stated value of the resistance of the resistor. [1]

   c   The student uses the criterion that if the true value of the resistance falls within the expected uncertainty, then the results are consistent with Ohm's law.

   During the experiment, they notice that the readings on the voltmeter and ammeter fluctuate above and below an average reading.

The student uses this to estimate the uncertainty of each reading. They take one more reading above the range of potential differences used in the graph. The readings and uncertainties of the final reading are shown below:

$V = 11.24 \pm 0.06$

$I = 0.52 \pm 0.02$

Use the student's criterion to determine whether the results are consistent with this relationship. [4]

[Total: 7]

> **REFLECTION**
>
> How did you verify your conclusions in experiments that you have conducted at school? Have a look back at your experimental write-ups and compare percentage differences with percentage uncertainty, or check whether your calculated values fall within the bounds of the expected uncertainty.

P1.10 Combining uncertainties

1   Calculate the value and the combined uncertainty for each of these sets of data and relationships.

   a $F = ma$

   $m = 1.00 \pm 0.02$ kg

   $a = 7.43 \pm 0.05$ m s^{-2}

   b $E_k = \frac{1}{2}mv^2$

   $m = 0.0042 \pm 0.0001$ kg

   $v = 14.8 \pm 0.2$ m s^{-1}

   c $\rho = \frac{m}{V}$

   $V = x^3$

   $m = 0.32 \pm 0.05$ kg

   $x = 0.050 \pm 0.001$ m

P1.11 Identifying limitations in procedures and suggesting improvements

1   A student has used a set linear air track and slider, pair of light gates and a set of masses to verify Newton's second law.

Figure P1.4 shows a diagram of the apparatus that they used.

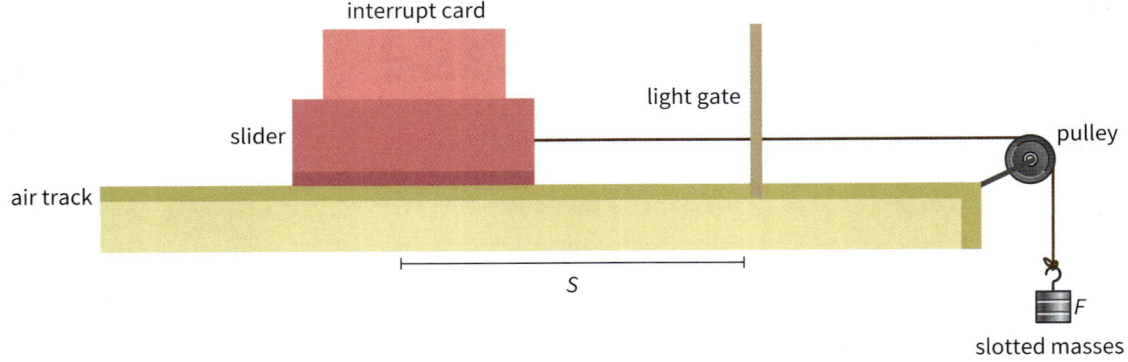

Figure P1.4

Here is a paragraph from the student's evaluation.

We used a range of masses on the mass hanger between 0.010 kg and 0.100 kg. We started from the highest mass and simply took them off for each experiment. We measured the final velocity once each time as we knew it was going to be very accurate.

The interrupt card was 5.0 cm long, which we measured with a millimetre ruler. The distance the slider travelled was 50.0 cm, although it was difficult to replace the slider exactly to the nearest millimetre in the same spot each time. We left a marker in the start position, so I think we certainly got it positioned right to the nearest 3 mm.

We input the length of the card, and the data logger calculated a speed for us each time to 5 decimal places! This is a very high resolution, but we were still surprised afterwards that our graph had a large amount of scatter from the line of best fit.

a   Suggest what the largest source of uncertainty will be. [1]
b   Justify your choice of the largest source of uncertainty given above. [2]
c   Suggest an improvement to the source of uncertainty that you identified above. [2]
d   Identify one source of systematic error in the student's experiment. Explain how they could improve this. [2]
e   Identify one source of random error in the student's experiment. Explain how they could improve this. [2]

[Total: 9]

> **UNDERSTAND THESE TERMS**
> - line of best fit
> - problem
> - improvement

Practical skills for AS Level

> **REFLECTION**
>
> Practical skills questions often require you to apply your practical skills knowledge to unfamiliar contexts. Were you able to successfully do this in the exam skills questions in this chapter? If not, make a note of why you dropped marks so you can avoid similar mistakes in the future.

SELF-ASSESSMENT CHECKLIST

Let's revisit the Knowledge focus and Exam skills focus for this chapter.

Decide how confident you are with each statement.

Now I can:	Show it	Needs more work	Almost there	Confident to move on
recognise random, systematic and zero errors	Categorise a range of causes of error as random, systematic and zero errors and learn appropriate responses to these errors for your answers.			
calculate uncertainties in measurements made with a range of instruments	Report results in practicals and questions with uncertainties calculated using either half a scale division or half the range of repeated measures.			
distinguish between precision and accuracy	Practise using the terms precision and accuracy in your answers.			
estimate absolute uncertainties and combine uncertainties when quantities are added, subtracted, multiplied and divided	Combine the uncertainties of calculated values by adding the percentage uncertainties and use these percentage uncertainties to calculate an absolute uncertainty for a calculated value.			
set up apparatus, follow instructions and make a variety of measurements	Look at pictures of apparatus to remind yourself what each one is for; revise the techniques suitable for measuring physical quantities in a range of experimental situations.			

CONTINUED

Now I can:	Show it	Needs more work	Almost there	Confident to move on
present data in an adequate table, produce best fit straight-line graphs and obtain the intercept and gradient	Practise recording, processing, and graphically analysing a range of different data types which arise in experiments and in questions.			
use readings to draw conclusions from an experiment and to test a relationship	Revise the equations of lines of best fits and how to apply these to experimental data.			
identify limitations in an experiment and identify the main sources of uncertainty	Write detailed evaluations for practical experiments, including identifying which improvements will have the greatest effect on the uncertainty of the final result.			
suggest changes to an experiment to improve accuracy and extend an investigation	Practise coming up with practical improvements which will result in an outcome being closer to a true value. Suggest further and related studies to experiments.			
apply my knowledge of practical skills to varied and unfamiliar contexts	Review questions in the practical skills chapters and list all the similarities in methods, apparatus and measurements.			

16 Circular motion

KNOWLEDGE FOCUS

In this chapter you will answer questions on:
- describing circular motion
- angles in radians
- steady speed, changing velocity
- angular speed
- centripetal forces
- calculating acceleration and force
- the origins of centripetal forces.

EXAM SKILLS FOCUS

In this chapter you will:
- show that you understand the 'state' command word and can answer 'state' questions.

'State' questions ask you to provide a fact or short answer to a question. For example, in this topic you may be asked to state the force acting on an object. The 'state' command word is often used for short answer questions. But you may need to refer back to an earlier part of the question that contains the answer already. This is different to a 'calculate' question, which will definitely require some steps of working to make sure you gain full credit for the answer. 'State' questions will usually only be worth one mark. It is important not to provide too much information or detail when you answer these questions. You are not expected to provide detailed explanations or descriptions for this command word. This command word is often combined with another word, such as 'explain' or 'suggest'. When you come across questions with two command words make sure you include answers to both command words in your answer.

State	express in clear terms

16.1 Describing circular motion and
16.2 Angles in radians

> **UNDERSTAND THIS TERM**
> - angular displacement

1 a A pizza company is looking at the position of a heater in their ovens and wondering why some of the toppings are not cooking evenly.

They decide to rotate the pizzas on a turntable that completes a rotation in 10 seconds.

   i What is the circumference of a 7 inch pizza in cm? (assume the pizza is circular and use 1 inch = 2.45 cm)
   ii What is the circumference of a 12 inch pizza?

   b i What is the angular displacement of the 7 inch pizza after 5 seconds?
   ii What is the angular displacement of the 12 inch pizza after 5 seconds?

> **« RECALL AND CONNECT 1 «**
>
> Think back to Chapter 1 and the ideas of vectors and scalars and the difference between distance and displacement. Can you state the difference between a scalar and a vector and make a table of examples of scalars and vectors?

2 a Look back at question 16.1.1b. Write your answers in radians.
   b How many rotations would the pizza have made if it had an angular displacement of
      i 2π radians
      ii 3π radians
      iii 10 radians

> **UNDERSTAND THIS TERM**
> - radian

> **REFLECTION**
>
> How will you remember that 360° = 2π radians? Try to use the definition of the radian and use $\frac{2\pi r}{r}$ as the arc length, because, for 360°, the arc length is the circumference.

16.3 Steady speed, changing velocity

1 Look back at question 16.1.1.

   Can you work out the speed of the 12 inch pizza as it rotates?

2   a   Explain how an object can be moving at a steady speed but still be
        accelerating. [3]
    b   State what provides the force in the following examples of circular motion.
        i   A ball on a string. [1]
        ii A satellite orbiting the Earth. [1]
        iii A car turning around a bend. [1]

[Total: 6]

> ≪ RECALL AND CONNECT 2 ≪
>
> In Chapter 13, you learnt about waves. Can you explain why there are areas
> of maximum and minimum intensity when two coherent waves meet?

16.4 Angular speed

UNDERSTAND THIS TERM
- angular speed

1   Calculate the angular speed of the:
    a   hour hand on a clock
    b   minute hand on a clock
    c   second hand on a clock.

2   Vinyl records are circular plastic discs on which music is recorded and can be
    played back. These discs are available in various diameters, including 17.8 cm
    and 25.4 cm.

    The records are played on a turntable, which rotates at a constant speed.
    a   A 25.4 cm diameter disc is played and takes 10 s to complete one rotation.
        i   Show that the angular speed of the disc is 0.63 rad s^{-1}. [1]
        ii Calculate the speed of a point at the outer edge of this disc. [2]
    b   A 17.8 cm diameter disc also takes 10 s to complete one rotation.
        Explain, without a calculation, how the speeds of a point
        on the outer edges of the two discs compare. [2]

[Total: 5]

3   The radius of the Earth is 6400 km.

    Assuming 1 year = 365.25 days, calculate:
    a   the angular speed, ω, of the Earth [2]
    b   the linear speed, v, of a point on the Earth's surface at the equator. [2]

[Total: 4]

16.5 Centripetal forces and
16.6 Calculating acceleration and force

> **UNDERSTAND THESE TERMS**
> - centripetal force
> - Newton's first law (of motion)

1. A ball is being swung around in a horizontal circle.

   a By considering the force that is keeping it in circular motion, describe what happens when the speed increases too much and when the string breaks.

   b Describe in which direction the ball goes.

2. The London Eye is an observation wheel that has a circumference of 434 m. Passengers can ride in a pod attached to the wheel. One complete tour takes 30 minutes to complete.

   Calculate the following:

   a the radius of the London Eye
   b the angular speed of a passenger at the end of one of the capsules.
   c the linear speed of the passenger
   d the centripetal acceleration of the passenger.

3. The rotation of the Earth could be fast enough for objects on the equator to become weightless.

   a Show that, by equating the weight of the object and the centripetal force due to the rotation, that $g = r\omega^2$ [2]

   b Calculate the period of rotation (in minutes) that would be required for this to happen? [3]

   [Total: 5]

> **UNDERSTAND THESE TERMS**
> - centripetal acceleration
> - Newton's second law (of motion)

REFLECTION

Did you notice that circular motion questions are usually based around the calculation of ω and how the linear speed, centripetal acceleration and centripetal force all depend on this key value? Can you see how this leads to objects rotating on a turntable will have similar angular speeds, but very different linear speeds depending on the position along the radial arm of each rotation?

16.7 The origins of centripetal force

1 A force diagram for a fairground ride is shown in Figure 16.1.

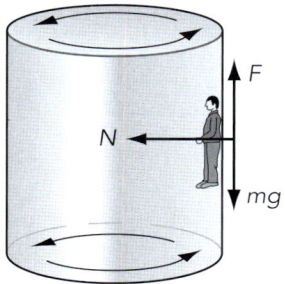

Figure 16.1

The radius of the ride is 5.2 m, the period of rotation is 2.5 seconds, and the mass of the person is 75 kg.

Calculate:

a   the frictional force, F [2]
b   the normal reaction force, N. [2]

[Total: 4]

2 A ball ($m = 0.2$ kg) is swung around a vertical circle.

The string is 0.5 m long. 20 rotations are timed to take 8.4 seconds.

a   State the force that is keeping the ball in a circle. [1]
b   Calculate the centripetal force for this rotation. [2]
c   Draw a free-body force diagram for the ball at:
   i   the top of the circle [1]
   ii the bottom of the circle. [1]
d   Calculate the maximum tension in the string. [3]

[Total: 8]

REFLECTION

Calculate questions will usually require you to show your workings. It is possible to score marks for workings, even if your final answer is wrong. Did you clearly set out your workings when answering the calculate questions in this chapter?

CAMBRIDGE INTERNATIONAL AS & A LEVEL PHYSICS: EXAM PREPARATION AND PRACTICE

SELF-ASSESSMENT CHECKLIST

Let's revisit the Knowledge focus and Exam skills focus for this chapter.

Decide how confident you are with each statement.

Now I can:	Show it	Needs more work	Almost there	Confident to move on
express angular displacement in radians	By using the equivalence of 360° = 2π radians, practise converting units from degreed to radians, and vice versa.			
solve problems using the concept of angular speed	Calculate angular speeds of objects in circular motion by considering the time period, T, and the circumference of the orbit, or by using 2π radians. This can be the hands of a clock or the International space station.			
describe motion along a circular path as due to a perpendicular force that causes a centripetal acceleration	Think about the idea that the speed can be constant but there is an acceleration leads to the idea that there must a force acting to change the velocity. The only possible explanation is a force acting perpendicularly to the velocity. You can identify the source of this force in different examples.			
show that I understand the 'state' command word and can answer 'state' questions	Write a 'state' question for this topic and an accompanying mark scheme.			

17 Gravitational fields

KNOWLEDGE FOCUS

In this chapter you will answer questions on:
- representing a gravitational field
- gravitational field strength, g
- energy in a gravitational field
- gravitational potential
- orbiting under gravity
- the orbital period
- orbiting the Earth.

EXAM SKILLS FOCUS

In this chapter you will:
- show that you understand the 'show (that)' command word and can answer 'show (that)' questions.

This chapter has a lot of 'show (that)' questions. When working through this type of question, make sure you show all steps of the calculation, as each step in a calculation will show you can successfully use the correct equation or formula to answer the question. If you do not think you have the correct answer after performing the calculations, do not panic. Go back through your working and try to find the incorrect step. If you still cannot find the error, leave your working, as you may gain marks for using the correct method or successfully using the correct equation.

| Show (that) | provide structured evidence that leads to a given result |

17.1 Representing a gravitational field

1   a   Calculate the force of gravitational attraction of:
        i   two protons in the nucleus that are 1 femtometre apart
        ii two students each of 60 kg sat 2 m apart in class
        iii the Earth ($m = 6.0 \times 10^{24}$ kg) on the Moon ($m = 7.4 \times 10^{22}$ kg); assume an orbit of 385 000 km.
    b   If the gravitational attraction on a girl of mass 55 kg is 539 N, show that the gravitational constant, G, is 6.7×10^{-11} N m² kg⁻².

2   Use Newton's law of gravitation formula to show that the base units for the gravitational constant, G, are kg⁻¹ m³ s⁻².

3   a   Define Newton's law of gravitation. [1]
    b   The gravitational force between two objects which are 4 m apart is 5 N. Calculate the force between them if the distance between them changed to:
        i   8 m [1]
        ii 0.04 m [1]
        iii infinity. [1]

[Total: 4]

> **UNDERSTAND THESE TERMS**
> - Newton's law of gravitation
> - gravitational field

17.2 Gravitational field strength, g

1   a   Calculate the gravitational field strength, g, at the Earth's surface.
        (mass of the Earth = 6×10^{24} kg, radius of the Earth = 6400 km)
    b   The units for 'g' can be given as N kg⁻¹ or m s⁻².
        By using base units, show that these are the equivalent unit.

2   a   A planet has half the mass of the Earth and a quarter of the radius.
        Show that the gravitational field strength on this planet is approximately 80 N kg⁻¹. [2]
    b   A different planet has double the radius of the Earth, and the density of the planet is half the density of the Earth.
        Calculate an approximate value for gravitational field strength on the surface of this planet. [2]

[Total: 4]

17 Gravitational fields

17.3 Energy in a gravitational field

1   a   By using the equations for work done and gravitational force (from 17.1) deduce a formula for gravitational potential energy E_p in terms of G, m_1, m_2 and r.
    b   i   Use the formula in part **a** to work out the E_p of an object of mass = 3 kg, lifted 10 m above the Earth's surface.
        ii Calculate the E_p of the object using $E_p = mgh$ ($g = 9.81$ m s^{-2}).
        iii Why are these values different?
        iv By considering the E_p on the Earth's surface, calculate the change in E_p using the formula in part **b i** (note: work to the 8 s.f.).

2   The escape velocity for a rocket can be calculated by equating the kinetic energy of a rocket to the E_p on the surface of a planet.
    a   Show that:
        $$v = \sqrt{\frac{2GM}{r}}$$
        where, M is the mass of the Earth, r is the radius, and v is the escape velocity. [2]
    b   Calculate the escape velocity for the SpaceX rocket Falcon 9 (mass = 550 000 kg) from the Earth. [2]

[Total: 4]

> **« RECALL AND CONNECT 1 «**
>
> In Chapter 5 you looked at the energy changes between E_p and E_k for a falling object.
>
> Calculate the speed of a 2 kg rock and a 4 kg rock hitting the ground from a height of 2 m. Ignore air resistance.

UNDERSTAND THIS TERM

- gravitational field strength

17.4 Gravitational potential

1   a   What are the base units for $\varnothing$?
    b   Find the gravitational potential of the 3 kg ball on the surface of the Earth.
    c   Find the change in gravitational potential if it is moved to 10 m off the surface.

> **« RECALL AND CONNECT 2 «**
>
> In Chapter 1 you looked at base units and how to show that both sides of an equation are homogeneous. Write down two different versions of an energy equation and show that both forms will come down to the base unit for the joule; kg m² s^{-2}.

149

> CAMBRIDGE INTERNATIONAL AS & A LEVEL PHYSICS: EXAM PREPARATION AND PRACTICE

> **REFLECTION**
>
> By now, you will have seen that the equations for gravitational potential and gravitational field strength only rely on the mass of the bigger body, such as the planet. In exam questions, there may be a distractor which is the mass of the object being asked about. How will you identify these distractors and make sure you make the correct calculations?

> **UNDERSTAND THIS TERM**
>
> - gravitational potential at a point

17.5 Orbiting under gravity and
17.6 The orbital period

1   The International Space Station (ISS) orbits the Earth approximately every 90 minutes at a distance of 400 km from the Earth's surface.

   a Show that the speed of the International Space Station is approximately 8000 m s^{-1}. [2]

   b Use the speed calculated in part **a** to find the mass of the Earth. [3]

   c When an astronaut is on a spacewalk, show that the speed of the astronaut is the same as the ISS. [2]

[Total: 7]

2   **a** Write down the formula for Newton's law of gravitation for two objects of respective masses m and M, at a distance of r apart.

   b Write down the formula for the centripetal force of an object of mass, m, moving in a circle of radius r.

   c By using the fact that the centripetal force for an object orbiting the Earth is equal to the force calculated in Newton's law of gravitation, show that:

$$T^2 = \left(\frac{4\pi^2}{GM}\right)r^3$$

3   **a** Use the formula $T^2 = \left(\frac{4\pi^2}{GM}\right)r^3$ to show that the orbital period for the ISS is approximately 90 minutes.

   b Calculate the orbital period for a space probe orbiting a planet at 400 km from the surface with a mass four times the mass of the Earth but with a radius of half of the Earth.

> **UNDERSTAND THIS TERM**
>
> - orbital period

17.7 Orbiting the Earth

1 The average distance from the Earth to the Sun is 1.5×10^8 km.

Find the distance from the Sun of:

    a Neptune (1 year on Neptune = 165 years on Earth)
    b Mars (1 year on Mars = 1.9 years on Earth)
    c Venus (1 year on Venus = 0.6 years on Earth)

2 **a** Use this equation $T^2 = \left(\dfrac{4\pi^2}{GM}\right)r^3$ to calculate the mass of the Sun.

       The average distance between the Sun and the Earth is 1.5×10^8 km. [2]

    b Show that both sides of the equation are homogeneous. [3]

                                                                                  [Total: 5]

3 Two of the moons of Saturn are Phoebe and Titan.

Assuming their orbits are circular, Phoebe has an orbital radius of 13 million km, and Titan has an orbital radius of 1.2 million km.

    a By considering the forces acting on the moons show that the masses of the moons are not necessary to calculate the angular speed of orbit. [2]

    b Calculate the ratio: $\dfrac{\text{orbital period of Phoebe}}{\text{orbital period of Titan}}$ [2]

                                                                                   [Total: 4]

4 A satellite is put into geostationary orbit at a distance of 36 000 km from the Earth's surface.

    a Write down two features of a geostationary orbit. [2]
    b Use this to show that the mass of the Earth is approximately 6×10^{24} kg. [4]
    c Calculate the change in the gravitational potential of the satellite if its mass is 2000 kg. [2]
    d Calculate the angular speed of the satellite. [2]

                                                                                   [Total: 10]

REFLECTION

There were a lot of 'show (that)' questions and 'calculate' questions in this chapter. Are you confident you know the difference between these two command words and what is expected from each?

SELF-ASSESSMENT CHECKLIST

Let's revisit the Knowledge focus and Exam skills focus for this chapter.

Decide how confident you are with each statement.

Now I can:	Show it	Needs more work	Almost there	Confident to move on
describe a gravitational field as a field of force and define gravitational field strength g	Write down a description of a gravitational field and define it as the region in space where a mass feels a gravitational force.			
represent a gravitational field using field lines	Practise drawing radial fields; show that it appears as parallel lines near the surface of a planet.			
understand the meaning of centre of mass and use the concept in problems involving uniform spheres	Practise using the volume of a sphere equation to solve problems involving the density of planets.			
recall and use Newton's law of gravitation	Write the equation $F = \dfrac{Gmm}{r^2}$ in words to describe the force as the product of the masses and the inverse square of the distance between them.			
solve problems involving the gravitational field strength of a uniform field and the field of a point mass	Practise using this formula: $g = \dfrac{Gm}{r^2}$ Try rearranging and substituting different values.			
understand how the gravitational potential energy, $E = -\dfrac{Gm_1 m_2}{r}$, of two point masses is a consequence of gravitational potential	Make flashcards with gravitational potential (and other difficult terminology from this chapter) and its definition. Include the formulae in symbols and written out in words.			
define and solve problems involving gravitational potential	Practise questions where you have to calculate gravitational potential for an object, given the mass of the planet and the distance from its centre.			

17 Gravitational fields

CONTINUED				
Now I can:	Show it	Needs more work	Almost there	Confident to move on
analyse circular orbits in an inverse square law field, including geostationary orbits	Use the circular motion equation for centripetal force $F = \dfrac{mv^2}{r}$ and equate this to Geostationary orbits are orbits that have a time period, T, equal to 1 day and the orbits are always over the same place on the equator.			
show that I understand the 'show (that)' command word and can answer 'show (that)' questions	Answer some 'show (that)' questions, swap your answers with a friend and feed back on each other's work.			

18 Oscillations

> **KNOWLEDGE FOCUS**
>
> In this chapter you will answer questions on:
> - free and forced oscillations
> - observing oscillations
> - describing oscillations
> - simple harmonic motion
> - representing s.h.m. graphically
> - frequency and angular frequency
> - equations of s.h.m.
> - energy changes in s.h.m.
> - damped oscillations
> - resonance.

> **EXAM SKILLS FOCUS**
>
> In this chapter you will:
> - show that you understand the 'sketch' command word and can answer 'sketch' questions.

It is important to revisit command words in different topics so that you gain practice answering questions across many different topics in physics and to understand what depth of answer is required. In this chapter, you will find lots of questions that require you to sketch graphs. In the oscillations topic, sketch graphs usually include a wave, such as *displacement* against *time*. The important thing is to get the shape correct – remember that sketches should be simple and not too detailed.

| Sketch | make a simple freehand drawing showing the key features |

18 Oscillations

18.1 Free and forced oscillations

1 Write down why these are examples of *free* oscillations.

    a A child on a swing is pulled back from the equilibrium position and then released.

    b The vibration of a drum skin after it has been hit.

2 Write down why these are examples of *forced* oscillations.

    a A piston connects a cylinder in a car engine to a drive shaft.

    b A loudspeaker cone produces a sound of frequency 2 kHz.

3 State the requirement for a simple harmonic oscillator to oscillate at its natural frequency. **[Total: 1]**

REFLECTION

Think about oscillations that you come across in your day-to-day life. Do you feel confident you could categorise them into free or forced oscillations? What could you do to increase your confidence?

UNDERSTAND THESE TERMS

- oscillation
- frequency

18.2 Observing oscillations

1 How could you accurately measure the time period of these simple harmonic oscillations?

    a A swing in a play park.

    b A ruler vibrating freely from the edge of a desk.

    c A 20 cm long pendulum.

2 A student notices an object floating in the waves as they approach a beach. The object appears to bob up and down in the water.

    a Suggest how the student could check whether this motion has a constant frequency. **[2]**

    b The student notices that the amplitude of the oscillation does change with each subsequent wave.

        Explain why this does not necessarily stop the oscillation from being simple harmonic motion. **[1]**

        [Total: 3]

18.3 Describing oscillations

UNDERSTAND THESE TERMS
- displacement
- amplitude
- period

1 Use the displacement–time graph for an oscillator (Figure 18.1) to answer the following questions

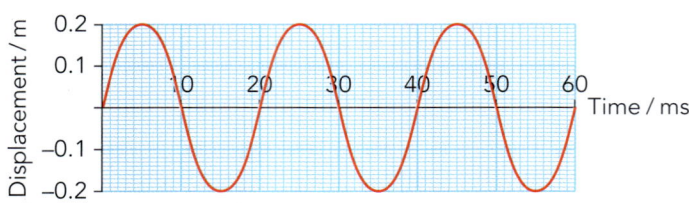

Figure 18.1

   a   What is the amplitude of the oscillation?
   b   What is the time period of the oscillation?
   c   What is the displacement at time 32 ms?

2 What is the phase difference between the two oscillations at the same frequency in Figure 18.2?

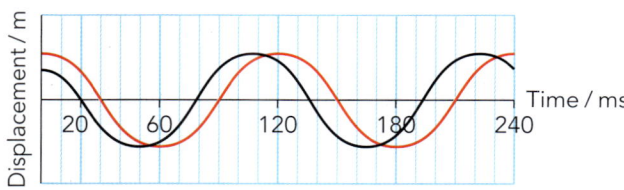

Figure 18.2

3 Two identical twin children decide to have a race on the swings.

   One child starts with the swing as far forward as possible, and the other child starts with the swing as far back as possible.

   The winner will be the child that catches up with the other child.

   a   Define the term phase difference and give a possible unit of phase difference. [2]
   b   Figure 18.3 shows the displacement against time graphs for the two swings.
       Give the phase difference between the two oscillators. [1]

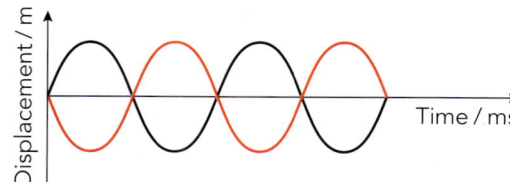

Figure 18.3

c Explain why neither child can win the 'race' if they do not have an external force pushing them on the swing. [2]

d Later, the two children have another 'race' but start at different positions. At one time, they swing with a constant maximum displacement of 3 m from the equilibrium position.

Sketch a displacement–time graph for two oscillators with a phase difference of 30°. [2]

e During this movement, the two children notice that they cross at the same position on each swing.

Calculate the displacement at which they cross. [3]

[Total: 10]

> **UNDERSTAND THESE TERMS**
> - phase
> - phase difference

18.4 Simple harmonic motion

> **‹‹ RECALL AND CONNECT 1 ‹‹**
>
> What does 'directly proportional' mean? Sketch a graph to illustrate your answer.

1 a What is the defining relationship for s.h.m.?

b Sketch a graph of acceleration against displacement for a simple harmonic oscillator.

2 A windscreen wiper is a rubber blade that moves across a vehicle window to remove raindrops.

The windscreen wiper of a particular car moves across the window at constant speed in one direction and then returns to its original position at the same constant speed.

a Explain why the windscreen wiper is **not** moving with simple harmonic motion. [2]

b An electric motor can be used to create a wiper motion which is a simple harmonic motion.

In this case, the rotational motion of the motor is translated into two reciprocating motion, which is attached to the wiper blades. State the position at which the wiper would have:

  i highest speed [1]
  ii highest acceleration. [1]

c Suggest reasons why this would not be an appropriate design for a windscreen wiper. [2]

[Total: 6]

> CAMBRIDGE INTERNATIONAL AS & A LEVEL PHYSICS: EXAM PREPARATION AND PRACTICE

> **REFLECTION**
>
> How confident are you that you can derive the s.h.m. graphs and equations from the definition of s.h.m.? How will you make sure you remember them?

> **UNDERSTAND THIS TERM**
>
> - simple harmonic motion (s.h.m.)

18.5 Representing s.h.m. graphically

> **« RECALL AND CONNECT 2 «**
>
> How do the velocities of an object relate to the shape of a displacement–time graph?
>
> How do the accelerations relate to the shape of a velocity–time graph?

1   For the same simple harmonic oscillator with a time period of 40 ms. Draw two full cycles for each.

    a Sketch a displacement against time graph.
    b Sketch a velocity against time graph.
    c Sketch an acceleration against time graph.

2   Figure 18.4 shows a displacement–time graph for a simple harmonic oscillator of mass 15 g.

    a Sketch an acceleration–time graph for the same oscillator. You do not need to calculate an acceleration or add a scale to the vertical axis. [1]
    b Use the displacement–time graph to show that the highest speed of the oscillator is 0.31 m s^{-1}. [3]
    c Calculate the total energy in the system. [2]

                                                                                                            [Total: 6]

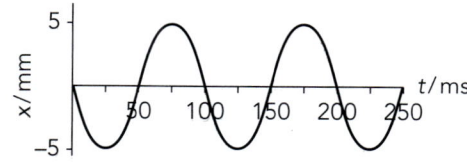

Figure 18.4

18.6 Frequency and angular frequency

1   Copy this table and write in the correct values for cells **a–g**.
    Give all your answers to two significant figures.

Time period / s	Frequency / Hz	Angular frequency / rad s^{-1}
0.35	a	b
c	24	d
e	f	240
1.4×10^{-15}	7.4×10^{14}	g

2   Work out the angular frequency of these oscillations:
    a   A long pendulum which, when released from one side of the room, takes 0.72 s to first reach its equilibrium position.
    b   A steam piston produces 25 full oscillations per minute.

3   A simple pendulum has a length of 40 cm. A student uses an ultrasound position sensor to record the position of the pendulum over four full oscillations. Figure 18.5 shows the displacement–time graph for the pendulum.

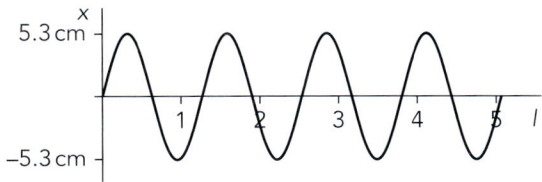

Figure 18.5

a   Use the graph to determine the time period of the pendulum. [2]
b   Show that the angular frequency of the pendulum is 5.0 rad s^{-1}. [2]
c   Calculate the maximum velocity of the pendulum. [2]

[Total: 6]

UNDERSTAND THIS TERM

- angular frequency

18.7 Equations of s.h.m.

1   $a \propto -x$ is the definition of s.h.m. How does the acceleration – displacement graph for a simple harmonic oscillator in Figure 18.6 show this?

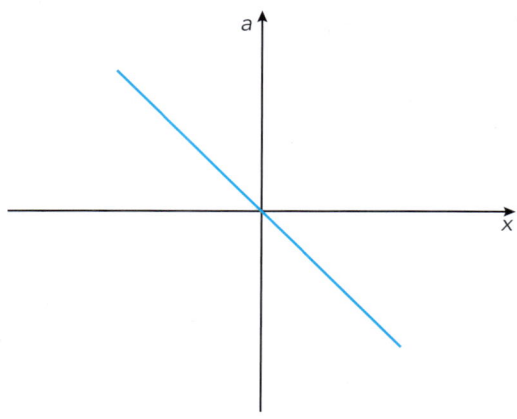

Figure 18.6

2   a   What is the equation relating displacement to time for an oscillator in s.h.m.?
    b   What is the equation relating velocity to displacement for an oscillator in s.h.m.?
    c   What is the equation relating maximum speed to maximum displacement for an oscillator in s.h.m.?

3   The vibrations of the particles in a solid can be modelled as simple harmonic motion. The particles in a particular solid vibrate with a frequency of 10 THz at a certain temperature. The amplitude of the oscillations of the particles is 10 pm.

   a   Calculate the maximum speed of the particles. [2]
   b   Calculate the maximum acceleration of the particles. [2]

   [Total: 4]

18.8 Energy changes in s.h.m.

1   a   Sketch a graph of kinetic energy, potential energy and total energy against displacement for a simple harmonic oscillator.
    b   Sketch a graph of kinetic energy, potential energy and total energy against time for a simple harmonic oscillator.
    c   What is the equation linking total energy in the system to mass, angular frequency and amplitude?

2   A student sets up a linear air track with a slider attached to either end by springs.

They use video analysis to track the position of the slider for the three full oscillations. Figure 18.7 shows a graph of their results.

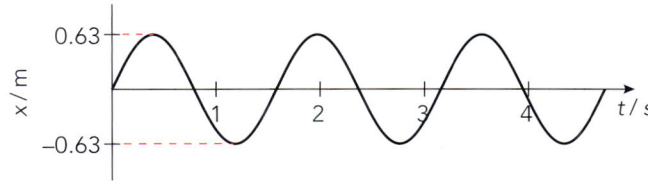

Figure 18.7

The slider has a mass of 400 g.

a   Show that the total energy of this oscillator is equal to 1.3 J. [4]
b   Show that the velocity of the oscillator at time $t = 1$ s is equal to -1.7 m s^{-1}. [3]
c   Calculate the potential energy at time $t = 1$. [2]
d   Explain why the amplitude of the oscillation is unchanged throughout the first three oscillations. [2]

[Total: 11]

REFLECTION

There are 11 marks for the exam skills question in this section, spread across three different command words. The most common command words in physics, are 'describe', 'explain', and 'calculate'. But it is important that you are able to answer all of the command words well. As you revise, how will you keep track of your abilities to answer all of the command words that come up? What will you do next to practise and improve your answers to the ones you find more difficult?

18.9 Damped oscillations

1   a   Write definitions for three types of damping.
    b   On the same axes, sketch a characteristic graph for each type of damping.

2   A student builds a model building. When knocked, the model moves freely in simple harmonic motion.

The student measures the displacement against time for their building using video tracking software. They notice that the peak amplitude decreases with each oscillation.

They then add a damping mechanism to their model. They record displacement against time again.

UNDERSTAND THESE TERMS

- light damping
- heavy damping

This table shows the results for the highest displacement in each subsequent oscillation for the building with and without the damping mechanism.

Oscillation number	Maximum displacement / cm	
	Without damping mechanism	With damping mechanism
0	6.0	5.0
1	4.0	2.7
2	2.7	1.6
3	1.9	1.0
4	1.3	0.5
5	0.8	0.3
6	0.5	0.2

a Add their results to a pair of axes, as shown in Figure 18.8. Draw lines of best fit for the two sets of results.. [4]

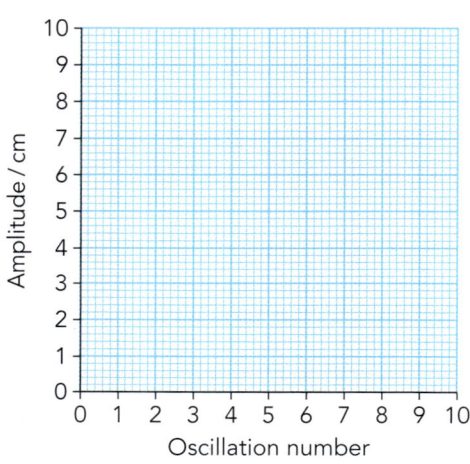

Figure 18.8

b Explain what is meant by the term damping. [2]

c The student has used a mass on a spring as a damping mechanism.

Suggest an alternative simple harmonic oscillator that could be used as a damping mechanism. [1]

d Describe the trend shown in the results above and use the data to compare the motion of the building with and without the damping mechanism. [3]

[Total: 10]

18.10 Resonance

1. Write two sentences to describe resonance.

2. A group of students conduct an experiment with a mass–spring system attached to a signal generator. They vary the frequency and measure the amplitude of the oscillations. They plot a graph of driving frequency against amplitude.

   They expect to observe resonance.

   Figure 18.9 shows the graph of their results.

   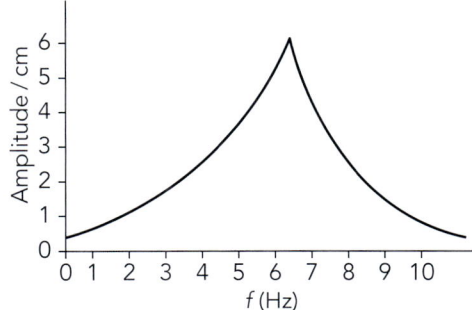

   Figure 18.9

   a Explain what is meant by the term resonance. [2]
   b Determine the natural frequency of the mass–spring system. [1]
   c Determine whether the graph shows resonance. [2]
   d The students then add more mass to their oscillator.
      Predict the shape of the graph that they would expect to see if they repeated their method with this new oscillator. [2]

   [Total: 7]

> **UNDERSTAND THESE TERMS**
> - resonance
> - critical damping

> **REFLECTION**
>
> How neatly did you sketch the graphs when working through questions in this chapter? How will you ensure you can sketch graphs neatly **and** quickly in an exam?

SELF-ASSESSMENT CHECKLIST

Let's revisit the Knowledge focus and Exam skills focus for this chapter.

Decide how confident you are with each statement.

Now I can:	Show it	Needs more work	Almost there	Confident to move on
give examples of free and forced oscillations	Sort a list of oscillations into examples of free and forced oscillations.			
use appropriate terminology to describe oscillations	Use the terms amplitude, period and phase in describing the motion of a simple harmonic oscillator, for example a pendulum.			
use the equation $a = -\omega^2 x$ to define simple harmonic motion (s.h.m.)	With reference to the equation $a = -\omega^2 x$ explain why the motion of a pendulum can be defined as s.h.m.			
recall and use equations for displacement and velocity in s.h.m.	Practise calculating velocities and displacements at given times using the equations for s.h.m. of a given frequency or time period.			
draw and use graphical representations of s.h.m.	Sketch a graph of displacement, velocity and acceleration against time for the same simple harmonic oscillator during the same period of time.			
describe energy changes during s.h.m.	Identify positions of maximum potential energy and maximum kinetic energy for a range of simple harmonic oscillators.			
recall and use $E = \frac{1}{2}m\omega^2 x_0$ where E is the total energy of a system undergoing simple harmonic motion	Calculate the total energy of a simple harmonic oscillator if given its mass, angular frequency and maximum displacement.			

CONTINUED

Now I can:	Show it	Needs more work	Almost there	Confident to move on
describe the effects of damping on oscillations and draw graphs showing these effects	Sketch graphs to illustrate under damping, critical damping and over damping.			
understand that resonance involves a maximum amplitude of oscillation	Identify resonance when given graphical examples of amplitude against frequency or when given descriptions of situations with rapid increases of amplitude towards a maximum.			
understand that resonance occurs when an oscillating system is forced to oscillate at its natural frequency	Explain what causes resonance and give examples of resonance.			
show that I understand the 'sketch' command word and can answer 'sketch' questions	Write a list of the things you need to include on a sketch graph.			

19 Thermal physics

KNOWLEDGE FOCUS

In this chapter you will answer questions on:
- changes of state
- energy changes
- internal energy
- the meaning of temperature
- calculating energy changes.

EXAM SKILLS FOCUS

In this chapter you will:
- show that you understand the 'describe' command word and can answer 'describe' questions.

In this chapter, there are lots of questions where you are asked to describe something. In physics, the word 'describe' has a specific meaning: you will need to give the main features of a process or concept in your answer.

| Describe | state the points of a topic / give characteristics and main features |

You are often asked to describe experiments in an examination. Start by writing down the relevant equation, or try to visualise doing the experiment. State what you want to measure and with what instrument (for example, 'you need to measure the current using an ammeter'). It is good practice to plot a graph and often you will need to use the gradient of that graph in calculations.

19 Thermal physics

19.1 Changes of state

1   Copy and complete Table 19.1 to summarise the arrangement of the molecules in solids, liquids and gases.

	Separation of particles	Arrangement of particles	Motion of particles
solid			
liquid			
gas			

Table 19.1

19.2 Energy changes

1   a   Sketch the cooling curve for a substance that goes through all the changes of state from gas to solid. Label the sketch with the states of matter as well as the melting and boiling points.

    b   What is taking place in the horizontal sections?

    c   What is taking place in the sloping sections?

> **UNDERSTAND THIS TERM**
> - evaporation

« RECALL AND CONNECT 1 «

Recall, from your earlier physics studies, the definition of internal energy and how it differs from thermal energy or heat.

19.3 Internal energy

1   Using the idea of gas trapped in a syringe, outline why the work done on or by a gas is: pressure × change in volume.

> **UNDERSTAND THESE TERMS**
> - internal energy
> - isothermal change

REFLECTION

How will you remember the sign convention for the first law of thermodynamics?

19.4 The meaning of temperature and 19.5 Thermometers

1   a   Why is the thermodynamic temperature scale so important?
    b   A temperature scale requires two fixed points. What are they for the thermodynamic temperature scale (Kelvin scale)?
    c   What features do all thermometers share?

> **« RECALL AND CONNECT 2 «**
>
> Recall, from your previous physics studies, the principle of conservation of energy and relate it the first law of thermodynamics.

UNDERSTAND THESE TERMS
- thermal energy
- thermal equilibrium
- thermodynamic scale
- absolute zero

UNDERSTAND THIS TERM
- thermocouple

19.6 Calculating energy changes

1   Some substances have been heated so that their temperature rises from a 'cold' value to a 'hot' value.

Use the information in Table 19.2 to calculate the missing values, **A–E**.

Some of the substances are fictional.

Substance	Mass	Specific heat capacity / $J\ kg^{-1}\ K^{-1}$	T_{cold} / °C	T_{hot} / °C	Thermal energy
adamantium	12 mg	13 500	13 300	27 500	A
aluminium	2.3 kg	880	1000	B	3.04 MJ
carbonite	23 mg	43	C	16 500	0.989 J
copper	10.3 g	D	1339	1885	2137.04 J
ice	E	2100	−200	−135	58.70 kJ

Table 19.2

2   Figure 19.1 shows the heating curve for a mystery substance X.

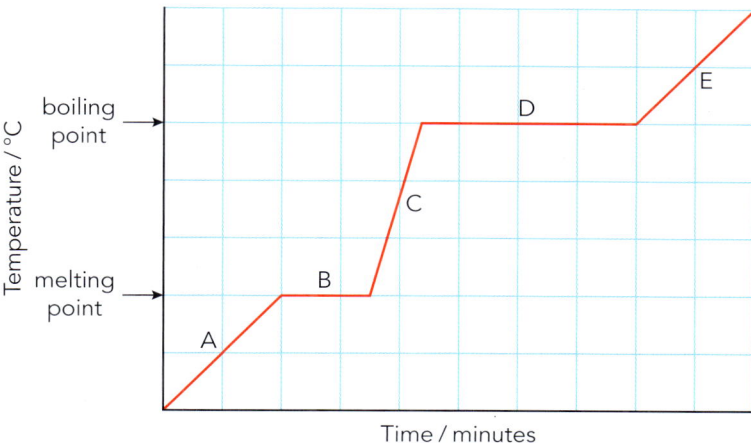

Figure 19.1

Each section of the curve is labelled with a different letter, A to E.
Another mystery substance labelled Y is tested.

   a   Compared with substance X, substance Y has a smaller specific latent heat of fusion but a bigger latent heat of vaporisation.
       Use letters to identify which sections will change and say in what way each will change.
   b   Compared with substance X, substance Y has a smaller specific heat capacity when in its solid state and a bigger specific heat capacity when in its liquid state.
       Use letters to identify which sections will change and say in what way each will change.

3 a   Describe an experiment to determine the specific capacity c of a metal block.   [6]
   b   State **one** assumption.   [1]
   c   Suggest **one** precaution that could reduce experimental error.   [1]

   [Total: 8]

4   The following data were recorded in order to find the specific heat capacity of a liquid.
    The 14.8 g of liquid was heated using a heating element.
    The temperature of the liquid increased from 17.6 K to 73.2 K in half an hour.
    The current through the element was 18.82 A, and the voltage across it was 2.93 V.
    a   Calculate the specific heat capacity of the liquid.   [3]
    b   List any assumptions that were made.   [2]

   [Total: 5]

5   a   Describe an experiment to determine the specific latent heat
        of vaporisation L of a liquid. [5]
    b   State **one** precaution you should take to reduce experimental error. [1]
    c   Describe how to modify the arrangement to determine the specific
        latent heat of fusion of ice. [2]
    d   Suggest why the value for the specific latent heat of vaporisation
        is likely to be too high, and the value for the specific latent heat
        of fusion is likely to be too low. [2]

    [Total: 10]

6   An unknown substance has been sent to a laboratory for analysis.

    As part of the investigation, a solid 0.2 kg sample was heated for 100 minutes,
    and its temperature was recorded as it changed state.

    The resulting heating curve is shown in Figure 19.2.

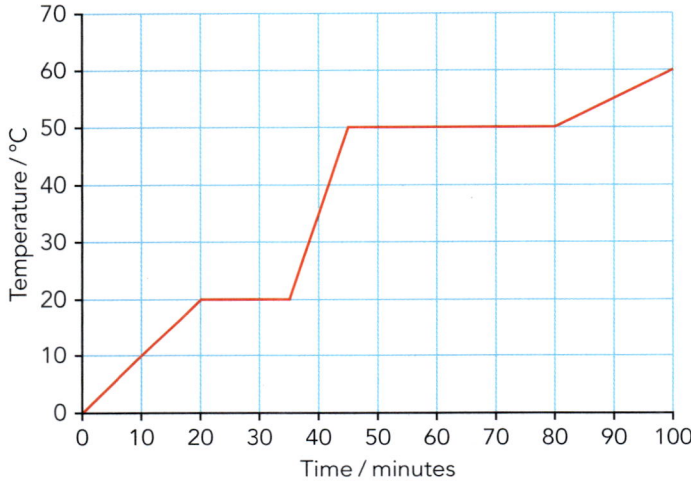

Figure 19.2

A current of 1.2 A was passed into the electrical heater, and there was
a voltage of 12 V across it.

a   Show that the power output of the electrical heater was 14.4 W. [1]
b   State the melting point of the substance. [1]
c   State the boiling point of the substance. [1]
d   Show that the specific heat capacity of the substance in its solid state
    is approximately 4300 J kg^{-1} °C^{-1}. [3]
e   Show that its specific latent heat of fusion is 64.8 kJ kg^{-1}. [3]
f   Calculate the specific heat capacity of the substance when it is in its
    liquid state. [2]
g   Calculate the specific latent heat of vaporisation of the substance. [2]
h   Calculate the specific heat capacity of the substance in its gaseous state. [2]

[Total: 15]

UNDERSTAND THESE TERMS

- specific heat capacity
- specific latent heat of fusion
- specific latent heat of vaporisation

19 Thermal physics

REFLECTION

How will you remember how to describe an experiment? What will you write down first? What do you need to look out for? Perhaps you could work with a classmate to analyse each other's experiment descriptions. How can they improve? How do they suggest you could improve?

SELF-ASSESSMENT CHECKLIST

Let's revisit the Knowledge focus and Exam skills focus for this chapter.

Decide how confident you are with each statement.

Now I can:	Show it	Needs more work	Almost there	Confident to move on
relate a rise in temperature of an object to internal energy, the sum of the random distribution of kinetic and potential energies of the molecules in a system	Try and relate theory to real life. When family or friends make a cup of coffee, explain to them what is happening to the internal energy of the water.			
recall and use the first law of thermodynamics	Relate it to the principle of conservation of energy. Write it on a flash card so that it is recalled frequently, paying particular attention to the sign of each term.			
calculate the work done when the volume of a gas changes at constant pressure	Get a syringe (with the needle removed) or visualise what is happening when you move the piston and relate this to the equation.			
measure temperature using a physical property and state examples of such properties	Commit some examples to a flash card. Research other examples.			

CONTINUED

Now I can:	Show it	Needs more work	Almost there	Confident to move on
use the thermodynamic scale of temperature, and understand that the lowest possible temperature is zero kelvin and that this is known as absolute zero	Regularly practise converting between the Celsius and Kelvin temperature scales for some well-known temperatures like the freezing and boiling point of water. Convert temperatures on weather forecasts to kelvin.			
relate transfer of (thermal) energy as being due to a difference in temperature and understand thermal equilibrium	Think of everyday examples of heat transfer and our efforts to slow it down using insulation.			
define and use specific heat capacity and specific latent heat, and outline how these quantities can be measured.	Commit this information to a flashcard and cycle through it frequently so that it is committed to long-term memory. Interpret heating and cooling curves in terms of these concepts.			
show that I understand the 'describe' command word and can answer 'describe' questions	Write down a definition of the 'describe' command word.			

Exam practice 5

This section contains past paper questions from previous Cambridge exams, which draws together your knowledge on a range of topics that you have covered up to this point. These questions give you the opportunity to test your knowledge and understanding. Additional past paper practice questions can be found in the accompanying digital material.

The following question has an example student response and commentary provided. Once you have worked through the question, read the student response and commentary. Are your answers different to the sample responses?

1   a   State what is meant by *centripetal* acceleration. [1]

   b   An unpowered toy car moves freely along a smooth track that is initially horizontal. The track contains a vertical circular loop around which the car travels, as shown in Fig. 1.1.

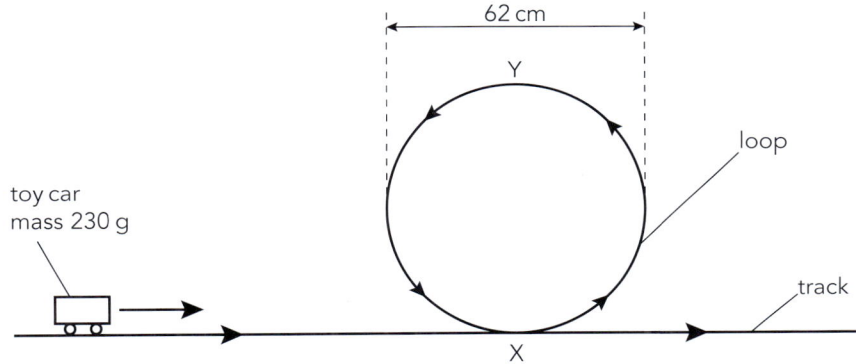

Fig. 1.1

The mass of the car is 230 g and the diameter of the loop is 62 cm. Assume that the resistive forces acting on the car are negligible.

   i   State what happens to the magnitude of the centripetal acceleration of the car as it moves around the loop from X to Y. [1]

   ii Explain, if the car remains in contact with the track, why the centripetal acceleration of the car at point Y must be greater than 9.8 m s^{-2}. [2]

   c   The initial speed at which the car in **b** moves along the track is 3.8 m s^{-1}. Determine whether the car is in contact with the track at point Y. Show your working. [3]

   d   Suggest, with a reason but without calculation, whether your conclusion in **c** would be different for a car of mass 460 g moving with the same initial speed. [1]

[Total: 8]

Cambridge International AS & A Level Physics (9702) Paper 42, Q1, November 2021

Example student response	Commentary
a Acceleration in a circle	The student needs to refer to the fact that the acceleration is perpendicular to the velocity for centripetal acceleration to occur. *This answer is awarded 0 out of 1 mark.*
b i decreases	The student answer is correct. *This answer is awarded 1 out of 1 mark.*
ii The centripetal force must be greater than the weight otherwise the car will fall off.	This is correct, but the second marking point is missing; there needs to be a reference to the contact force from the track. *This answer is awarded 1 out of 2 marks.*
c E_k at bottom = E_p at top + E_k at top E_k at top = E_k at bottom − E_p at top $\frac{1}{2}mv^2 = \frac{1}{2}mv^2 - mgh$ $= 0.5 \times 0.23 \times 3.8^2 - 0.23 \times 9.81 \times 0.62$ $= 0.26$ Therefore $v = 1.5$ m s^{-1} So it is not in contact.	The student gets a mark for the first line of the working, $\frac{1}{2}mv^2 = \frac{1}{2}mv^2 - mgh$. The rest does not gain credit even though the velocity is correct at the top. The remaining 2 marks were for applying $a = \frac{v^2}{r}$, and solving to find that a is less than 9.8 m s^{-2} *This answer is awarded 1 out of 3 marks.*
d As $F = ma = \frac{mv^2}{r}$ the mass is only relevant for the force not the acceleration.	The answer is correct but the use of the phrase 'independent of mass' would be better. *This answer is awarded 1 out of 1 mark.*

2   Now you have read the sample answer and commentary, write a question, and mark scheme, which asks students to apply the same understanding and skills as question **1**.

The following question has an example student commentary and answer provided. Work through the question first, then compare your answer with the sample answer and commentary. Are your answers different to the sample responses? What information does this give you about your understanding of this topic?

3   A fixed mass of an ideal gas has a volume V and a pressure p.

The gas undergoes a cycle of changes, X to Y to Z to X, as shown in Fig. 3.1.

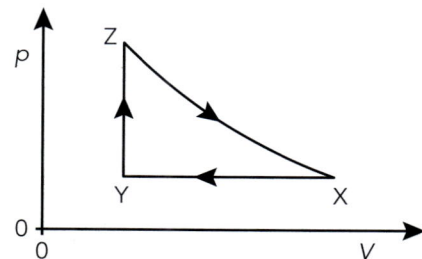

Fig. 3.1

Table 3.1 shows data for p, V and temperature T for the gas at points X, Y and Z.

	p / 10^5 Pa	V / 10^{-3} m^3	T / K
X	1.5	4.2	540
Y			230
Z	5.1		782

Table 3.1

a State the change in internal energy ΔU for one complete cycle, XYZX. [1]

b Calculate the amount n of gas. [2]

c Complete Table 3.1. [2]

d i The first law of thermodynamics for a system may be represented by the equation:

$$\Delta U = q + W.$$

State, with reference to the system, what is meant by:

ΔU:

q:

W: [3]

ii Explain how the first law of thermodynamics applies to the change Z to X. [2]

[Total: 10]

Cambridge International AS & A Level Physics (9702) Paper 42, Q2, March 2022

Example student response	Commentary
2 a 0	The student answer is correct. The system returns to its starting point. *This answer is awarded 1 out of 1 mark.*
b $pV = nRT$ Rearranged in terms of n: $n = \dfrac{pV}{RT}$ $n = \dfrac{1.5 \times 10^5 \times 4.2 \times 10^{-3}}{8.31 \times 540}$ $n = 0.14$	The students gets one mark for identifying the correct equation and rearranging it. And gets a second mark for the correct substitution and calculating the correct value. *This answer is awarded 2 out of 2 marks.*

Example student response	Commentary
c 		p / 10^5 Pa	V / 10^{-3} m³	T / K
---	---	---	---
X	1.5	4.2	540
Y	**1.5**	**1.8**	230
Z	5.1	1.8	782 | At Y, $p = 1.5 \times 10^5$ Pa $V = \dfrac{nRT}{P}$ $= \dfrac{0.14 \times 8.31 \times 230}{1.5 \times 10^5}$ $= 1.78 \times 10^{-3} \times$ m³ At Z, $V = 1.78 \times 10^{-3}$ m³	The students gets one mark for correctly working out the volume at Y. And gets a second mark for reading off the other values (e.g. pressure at Y and for a volume at Z = the volume at Y). *This answer is awarded 2 out of 2 marks.*

d i ΔU: change in internal energy
 	
       Q: thermal energy (heat)
 	
       W: work done
	The student needs to be more precise here and include more detail.
	
	For example, is the internal energy increasing? For ΔU to increase, is the thermal energy being applied to the system? Is the work being done on the system?
	
	It might be helpful for the student to state the conditions for the terms to be positive or negative.
	
	This answer is awarded 1 out of 3 marks.

ii The gas is expanding so it is doing work on its surroundings. The product $p\Delta V$ falls from 908 J to 630 J as the system moves from Z to X.	'The gas is expanding so it is doing work on its surroundings' gains one mark. The second mark is for recognising that this is an ideal gas and therefore the internal energy depends only on its kinetic energy. *This answer is awarded 1 out of 2 marks.*

4   Now write improved answers to any parts of question **3** where you did not score well. Use the commentary to guide you as you answer.

The following answer has an example student response and commentary provided. Once you have worked through the questions, read the student response and commentary and compare your answers. Are your answers different from the sample responses? If so, how are they different?

5 By reference to the first law of thermodynamics, state and explain the change, if any, in the internal energy of:

   a   a lump of solid lead as it melts at constant temperature [3]

   b   some gas in a toy balloon when the balloon bursts and no thermal energy enters or leaves the gas. [3]

   [Total: 6]

Cambridge International AS & A Level Physics (9702) Paper 42, Q3, June 2020

	Example student response	Commentary
a	The internal energy is the sum of the total kinetic and total potential energy of all the particles in a substance. Internal energy increases because of an increase in potential energy. This is because the interatomic forces between the particles are weakened as the substance melts. The temperature has not increased as the kinetic energy of the particles has not increased.	The student might have gained one mark for reasoning that the internal energy increased. However, the other marks could not be awarded because the student did not answer the question in terms of the first law of thermodynamics as required in the question. *This answer is awarded 1 out of 3 marks.*
b	According to the first law of thermodynamics, an increase in the internal energy of a system is the sum of the thermal energy supplied to it and the work done on the system. Work is done on the system when the gas expands and the balloon shrinks. Therefore, the internal energy decreases.	The student might have scored one mark for recognising that the internal energy would have decreased if work had been done on the gas. However, they confused the fabric of the balloon with what was happening to the gas inside. *This answer is awarded 1 out of 3 marks.*

6 Now write improved answers to any parts of question **5** where you did not score well. Use the commentary to guide you as you answer.

20 Ideal gases

KNOWLEDGE FOCUS

In this chapter you will answer questions on:
- particles of a gas
- explaining pressure
- measuring gases
- Boyle's law
- changing temperature
- ideal gas equation
- modelling gases: the kinetic model
- temperature and molecular kinetic energy.

EXAM SKILLS FOCUS

In this chapter you will:
- show that you understand the 'comment' command word and can answer 'comment' questions.

If you are asked to 'comment', you need to perform a calculation or comparison and then provide a written statement – usually one or two short sentences.
The final mark of any 'comment' question will always be for that written statement. You may need to use your own knowledge of the topic in order to successfully answer a 'comment' question.

| Comment | give an informed opinion |

20 Ideal gases

20.1 Particles of a gas and
20.2 Explaining pressure

1   a   Describe the motion of gas particles in a container.
    b   Describe the arrangement of gas particles in a container.
    c   What do we mean by 'particle' in the kinetic theory of gases?

2   a   What is the approximate speed for particles of a gas at standard temperature and pressure?
    b   Why is it that you could have an average speed of the particles similar to your answer to the above, but some of the particles could be going above the escape velocity of the Earth?

> ### REFLECTION
>
> It is important that you review all chapters when revising – but you don't have unlimited time! So, you need to prioritise. How will you decide which topics to spend the most time reviewing? Where does this topic rank on your priority list? Is it one of the easiest chapters or one of the most difficult for you?

3   A student inverts a test tube and pushes it, open end first, into a deep tray of water.

   They observe that the test tube displaces water beneath it rather than fills it with water.

   a   Explain, in terms of the kinetic model of matter, why the test tube does not fill with water. [3]
   b   The student repeats this with a measuring cylinder. They notice that some water does enter the container. The volume of the trapped air is 180 cm³.

   The student then moves the upright cylinder deeper into the water to a depth of 40 cm.

   Calculate the new volume measured on the scale of the measuring cylinder.

   Assume atmospheric pressure to be 100 kPa.
   The density of water is 1000 kg m⁻³. [4]

   [Total: 7]

> ### « RECALL AND CONNECT 1 «
>
> In Chapter 6 you learned about energy and momentum in collisions. This is going to be usefully applied in this chapter. What is the difference between an elastic and an inelastic collision?

20.3 Measuring gases

1. In Chapter 1, you learned that one of the seven base units is the mole, used to measure the amount of substance.

   a How many particles are there in 22 moles of a substance?

   b How many moles are there if there are 4.63×10^{27} molecules?

2. Copy and complete Tables 20.1 and 20.2 to check that you can work with amounts of gas.

Substance	Mass of one atom or molecule / u	Mass of one atom / kg
Argon (Ar)	39.9	6.62×10^{-26}
Oxygen gas (O_2)		5.31×10^{-26}
Chlorine (Cl_2)	70.9	
Carbon dioxide (CO_2)		1.26×10^{-25}

Table 20.1

Substance	Mass of gas	Number of particles	Amount / moles
Argon (Ar)	17.0 g		
Oxygen gas (O_2)		5.08×10^{26}	
Chlorine (Cl_2)	240×10^3 kg		
Carbon dioxide (CO_2)			5.53

Table 20.2

> **UNDERSTAND THESE TERMS**
> - Avogadro constant
> - mole

20.4 Boyle's law

1. Copy and complete these sentences applying Boyle's law.

   a A balloon of trapped gas is kept at a constant temperature. The pressure of the gas in the balloon is halved, and its volume will ....

   b A trapped gas is kept at a constant temperature, and its volume is reduced to a quarter of the original value its pressure is .... by ....

   c A trapped gas is kept at a constant temperature, its volume is reduced by 10%, and its pressure is .... by ....

2 Robert Boyle's model described the particles of air as being surrounded by tiny springs.

In his model, the particles of air were in contact with each other.

    a Comment whether the model agrees with the four assumptions of kinetic theory. [4]

    b Here are some of Robert Boyle's data. Use the data to predict what the pressure would be at a volume of 60. [2]

Volume / arbitrary units	Pressure / arbitrary units
12	118
24	59
36	39
48	29

    c Comment on the precision of the data and suggest a possible reason for inaccuracy in the data. [4]

[Total: 10]

REFLECTION

In question 20.4.2d, you were asked to comment and suggest as part of your answer. How did you apply the information about the available marks [4] to help you write your answer? Did you think carefully about the meaning of the command words to help you ensure you included the correct level of detail? Did you notice in the mark scheme that there were more than one way to score three of the marks?

20.5 Changing temperature

1 a Sketch a graph of temperature / °C against pressure / Pa.

    b How could you use an accurately plotted graph of pressure / Pa against temperature / °C to find a value for absolute zero?

2 A student is using the apparatus shown in Figure 20.1 to vary the temperature and measure pressure.

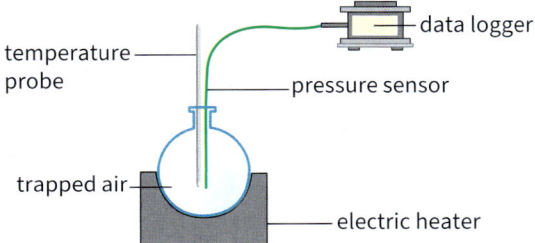

Figure 20.1

a   The round bottomed flask has a fixed volume.
    State the other control variable for this practical. [1]

b   Here are their results.

Temperature / °C	Pressure / kPa
25	101
37	105
52	109
73	116
95	123
110	130

Copy the axes provided in Figure 20.2 and plot these results. [2]

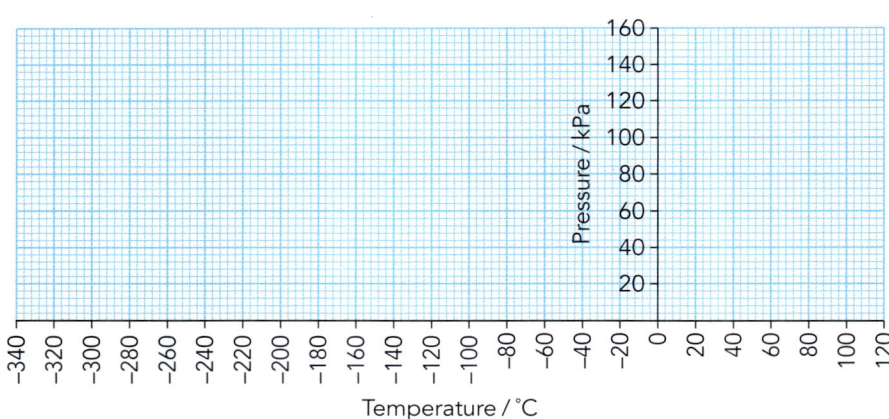

Figure 20.2

c   Use your graph to determine a value for absolute zero. [2]
d   Calculate a percentage difference for their final value.
    Suggest improvements to the practical to increase the accuracy
    of the final value for absolute zero. [2]

[Total: 7]

UNDERSTAND THIS TERM
- ideal gas

20.6 Ideal gas equation

1   Calculate the following values.

   a   The volume of a gas with 22 moles at a pressure of 200 kPa and a temperature of 390 K.
   b   The volume of a gas with 5.5 moles, at a pressure of 320 kPa and a temperature of 200 °C.
   c   The pressure of a gas of mass 750 g, molar mass 40 g mol^{-1}, at a volume of 6.0 m^3 and a temperature of 80 °C.

d The volume of a gas with 1.2×10^{24} particles at a pressure of 50 kPa and a temperature of 150 K.

e The volume of a gas with 3.8×10^{25} particles at a pressure of 1.6 MPa and a temperature of 1500 °C.

f The pressure of 22 g of helium at a volume of 2.7 m³ and a temperature of 80 °C. Helium has a mass of 6.646×10^{-27} kg.

> **UNDERSTAND THIS TERM**
> - equation of state

≪ RECALL AND CONNECT 2 ≪

Think back to Chapter 6, when you learned about how momentum is related to forces. Accurately write out Newton's second law in terms of momentum in words and in algebra.

20.7 Modelling gases: the kinetic model

1 What are the four assumptions of the kinetic theory of gases?

2 A simple model of the atmosphere consists of a number of layers of gas at different densities.

Here are some data about the atmosphere at different heights above sea level in our atmosphere.

Height above sea level / m	Density / kg m⁻³	Temperature / °C	Pressure / kPa
0	1.23	15	100
5000	0.74	−17	54
10 000	0.42	−50	27

a Calculate the root mean square (r.m.s.) speed of particles at a height of 10 000 m. [3]

b The atmosphere in the troposphere consists of mainly nitrogen, and about 20% oxygen.

The troposphere extends to about 11 km above sea level.

Molecular nitrogen has a mass of 28 u, and molecular oxygen has a mass of 32 u.

Without further calculation, comment on the r.m.s. speeds of the two molecules. [2]

c A student concludes that the data in the table do not show that pressure is proportional to the temperature. Use the data to justify the student's conclusion. [2]

[Total: 7]

> **UNDERSTAND THIS TERM**
> - the kinetic model

20.8 Temperature and molecular kinetic energy

1 a Work out the root mean square speed for the molecules in the table.

Temperature / °C	Mass of one molecule / u	Root mean square speed / m s^{-1}
20	2	
700	28	
45	44	

b Correct this student's derivation of the equation for the pressure of an ideal gas.

For one molecule in a cubic container		
	Student's derivation	Corrected version
We know that:	$F = \dfrac{\Delta p}{\Delta t}$	
We also know that:	$\Delta t = \dfrac{2l}{c}$ and $\Delta p = mc$	
Substituting gives:	$F = \dfrac{mc}{\left(\dfrac{2l}{c}\right)} \Rightarrow F = \dfrac{mc^2}{2l}$	
We know that:	$p = \dfrac{F}{A}$ and $A = l^2$	
Substituting gives:	$p = \dfrac{mc^2}{2l^3}$	
For N molecules		
We know that:	$l^3 = V$	
Substituting gives:	$p = \dfrac{m}{2V}(c^2)$	

> **UNDERSTAND THESE TERMS**
> - Boltzmann constant
> - root mean square speed

2 Calculate the mean translational kinetic energy of a molecule at temperature 20 °C. Choose the correct value from the options below.

A 4.14×10^{-22} J

B 6.07×10^{-21} J

C 6.0×10^{-21} J

D 5.2×10^{-21} J

SELF-ASSESSMENT CHECKLIST

Let's revisit the Knowledge focus and Exam skills focus for this chapter.

Decide how confident you are with each statement.

Now I can:	Show it	Needs more work	Almost there	Confident to move on
measure amounts of a substance in moles and find the number of particles using molar quantities	Practise converting between mass in grams, number of moles and number of particles.			
solve problems using the equation of state $PV = nRT$ for an ideal gas	Practise a set of questions using the ideal gas equation.			
deduce a relationship between pressure, volume and the microscopic properties of the molecules of a gas, stating the assumptions of the kinetic theory of gases	Use the assumptions of the kinetic theory of gases to discuss changes in pressure and volume for examples in everyday life, for example, refrigerators, car tyres and sealed food packages.			
relate the kinetic energy of the molecules of a gas to its temperature and calculate root mean square speeds	Use the relationship between temperature and average kinetic energy of the molecules of a gas to calculate the root mean square (r.m.s.) speed for particles in some examples of gases.			
show that I understand the 'comment' command word and can answer 'comment' questions	Practise giving an informed judgement as part of your answer to comment questions; you could try 'commenting' on other questions, too.			

21 Uniform electric fields

> **KNOWLEDGE FOCUS**
>
> In this chapter you will answer questions on:
> - attraction and repulsion
> - the concept of an electric field
> - electric field strength
> - force on a charge.

> **EXAM SKILLS FOCUS**
>
> In this chapter you will:
> - understand how to answer synoptic questions.

Questions that require to you demonstrate knowledge from different topics and the connections between them are called synoptic questions. You need to make sure that you recognise these questions and how to show these connections in your answers. For example, questions on topics in this chapter are often used to make synoptic links to topics you have studied in Chapter 8.

It is worth pausing and thinking about the areas of physics you will need to recall in order to tackle a challenging synoptic question *before* you start writing your answer. You will need to be confident in your understanding of this topic in order to do so. As you work through the questions in this chapter, see if you can spot the synoptic questions and think carefully about how best to answer them.

21 Uniform electric fields

21.1 Attraction and repulsion

1. Why does a poly(ethene) rod become negatively charged when rubbed with a cloth?

2. What are two ways that you could practically demonstrate the presence of a uniform electric field?

3. Figure 21.1 shows an insulating sphere hanging between two metal plates.

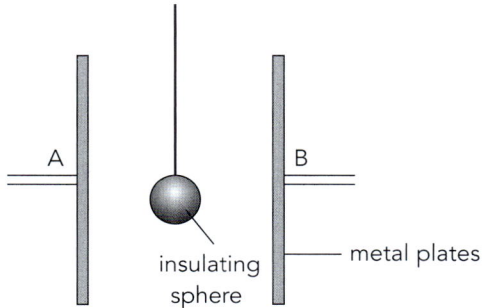

Figure 21.1

   a Initially, only plate A is charged. Explain why the insulating ball is attracted to plate A. [2]

   b Plates A and B are then connected to opposite sides of an a.c. signal at low frequency. Suggest and explain what is likely to be observed next. [3]

[Total: 5]

> **UNDERSTAND THESE TERMS**
> - electric charge
> - electric field

« RECALL AND CONNECT 1 «

Chapter 8 was about currents and potential differences. Write down:

- an equation which defines the potential difference in terms of energy and charge
- an equation which defines current in terms of charge and time.

21.2 The concept of an electric field

1. Imagine you are trying to get a primary school student to understand that all the forces they use to play sports are actually due to electric fields. What key information would you need them to understand?

2 Copy and complete the three electric field diagrams shown in Figure 21.2.

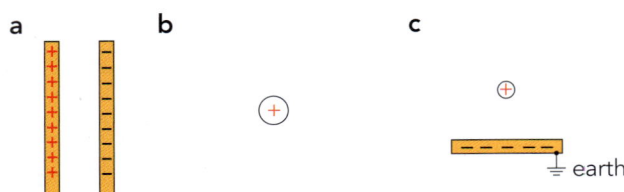

Figure 21.2

UNDERSTAND THESE TERMS
- field of force
- field lines

3 In a linear accelerator, charged particles are accelerated in the gaps between charged drift tubes. Figure 21.3 shows the drift tube arrangement of the drift tubes in a linear accelerator and their connection to an alternating potential difference supply.

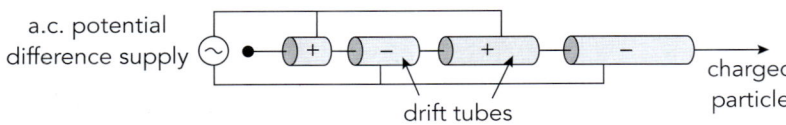

Figure 21.3

a Explain why the particle will accelerate in the gap between the drift tubes but not within them. [2]

b Explain why changing the spacing between the drift tubes would not affect the final velocity of the charged particle after it passes through the accelerating electric field. [4]

c A proton has a kinetic energy of 5.1×10^{-15} J after being accelerated through a uniform electric field.

Determine the potential difference between the plates. [2]

[Total: 8]

≪ RECALL AND CONNECT 2 ≪

In Chapter 15, you learned how to use a non-SI unit to describe very small amounts of energy, for example, for individual radioactive emissions. Define the electron volt (eV).

21.3 Electric field strength

1. Work out the missing values, **a–f**, in these tables.

   Remember:

   $$E = \frac{F}{Q} \qquad E = \frac{V}{d}$$

Potential difference / V	Plate separation / m	Electric field strength / N C^{-1}
24	0.5	a
230	b	1.0×10^5
c	1.5×10^{-6}	500

Charge / C	Electric field strength / N C^{-1}	Force / N
1.6×10^{-19}	d	8.0×10^{-18}
6.0×10^{-3}	2.9×10^3	e
f	1.0×10^{-9}	3.2×10^{-28}

   ### ❮❮ RECALL AND CONNECT 3 ❮❮

   Think back to Chapter 2. Write down the three equations of uniform acceleration.

2. A student connects two parallel copper electrodes to either side of some conductive paper. They connect each side to either side of a d.c. power supply. They also connect a voltmeter between one of the electrodes and a moveable connector. Their set-up is shown in Figure 21.4.

   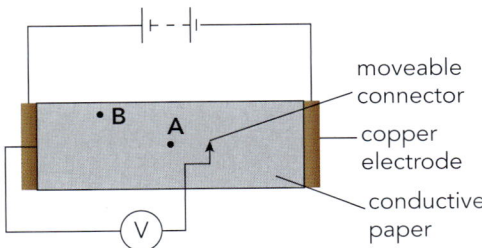

   Figure 21.4

   a. The student connects the moveable connector to point A, exactly halfway between the two electrodes. The connector reads 3 V.
      i. Determine the potential difference of the power supply. [1]

    ii The conducting paper measures 12 cm in length between the two electrodes. Point B is 3 cm from the left electrode.

       Calculate the reading on the voltmeter when the moveable connector is at point B. [1]

   iii Determine the direction of the force on a positive charge at point B. [1]

b In an electron gun, electrons are released by thermionic emission from a hot tungsten metal coil called a cathode. They are accelerated through a uniform electric field set up between two plates with a potential difference of 7.0 kV between them. The plates are spaced 3.0 cm apart.

   i Show that the electric field strength is $2.3\,\text{N}\,\text{C}^{-1}$. [1]

   ii Calculate the magnitude of the force on each electron. [1]

   iii Calculate the speed of the electron as it leaves the electric field. [2]

[Total: 7]

> **UNDERSTAND THIS TERM**
> - electric field strength

21.4 Force on a charge

1 Why will a particle moving perpendicular to a uniform electric field describe a parabolic path?

2 Calculate the force in each of these examples:

  a an electron in a uniform electric field of field strength $7\,\mu\text{N}\,\text{C}^{-1}$.

  b an electron between two parallel plates separated by 10 cm and with a potential difference of 600 V between them.

  c a 2+ ion between two charged plates separated by 5 cm. One is at a potential of $+1500\,\text{V}$ and the other $-1500\,\text{V}$.

3 Figure 21.5 shows an electron beam entering a uniform electric field between two parallel plates.

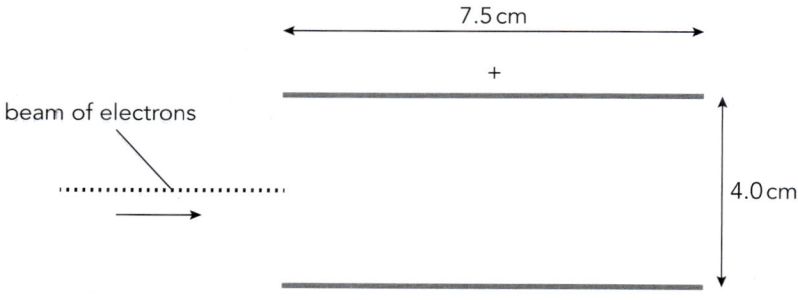

Figure 21.5

The spacing between the plates is 4.0 cm. Their length is 7.5 cm.

The electrons enter the field parallel to the plates midway between the plates with a kinetic energy of 5.0 keV.

Calculate the maximum potential difference between the plates so the electrons emerge from the electric field and do not contact the plates. [6]

[Total: 6]

21 Uniform electric fields

> **REFLECTION**
>
> Did you spot the synoptic links in the exam skills questions in sections 21.2 and 21.4? Particle physics is a context often used to make synoptic links between topics. Go back through the questions and practise your synoptic skills by identifying all of the topics that you use knowledge from to solve the problems in the questions.

SELF-ASSESSMENT CHECKLIST

Let's revisit the Knowledge focus and Exam skills Knowledge focus for this chapter.

Decide how confident you are with each statement.

Now I can:	Show it	Needs more work	Almost there	Confident to move on
show an understanding of the concept of an electric field	Explain some common effects of static electricity by reference to the electric fields around charged particles.			
define electric field strength	Write a definition of electric field strength and summarise this in a set of equations.			
draw field lines to represent an electric field	Sketch the fields around positively and negatively charged spheres and between parallel charged plates.			
calculate the strength of a uniform electric field	Practise calculating the electric field strengths in uniform electric fields.			
calculate the force on a charge in a uniform electric field	Practise calculating the force on charges in uniform electric fields.			
describe how charged particles move in a uniform electric field	Make a set of notes and diagrams to summarise the motion of charged particles in electric fields.			
understand how to answer synoptic questions	Look at some complex questions and try to identify which of them use knowledge and skills from more than one topic.			

22 Coulomb's law

KNOWLEDGE FOCUS

In this chapter you will answer questions on:

- electric fields
- Coulomb's law
- electric field strength for a radial field
- electric potential
- gravitational and electric fields.

EXAM SKILLS FOCUS

In this chapter you will:

- improve your technique when answering complex 'calculate' questions.

Certain 'calculate' questions will ask you to perform multi-step calculations, or calculations that require equations with many terms to answer the question successfully. Some of the information might come from the question itself, and other values might come from your formula sheet. Some data might need to be converted before it is put into the equation. Practise these skills and get used to checking through your working to identify errors. Often, it might be better to derive a new equation rather than make one calculation followed by a second calculation with that value.

| Calculate | work out from given facts, figures or information |

22 Coulomb's law

22.1 Electric fields

1 a Sketch the field around the positively charged sphere shown in Figure 22.1.

Figure 22.1

b What is shown by the direction of the field arrows in an electric field diagram?
c What is shown by the spacing of the field lines in an electric field diagram?
d Add lines of equipotential to the sketch of the field around the positively charged sphere that you drew in part **a**.

> **« RECALL AND CONNECT 1 «**
>
> Think back to Chapter 8, where you learnt that charge is quantised. Explain what is meant by the quantised nature of charge and give an equation to link total charge with the number of electrons.

2 It is possible to demonstrate the concept of electric fields by charging insulators using friction. A student uses a charged poly(ethene) rod to attract an aluminium can which rolls across the table.

a Define electric field strength. [2]
b Calculate the size of the force on an electron in an electric field of field strength $1.4 \times 10^{-5}\ \text{N C}^{-1}$. [1]
c When rubbed with a cloth, the rod carries a charge of in the order of $10^{-7}\ \text{C}$. Calculate the number of electrons that have been transferred from the rod to the cloth. [1]

[Total: 4]

22.2 Coulomb's law

1 a Link each part of the definition of Coulomb's law to the equation for Coulomb's law.

b Explain how the equation also includes the idea that like charges repel and unlike charges attract.

2   A student is investigating Coulomb's law. They are using a balloon and an insulating object. Their set-up is shown in Figure 22.2.

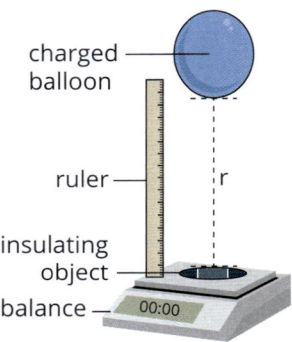

Figure 22.2

They charge the balloon by rubbing it on their clothes. The insulating object is placed on a mass balance to measure a 'force'.

Before bringing the charged balloon near the insulating object, they reset the mass balance to zero.

a   Predict the relationship between 'force' and distance that the student should expect in this experiment. [2]

b   Copy the table and complete the third column so that you can plot a graph of the student's results as a straight line. [6]

Distance cm	Reading on the mass balance / g	
70	0.15	
60	0.22	
50	0.27	
40	0.47	
30	0.82	
20	1.84	

c   Identify the main source of error in the student's investigation. [1]

d   Describe how the student should measure this quantity accurately. [2]

e   Explain why this experiment cannot lead to a value for the permittivity of free space. [1]

[Total: 12]

UNDERSTAND THIS TERM
- Coulomb's law

22.3 Electric field strength for a radial field

1. Copy and complete this table to calculate the strength of an electric field at different distances from a charged sphere.

Charge / nC	Distance / μm	Electric field strength / × 10⁹ N C⁻¹
35	100	
2.0		720
	14	390
0.43	70	

2. In Figure 22.3, two identical spheres on strings are held apart by the electrostatic force, F. The spheres have equal charge. The horizontal distance between the two spheres is 0.36 m. They are held apart at an angle of 23° from the vertical. The mass of each sphere is 6.2 g.

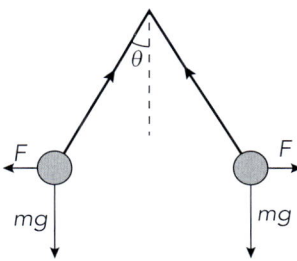

Figure 22.3

a Calculate the charges on the spheres. [4]

b A point charge, q, is held at equilibrium between two charged spheres. These are shown in Figure 22.4. The distance between the centres of charge A and B is 1.2 m.

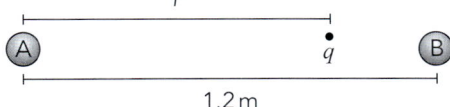

Figure 22.4

Sphere A has four times the charge of sphere B. Calculate the distance, r. [3]

[Total: 7]

> **REFLECTION**
>
> How did you do on this challenging mathematical question? Did you use derivation to work through an algebraic solution before inputting values? Or did you calculate, for example, the value of the weight and store that value in your calculator for use later? How will you keep practising to ensure that you can tackle these challenging questions?

22.4 Electric potential

1   a   What is meant by potential difference?

    b   Figure 22.5 shows a graph of electrical potential against distance in a uniform field. Calculate the potential gradient.

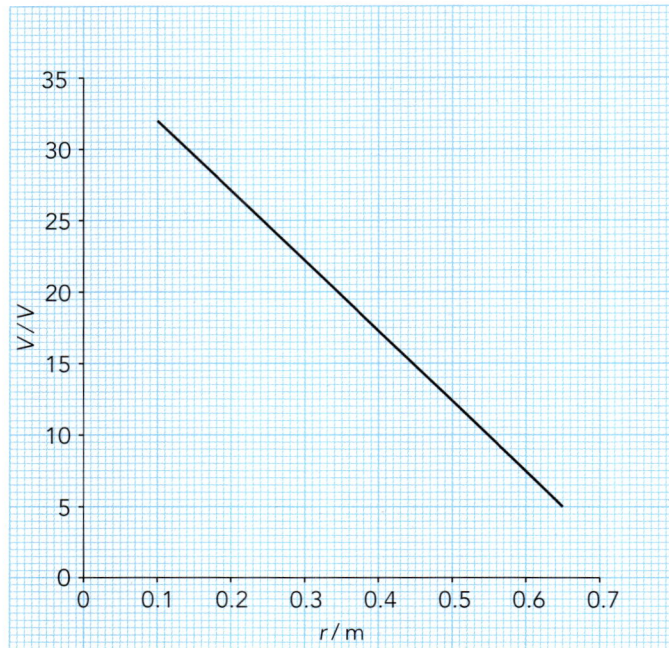

Figure 22.5

    c   Figure 22.6 shows a graph of electrical potential against distance in a radial field. Calculate the potential gradient at 20 m.

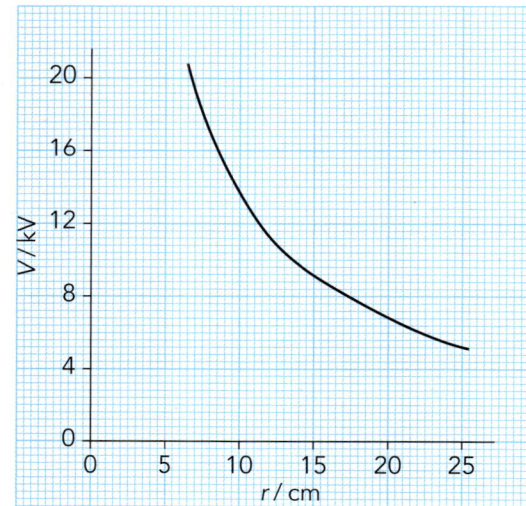

Figure 22.6

2   Figure 22.7 shows the radial field around a point charge.

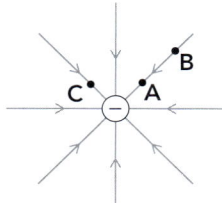

Figure 22.7

a   The electrical potential at point A is −4 V. Point B is twice as far from the centre of the charge.
    Calculate the potential at point B. [1]
b   Explain why no work is done in bringing a charge from point A to point C. [1]
c   A point charge of 6 nC is placed at point A.
    Calculate the change in electrical potential energy in moving the charge from point A to point B. [1]
d   Two charged spheres are separated by a distance of 0.36 m.
    They are shown in Figure 22.8.

Figure 22.8

The charge of sphere A is −6 nC, and the charge of sphere B is 12 nC.

Calculate the electrical potential at point X, 0.12 m from sphere B. [4]

[Total: 7]

UNDERSTAND THIS TERM

- electric potential

22.5 Gravitational and electric fields

> **« RECALL AND CONNECT 2 «**
>
> Think back to Chapter 17, when you learned about gravitational fields. Write out Newton's law of gravitation. Use this law to write down an equation for gravitational potential energy for two point masses.

1 Copy and complete this table to compare gravitational and electric fields.

Quantity	Gravitational fields	Electric fields
		$E = \dfrac{F}{Q} = \dfrac{V}{d}$ $E = \dfrac{Q_1}{4\pi\varepsilon_0 r^2}$
force		
potential		$V = \dfrac{Q_1}{4\pi\varepsilon_0 r}$
	$E = \dfrac{-Gm_1m_2}{r}$ $E = mgh$	

2 A student has written the following discussion of gravitational and electric fields:

Gravitational fields and electric fields are similar because they both have field strengths which are force per unit, and the quantity they act on. They are different because gravity acts on mass, and the electric field acts on charge.

In radial fields, both forces vary with the inverse square of the distance between two objects. The equations for potentials, however, vary with inverse distance. For this reason, they can both only have negative potentials. However, because electrical charge can be positive or negative electric potential is a vector, whereas gravitational potential can only be scalar.

    a   Identify the errors that the student has made. [2]

    b   An experiment using exotic helium atoms found the diameter of a nucleus of helium to be in the order of 2 fm (2×10^{-15} m).

        Compare the relative sizes of electric and gravitational forces between two protons in the nucleus. Treat each proton as a sphere of uniformly distributed mass and charge. [4]

    c   Comment on the forces involved in equilibrium in the nucleus. [1]

        [Total: 7]

22 Coulomb's law

SELF-ASSESSMENT CHECKLIST

Let's revisit the Knowledge focus and Exam skills focus for this chapter.

Decide how confident you are with each statement.

Now I can:	Show it	Needs more work	Almost there	Confident to move on
recall and use Coulomb's law	Write out Coulomb's law in both words and algebra.			
calculate the field strength for a point charge	Practise calculating electric field strength at various distances around a point charge.			
recognise that for the electric field strength for a point outside a spherical conductor, the charge on the sphere may be considered to be a point charge at the centre of the sphere	Use the centre of charge for spherical conductors as the start of the distance to any point in a radial field.			
define electric potential	Draw a diagram to illustrate the definition of electric potential and self-explain how you will use these in equations where this term appears.			
calculate potential due to a point charge	Practise calculating electrical potentials for positions in uniform and radial fields.			
relate field strength to the potential gradient	Sketch a graph to show how you would use a graph of potential vs distance to calculate a potential gradient.			
compare and contrast electric and gravitational fields	Outline some similarities and differences between gravitational and electric fields.			
use good technique when answering complex 'calculate' questions	Check your working for each calculation you performed in this chapter. Make a note of any errors you made and ensure you understand where you went wrong.			

23 Capacitance

KNOWLEDGE FOCUS

In this chapter you will answer questions on:
- capacitors in use
- energy stored in a capacitor
- capacitors in parallel
- capacitors in series
- comparing capacitors and resistors
- capacitor networks
- charge and discharge of capacitors.

EXAM SKILLS FOCUS

In this chapter you will:
- show that you understand the 'predict' command word and can answer 'predict' questions.

'Predict' questions require you to describe possible outcomes based on data or information given to you in the question, which may need to be combined with your own knowledge and understanding. When you are asked to make a prediction, you are expected to suggest what may happen based on available evidence. To do this successfully, it is important that you use all the information provided in the question to inform your answer.

'Predict' questions can be challenging. They require you to use knowledge and information from the question to produce an answer which is not always immediately obvious. This chapter will give you plenty of opportunities to practise the techniques to make sure you remember how to tackle a 'predict' question.

| Predict | suggest what may happen based on available information |

23 Capacitance

23.1 Capacitors in use

1. Calculate the charge stored in each capacitor.
   a. 12 V; 1000 μF
   b. 6 V; 4700 μF
   c. 230 V; 10 μF

2. A demonstration capacitor can be made using sheets of aluminium foil and a plastic sheet.

   The demonstrator uses a 1.0 kV EHT power supply.

   a. Describe the construction of a simple capacitor. [1]
   b. The demonstration capacitor is connected and charged through a data logging ammeter.

   Use Figure 23.1 to show that the total charge stored on the capacitor is approximately 3.3×10^{-5} C. [2]

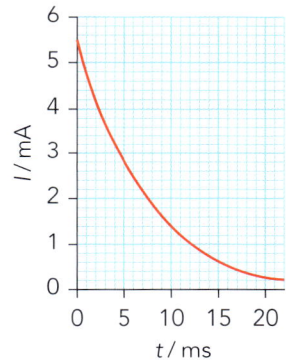

Figure 23.1

   c. Calculate the capacitance of the capacitor. [2]

   [Total: 5]

> ### « RECALL AND CONNECT 1 «
> In previous chapters, such as Chapter 18 on oscillations, you learned that exponential decay is often used as a model to solve physics problems. What is meant by exponential decay?

> ### REFLECTION
> How can you increase your confidence when using graphs to solve problems? Could you use the principles behind calculus to quickly figure out what is represented by the gradient of a graph and what is represented by the area under the graph?

UNDERSTAND THESE TERMS
- capacitance
- Farad

23.2 Energy stored in a capacitor

1. Copy and complete this table of values using the equations for energy stored in a capacitor.

p.d. / V	Charge / C	Capacitance / F	Energy stored in a capacitor / J
24		680×10^{-6}	
		2200×10^{-6}	1.2×10^{6}
	5.0×10^{-3}		3.8×10^{-3}
9		15×10^{-6}	

2. Use the graphs (Figure 23.2) to calculate the energy stored in each of the capacitors.

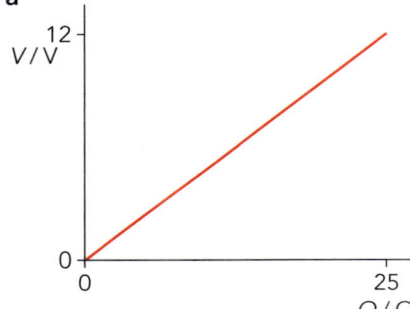
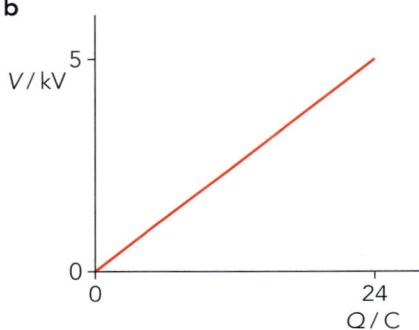

Figure 23.2

3. The circuit shown in Figure 23.3a is used to charge a capacitor.

   The capacitor is then discharged through a d.c. motor.

   Figure 23.3b shows the potential difference against charge graph for the capacitor.

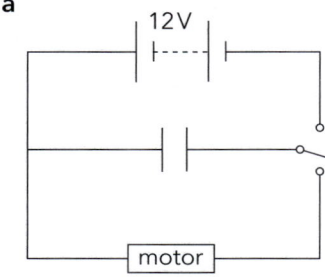
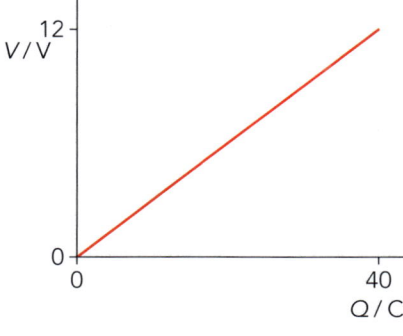

Figure 23.3

In reality, the motor will not be able to turn if the current falls beneath 0.60 A.

The motor has an effective resistance of 6.7 Ω.

You can assume all other resistances are negligible.

    a   Calculate the total energy supplied to the motor before it stops spinning. [3]

    b   The motor is used to lift a 50 g mass.

         Calculate the maximum possible height the motor could raise the mass. [2]

[Total: 5]

23.3 Capacitors in parallel

> ### ≪ RECALL AND CONNECT 2 ≪
>
> In Chapter 9, you learned about how to combine resistors in series and parallel. Remind yourself of the equations for resistors in series and parallel and how they were derived from the first principles.

1   Derive a formula for capacitors in parallel.

2   Calculate the effective capacitance of the networks of capacitors in Figure 23.4.

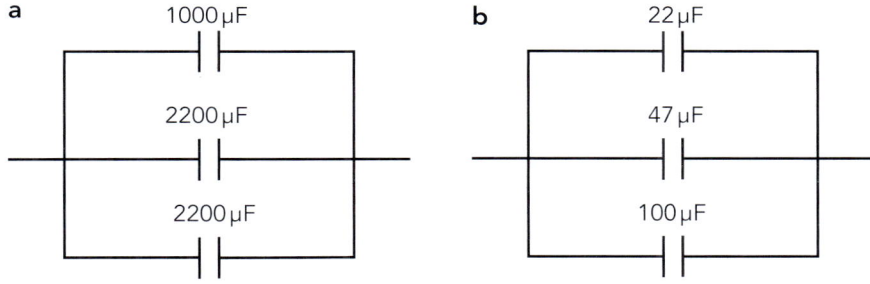

Figure 23.4

3   A lamp is connected in series with a 4700 μF. The capacitor is charged to 3 V.

    The capacitor is then discharged through a lamp. The lamp lights dimly and, after a short time, goes out.

    a   Calculate the total energy transferred to the lamp. [1]

    b   A second 4700 μF capacitor is connected in parallel with the first.

        The same potential difference is used to charge the capacitor.

        Explain why the lamp appears brighter initially. [2]

c   The total charge on the pair of capacitors is the sum of the charges on the individual capacitors.

Explain what other rule you need to use to derive an equation for capacitors in parallel. [1]

[Total: 4]

> **REFLECTION**
>
> Do you get confused by different parts of physics that follow similar rules? For example, students often mix up static electricity and magnetism. And the difference between current and potential difference and their relationship to electrical energy is a common area for misconceptions to arise. Capacitance and resistance are another example of this, especially given how similar the rules for series and parallel circuits seem at first glance. How will you make sure you are clear about the knowledge you need to apply when you are in an exam?

23.4 Capacitors in series

1   Derive a formula for capacitors in series.

2   Calculate the effective capacitance of the networks of capacitors in Figure 23.5.

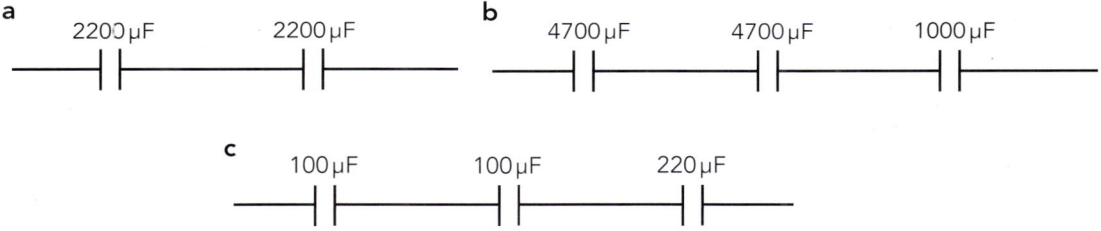

Figure 23.5

3   A circuit in an electrical appliance requires a charge store in the range $15 \pm 2\,\text{mC}$.

Three capacitors are linked together in a network of capacitors connected to an EMF of 6 V.

The values of the capacitors are 3300 µF, 3300 µF and 4700 µF.

   a   Draw the network of capacitors. [2]
   b   Predict how the store of charge would change if the appliance were connected to a 12 V power supply. [2]
   c   Explain how the network of capacitors could be altered to give approximately the same charge stored as before with the 12 V power supply. [2]

[Total: 6]

23.5 Comparing capacitors and resistors

1 Correct the student comparison of resistors and capacitors in series and parallel.

The formula for calculating the effective resistance of resistors in series is to add them up, which is the same as calculating the capacitance of capacitors in series.

When you add a resistor in parallel, the effective resistance always goes down. This is not the same as capacitors, as more capacitors in parallel always increase the overall capacitance. This is because when you add a resistor in parallel, you make it add up to a bigger gap between the parallel plates, whereas adding resistors in parallel always gives an extra route for the charge to flow.

2 The network of capacitors and resistors in Figure 23.6 gives a time constant, RC, of 1.2 s.

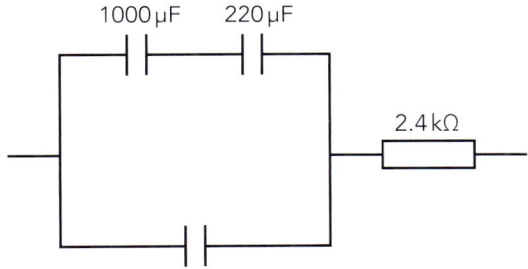

Figure 23.6

    a Calculate the capacitance of capacitor marked C. [3]

    b The capacitor is charged to a p.d. of 30 V and then discharged.
       Sketch a graph of *p.d.* against *time* for the capacitor and resistor network during this discharge. [2]

    c A second 2.4 kΩ resistor is added in parallel with the first.
       Predict the effect on the discharge of the capacitors. [4]

       [Total: 9]

23.6 Capacitor networks

1 a i Sketch the **four** ways that three capacitors of 1000 μF can be connected.

    ii Calculate the effective capacitance of each network.

b   Calculate the effective capacitance of the two capacitor networks in Figure 23.7.

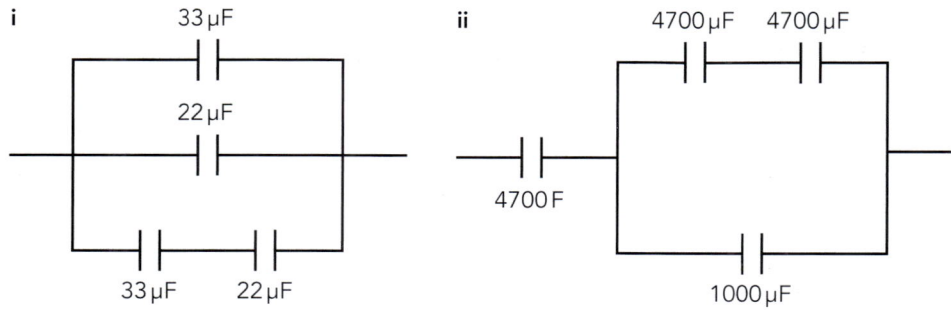

Figure 23.7

2   Figure 23.8 shows a potential difference–charge graph for a capacitor network.

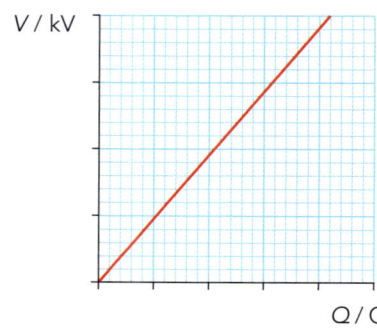

Figure 23.8

a   i   Calculate the effective capacitance of the network. [2]
    ii Calculate the work done in charging the capacitor network. [2]

b   Figure 23.9 shows the capacitor network.

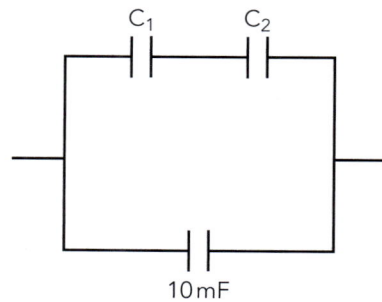

Figure 23.9

Capacitors C_1 and C_2 are identical. Calculate their capacitance. [2]

c   Predict the change on the time to fully discharge if a capacitor is added in series with the capacitor network. You do not need to include a calculation in your response. [3]

[Total: 9]

23.7 Charge and discharge of capacitors

1. Calculate the time constant for each of these circuits.
   a. 2 kΩ resistor and a 4700 µF capacitor
   b. 62 Ω resistor and a 22 mF capacitor
   c. 1 MΩ resistor and a 10 µF capacitor

2. Calculate the time taken to decay to the stated value in each of these situations.
   a. A 3300 µF capacitor charged to 3 V is discharged through a 22 kΩ resistor.
      Calculate the time to reach 1 V.
   b. A 1000 µF capacitor with 4 mC of charge on one plate is discharged through a 15 kΩ resistor.
      Calculate the time to reach 0.5 mC.
   c. A 47 mF capacitor with is discharged through a 100 Ω resistor.
      The initial current is 12 mA Calculate the time to reach a current of 2.0 mA.

3. A student conducts a practical to measure the current in a circuit as they discharge a capacitor.

   Table 23.1 shows their results.

Potential difference / V	Time / s
6.0	0
4.8	2
3.8	4
3.0	6
2.4	8
1.9	10
0.6	12

   Table 23.1

   a. Plot the results on a suitable axes on graph paper. [3]
   b. State the time constant for the decay. [1]
   c. The capacitor has a capacitance of 2200 µF.
      Calculate the resistance of the circuit. [1]

   [Total: 5]

> **UNDERSTAND THESE TERMS**
> - exponential decay
> - time constant

> **REFLECTION**
>
> Did you find the 'predict' questions in this chapter challenging? Were you able to use previous knowledge as well as information in the questions to correctly answer them? What could you do to increase your confidence in answering 'predict' questions?

SELF-ASSESSMENT CHECKLIST

Let's revisit the Knowledge focus and Exam skills focus for this chapter.

Decide how confident you are with each statement.

Now I can:	Show it	Needs more work	Almost there	Confident to move on
define capacitance	Self-explain how the definition of capacitance is related to the equation: $C = \dfrac{Q}{V}$			
solve problems involving charge, voltage and capacitance	Practise calculations using the equation: $C = \dfrac{Q}{V}$			
deduce the electric potential energy stored in a capacitor from a potential–charge graph	Sketch a graph of V against Q for a capacitor and label what is shown by the area under the graph.			
deduce and use formulae for the energy stored by a capacitor	From the formula: $W = \dfrac{1}{2}QV$ derive formulae relating energy stored in a capacitor to capacitance.			
derive and use formulae for capacitances in series and parallel	Memorise the steps to derive the formulae for capacitors in series and in parallel.			
recognise and use graphs showing variation of potential difference, current and charge as a capacitor discharges	Sketch the *current–time*, *potential difference–time* and *charge–time* for a discharging capacitor. Label a half-life for each and annotate the graphs with the equations for each exponential decay.			
recall and use the time constant for a capacitor–resistor circuit	Add to your graphs an explanation of what is meant by the time constant of the decay and how to calculate that from the details of a circuit.			

CONTINUED

Now I can:	Show it	Needs more work	Almost there	Confident to move on
use the equation for the discharge of a capacitor through a resistor	Practise using equations for exponential decay, including use of natural logarithms as the inverse of the exponential function.			
show that I understand the 'predict' command word and can answer 'predict' questions	Find and answer some 'predict' questions in past papers; remember to use all of the information provided in the question to make a prediction.			

Exam practice 6

This section contains past paper questions from previous Cambridge exams, which draws together your knowledge on a range of topics that you have covered up to this point. These questions give you the opportunity to test your knowledge and understanding. Additional past paper practice questions can be found in the accompanying digital material.

The following question has an example student response and commentary provided. Once you have worked through the question, read the student response and commentary. Are your answers different to the sample responses?

1   a   i   State what is meant by the *internal energy* of a system. [2]

    ii Explain why, for an ideal gas, the change in internal energy is directly proportional to the change in thermodynamic temperature of the gas. [3]

   b   A cylinder of volume 1.8×10^4 cm^3 contains helium gas at pressure 6.4×10^6 Pa and temperature 25 °C.

   Helium gas may be considered to be an ideal gas consisting of single atoms.

   Calculate the number of helium atoms in the cylinder. [3]

   [Total: 8]

Cambridge International AS & A Level Physics (9702) Paper 41, Q3, June 2018

		Example student response	Commentary
a	i	The internal energy is the sum of the potential and kinetic energies of the particles.	For the second mark, the student needs to mention that the particles are in random motion OR that they have a range of speeds and distances between them (in a Boltzmann distribution). *This answer is awarded 1 out of 2 marks.*
	ii	In a gas temperature is proportional to kinetic energy. Gases have the highest potential energies, and so increasing the kinetic energy of the particles simply increases the temperature and it's linear so that's proportional.	The student only scores the final mark out of three for stating that temperature is proportional to kinetic energy. (Note that this is, in fact, different to what you are told in the question, which states internal energy is directly proportional to temperature.) For the other two marks, they needed to: • state that there are negligible forces between the particles, so no potential energy • state that this means the energy is all kinetic. They are correct that gas, as a state of matter, has the highest potential energy; however, we treat that potential energy as zero potential energy. (Solid and liquid particles have negative potential energies.)

Exam practice 6

Example student response	Commentary
	Potential energy is due to the positions of particles and the forces between them. In a gas, we assume that they are far enough apart so as to be essentially unrelated to each other. It is an assumption of the kinetic model of gases that the forces between the particles are negligible. They, therefore must have zero potential energy. If you are struggling with this concept, you might need to revisit the ideas of potential energies in electric fields and gravitational fields. (Note: the student may have forgotten that 'linear' is not the same as 'directly proportional'. If they'd remembered, then they'd know that there must be zero potential energy in order for a *temperature–internal energy* graph to pass through the origin.) **This answer is awarded 0 out of 1 mark.**
b $pV = NkT$ $N = \dfrac{pV}{kT}$ $N = \dfrac{6.4 \times 10^6 \times 1.8 \times 10^2}{1.38 \times 10^{-23} \times 25}$ $N = 3.34 \times 10^{30}$	One mark has been awarded for providing the correct equation. However, the student has: - forgotten to convert into absolute temperature (kelvin); this is a very common mistake - converted cm^3 into m^3 with a factor of 100 rather than a factor of 1 000 000. This means they substituted the wrong values into the equation, which lost them the second mark. They then lost the third mark because they did not calculate an accurate answer (that is, the value on the mark scheme or one that rounds to it). (Note: you could solve this with a different, slightly longer method. Use the equation of state to calculate the number of moles and then use the Avogadro constant to calculate the number of atoms.) **This answer is awarded 1 out of 3 marks.**

2   Now that you've gone through the commentary, have a go at writing a full mark scheme for question **1**. This will check that you've understood exactly why each mark has (or has not) been allocated. The more often you do this, and the better you get to know the way mark schemes are written, the more confident you will feel about your answers in an exam.

The following question has an example student commentary and answer provided. Work through the question first, then compare your answer with the sample answer and commentary. Are your answers different to the sample responses? What information does this give you about your understanding of this topic?

3 a Explain what is meant by the *capacitance* of a parallel plate capacitor. [3]

b A parallel plate capacitor C is connected into the circuit shown in Fig. 3.1.

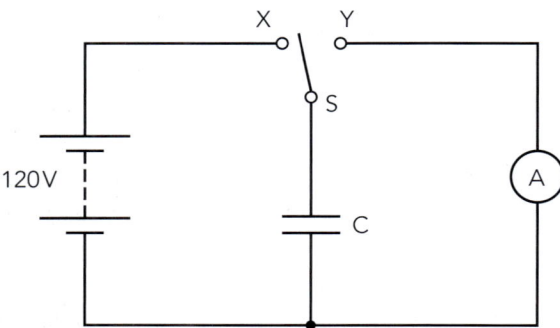

Fig. 3.1

When switch S is at position X, the battery of electromotive force 120 V and negligible internal resistance is connected to capacitor C.

When switch S is at position Y, the capacitor C is discharged through the sensitive ammeter.

The switch vibrates so that it is first in position X, then moves to position Y and then back to position X 50 times each second.

The current recorded on the ammeter is 4.5 µA.

Determine:

    i the charge, in coulomb, passing through the ammeter in 1.0 s [1]
    ii the charge on one plate of the capacitor, each time that it is charged [1]
    iii the capacitance of capacitor C. [2]

c A second capacitor, having a capacitance equal to that of capacitor C, is now placed in series with C.

Suggest and explain the effect on the current recorded on the ammeter. [2]

[Total: 9]

Cambridge International AS & A Level Physics (9702) Paper 41, Q7, June 2018

Exam practice 6

Example student response	Commentary
a Capacitance = $\dfrac{\text{charge}}{\text{p.d.}}$ There are two parallel plates which are insulated from each other by a material called a dielectric. They can be connected to either side of a source of e.m.f. Charge is stored in them when there's a potential difference across them.	The student has correctly written out the equation which defines capacitance, and they also discuss that the potential difference is across the two plates. For the third mark, the examiner wanted to see a recognition that the charge was equal to the charge on one of the plates. It is a common misunderstanding to imagine the charge being stored in the insulating gap. In a capacitor all of the charge on the positive plate is equal in magnitude to the charge on the negative plate. The Q in the equation $C = \dfrac{Q}{V}$ is in effect the magnitude of the charge on one plate. The detail the student gave about the material in between the two insulated plates is not necessary for any marks. The command word is *explain*. This detail would be useful if the question had asked: *describe the construction of a parallel plate capacitor*. When you are not sure what the extra marks might be for, look back carefully at the command words and the statements in the question. **This answer is awarded 2 out of 3 marks.**
b **i** $Q = It$ 4.5 μC	This is a tricky context but a simple application of the equation linking charge, current and time. The student has recognised this is a 1 mark question and so should be a simple piece of thinking and calculation. **This answer is awarded 1 out of 1 mark.**
ii 225 μC	The student has multiplied by 50 instead of dividing. This could have been avoided by using a 'sense check'. This means asking yourself if this value makes sense in the context of the question. **This answer is awarded 0 out of 1 mark.**
iii $C = \dfrac{225 \times 10^{-6}}{120} = 1.875 \times 10^{-6}\,\text{F}$	The student gains one mark for the correct substitution and one mark for the answer with the error carried forward from part **ii**. **This answer is awarded 2 out of 2 marks**
c $\dfrac{1}{C_T} = \dfrac{1}{C} + \dfrac{1}{C} = \dfrac{2}{C}$ $C_T = \dfrac{C}{2}$ Capacitance is halved. So time constant would be lower, so it would discharge more quickly so current would be higher.	The student scores the first mark for correctly working out the change to the overall capacitance. For the second mark, they needed to realise that the overall charge per second is halved, i.e. the current is halved. They have overcomplicated things and presumed this was about exponential decay. **This answer is awarded 1 out of 2 marks.**

Now you have read the commentary to the previous question, here is a question on a similar topic which you should attempt. Use the information from the previous response and commentary to guide you as you answer.

4 **a** State **two** different functions of capacitors in electrical circuits. [2]

  b Three uncharged capacitors of capacitances C_1, C_2 and C_3 are connected in series with a battery of electromotive force (e.m.f.) E and a switch, as shown in Fig. 4.1.

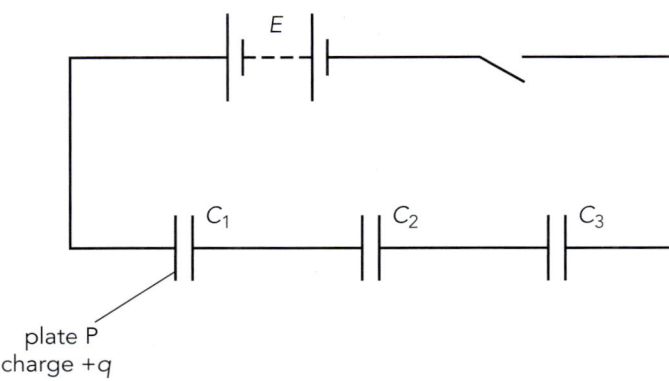

Fig. 4.1

When the switch is closed, there is a charge $+q$ on plate P of the capacitor of capacitance C_1.

Show that the combined capacitance C of the three capacitors is given by the expression:

$$\frac{1}{C} = \frac{1}{C_1} + \frac{1}{C_2} + \frac{1}{C_3}$$ [3]

  c A student has available four capacitors, each of capacitance 20 μF.

Draw circuit diagrams, one in each case, to show how the student may connect some or all of the capacitors to produce a combined capacitance of:

  i 60 μF [1]
  ii 15 μF. [1]

[Total: 7]

Cambridge International AS & A Level Physics (9702) Paper 41, Q6, June 2019

24 Magnetic fields and electromagnetism

KNOWLEDGE FOCUS

In this chapter you will answer questions on:
- producing and representing magnetic fields
- magnetic force
- magnetic flux density
- measuring magnetic flux density
- currents crossing fields
- forces between currents
- relating SI units
- comparing forces in magnetic, electric and gravitational fields.

EXAM SKILLS FOCUS

In this chapter you will:
- further practise answering 'explain' questions.

It is important to revisit command words in different topics so that you gain practice answering questions across many different topics in physics. In this chapter you will practise your understanding of the command word 'explain', which you practised in Chapter 4. As you work through the chapter, compare your answers with the 'explain' questions in this chapter to the answers you gave in Chapter 4. Do you feel you have improved your understanding of how to approach these questions?

24.1 Producing and representing magnetic fields and 24.2 Magnetic force

> **« RECALL AND CONNECT 1 «**
>
> Think back to Chapters 17 and 21. Write the definitions and equations for gravitational field strength and electric field strength.

1   Figure 24.1 shows four diagrams.

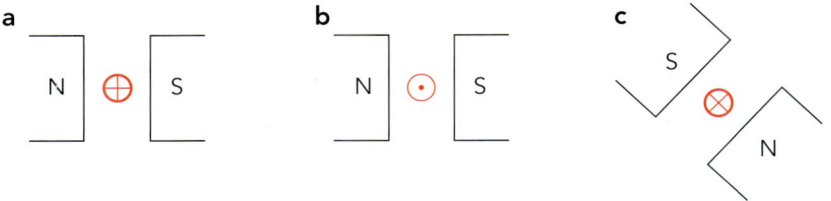

Figure 24.1

Each diagram shows either a current going into the page (a cross inside a circle) or a current coming out of the page (a dot inside a circle).

Each diagram also shows the poles of a magnet.

For each diagram, predict the direction that the wire moves.

Support each prediction with an explanation. **[Total: 6]**

2   Figure 24.2 shows four incomplete diagrams of current flowing in different directions through a solenoid.

Copy and complete each diagram, following the instructions underneath each one.

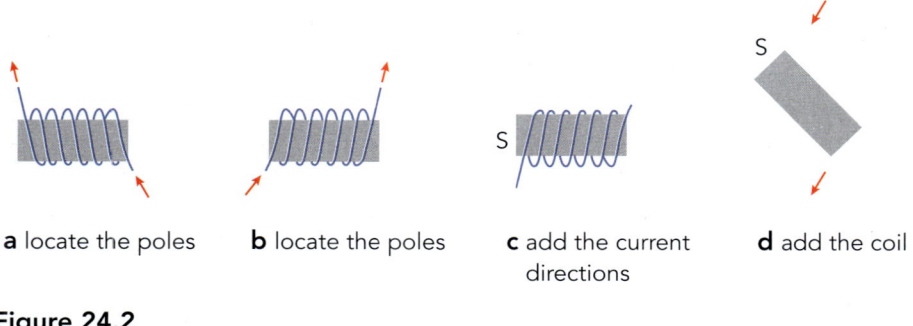

a locate the poles   **b** locate the poles   **c** add the current directions   **d** add the coil

Figure 24.2

> **UNDERSTAND THESE TERMS**
> - Fleming's left-hand rule
> - motor effect

24 Magnetic fields and electromagnetism

> **REFLECTION**
>
> How will you remember the various rules in this chapter, including the right-hand grip rule, Fleming's left-hand rule, and a method for working out the poles at each end of an electromagnet or solenoid?

24.3 Magnetic flux density

1. In the Northern Hemisphere, the Earth's magnetic field points from the geographical North Pole to the geographical South Pole.

   Electrical cables are held above the ground by pylons about 650 m apart. The cables carry a current of 100 A.

   a. If conventional current flows through the cables from West to East (left to right), determine the direction of the magnetic force. [1]
   b. State the equation for the force on a current-carrying conductor. [1]
   c. The local magnetic flux density is 40 µT.
      Calculate the force on a section of cable between each pair of pylons. [1]
   d. Give the units to your answer in part **c**. [1]
   e. This force would be equivalent to what change in mass on the Earth's surface?
      Comment on your answer. [2]

   [Total: 6]

   > **UNDERSTAND THIS TERM**
   >
   > - magnetic flux density

2. Use the equation for magnetic flux density to work out the missing values **A–E** in the table below.

Force	Magnetic flux density	Current	Length
A	2 T	0.20 A	2 m
4 N	B	100 A	1 km
60 mN	0.2 T	C	2 m
225 µN	150 mT	30 mA	D
E	6 T	60 mA	2 m

3. A 4 mm section of wire passes through a magnetic field that acts vertically upwards.

   The magnetic flux density is 4 T and a force of 54 mN pushes the wire due West.

   Calculate the direction and magnitude of the current through the wire.

24.4 Measuring magnetic flux density

1. Describe how the flux density can be measured using a current balance. **[Total: 5]**

2. A wire is clamped so that it cannot move, and a 4 cm section of it is passed between the poles of a magnet whose magnetic flux density is 15 mT as shown in Figure 24.3.

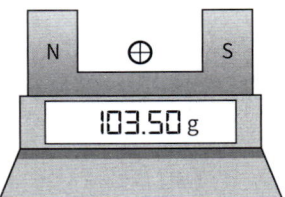

Figure 24.3

Before a current is passed through the wire, the reading on the mass balance is 103.50 g.

Calculate the reading on the balance when a current of 12 A is passed through the wire. **[Total: 6]**

3. A magnet is placed on top of a mass balance, which is then zeroed.

A wire is placed so that a 5.5 cm section passes perpendicular to the magnetic field.

A current of 1.65 A is passed through the wire, and the reading on the balance increases by 1.73 g.

What is the value of the magnetic field strength?

24.5 Currents crossing fields

1. Figure 24.4 shows the cross-section of a loudspeaker.

A coil of wire is wound around a cylinder. This is attached to the cone, which is free to move. The coil passes between the poles of a magnet, as shown.

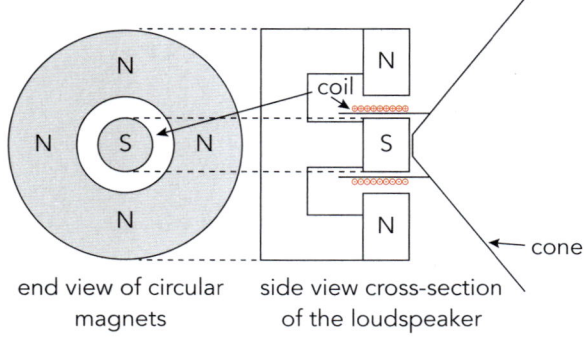

Figure 24.4

a   In the top half of the coil, the current goes into the page.
    Predict the direction the cone will move explain your answer. [2]
b   In the bottom half of the coil, the current is coming out of the page.
    Predict the direction the cone will move explain your answer. [2]
c   Suggest what will happen to the cone when the loudspeaker is operating normally.
    Explain your answer. [2]
d   The coil has 240 turns and has been wound onto a 1.2 cm diameter cylinder.
    Determine the length of the wire. [1]
e   The magnetic flux density of the magnets is 15 mT.
    When a current of 300 mA flows, determine the force on the coil. [2]
f   Give the units for your answer to part e. [1]

[Total: 10]

2   At a particular point on the Earth's surface, the Earth's magnetic field has a horizontal component of 16 µT due South and a downward vertical component of 39 µT.

Work out:

a   The magnitude of the Earth's magnetic field at this point and the inclination of its field lines (the angle from the horizontal).
b   The magnitude and direction of the force on a horizontal length of wire 365 m long and carrying a current of 100 A from East to West.

3   A 5 cm long conductor is spinning in a uniform magnetic field, as shown in Figure 24.5.

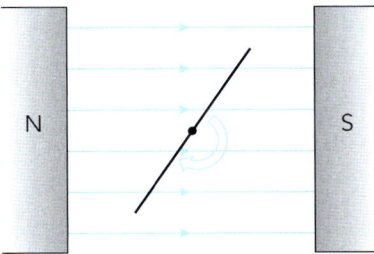

Figure 24.5

The force and torque on a current-carrying conductor vary depending on its angle with the magnetic field.

Copy and complete the table below by calculating the force and torque on a 5 cm long conductor where it has the angles with the magnetic field shown.

The first angle has been done for you. You may need to work out how to calculate torque from your previous studies.

The magnetic field density is 15 mT and a current of 2 A passes through the wire.

Angle / °	Force / 10^{-4} N	Torque / 10^{-6} N m
0	0	0
30		
45		
60		
90		

4 Figure 24.6 shows a square coil with sides of 4 cm within a uniform magnetic field.

The leads to the power supply are not shown. A current of 300 mA flows around the loop, and it is placed inside a uniform magnetic field whose field strength is 30 mT.

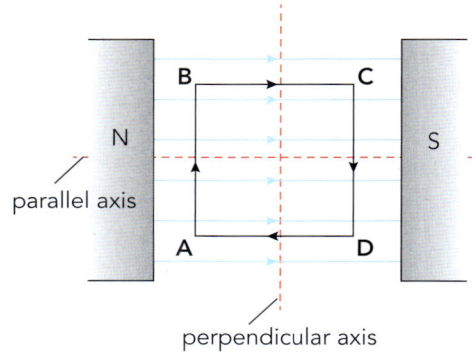

Figure 24.6

a   What is the force and torque on the sides:
   i   AB
   ii BC
   iii CD
   iv DA?

b   How would the force and torque vary on side AB if the coil was spinning about the axis that is perpendicular to the field lines?

c   How would the force and torque vary on side BC if the coil was spinning about the axis that is parallel to the field lines?

24.6 Forces between currents

1   Current passes through two parallel wires, wire L and wire R, in the same direction, as shown in Figure 24.7.

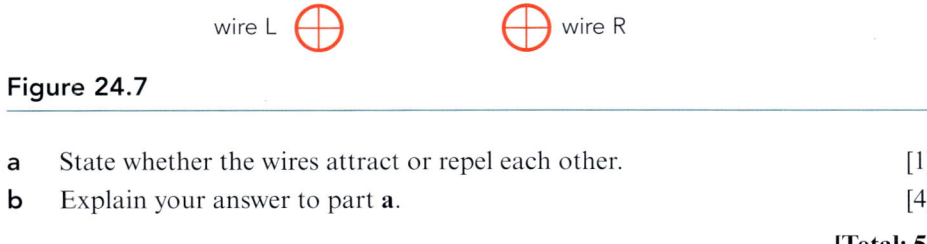

Figure 24.7

    a   State whether the wires attract or repel each other. [1]
    b   Explain your answer to part **a**. [4]

[Total: 5]

24.7 Relating SI units

1   The usual unit for magnetic flux density is the tesla. Express the magnetic flux density in base SI units.

> **REFLECTION**
>
> How do you recall the base SI units? What is your strategy for working out the base SI units for a given variable or whether a given equation is homogeneous?

24.8 Comparing forces in magnetic, electric and gravitational fields

1   What do all fields (electric, gravitational, magnetic) share in common?

UNDERSTAND THESE TERMS
- base units
- derived units

CAMBRIDGE INTERNATIONAL AS & A LEVEL PHYSICS: EXAM PREPARATION AND PRACTICE

SELF-ASSESSMENT CHECKLIST

Let's revisit the Knowledge focus and Exam skills focus for this chapter.

Decide how confident you are with each statement.

Now I can:	Show it	Needs more work	Almost there	Confident to move on
describe a magnetic field as an example of a field of force caused by moving charges or permanent magnets	Describe how moving charges is the source of permanent magnetism.			
use field lines to represent a field and sketch various patterns	Sketch the magnetic field pattern around a bar magnet, a current-carrying conductor and a solenoid.			
determine the size and direction of the force on a current-carrying conductor in a magnetic field	Write some questions along the lines of those in 24.3.2 and 24.3.3 and get your classmates to show you how they get the correct force and direction on the wire. Get them to write some questions for you.			
define magnetic flux density and know how it can be measured	Describe how a mass balance can be used to measure magnetic flux density, taking care to state how measurements are taken to calculate a value.			
explain the origin of the forces between current-carrying conductors and find the direction of these forces	Use the right-hand grip rule and Fleming's left-hand rule to show that parallel conductors attract when the current is in the same direction and repel when the currents are in opposite directions.			
answer a variety of 'explain' questions	Choose a command word and compare how you would answer a question using that command word and 'explain'.			

25 Motion of charged particles

KNOWLEDGE FOCUS

In this chapter you will answer questions on:
- observing the force
- orbiting charged particles
- electric and magnetic fields
- the Hall effect
- discovering the electron.

EXAM SKILLS FOCUS

In this chapter you will:
- plan and structure long-form responses.

You practised answering longer answer questions in Chapter 14. In this chapter, you will find several written questions worth 6 marks. Before you write your answer to these longer written questions, you should stop to think about the most logical steps to structure your response. Try to understand all of the instructions that you are given in the question – this will help you to spot the two or three parts that make up the long question. Use the knowledge and skills you practised in Chapter 14 to help you as your answer the questions in this chapter. Remember that useful information will be given in the other instructional text in these questions, which you practised identifying in Chapter 14.

25.1 Observing the force

1. Copy and complete the table stating whether each situation will cause the particle to move in a clockwise or anticlockwise direction.

Charge	Direction	Direction of the magnetic field	Clockwise or anticlockwise
Positive	From left to right	Out of the page	
Negative	From left to right	Into the page	
Positive	From top to bottom	Into the page	
Negative	From bottom to top	Out of the page	

2. Electron beam tubes can be used in a school laboratory to accelerate electrons to two-thirds of the speed of light.

   a Figure 25.1 shows an electron beam tube.

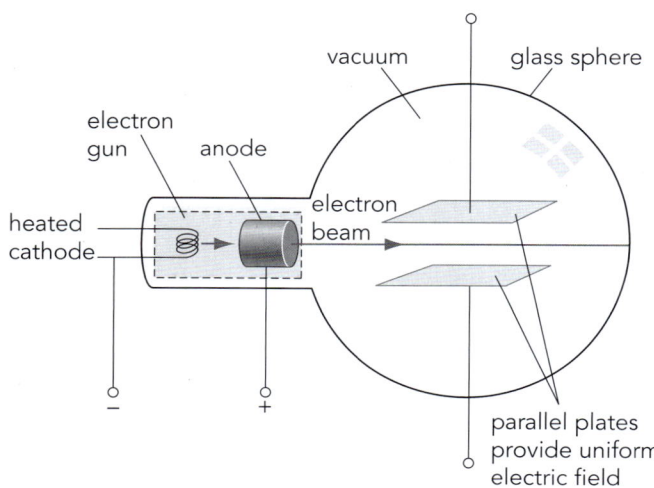

Figure 25.1

Explain how electrons are produced at the cathode and how the apparatus can be used to show that the electrons have mass and have a negative charge. [6]

   b An electron beam tube can also be used with a pair of Helmholtz coils. When a current is passed through a pair of Helmholtz coils, a magnetic field is created perpendicular to the plane of the uniform electric field.

   The Helmholtz coils are set a fixed distance apart on either side of the vacuum tube. They produce a field strength per ampere of approximately 7.5×10^{-4} T A^{-1}.

   Calculate the size of the force on the electron when a 0.30 A current is passed through the Helmholtz coils. [3]

   [Total: 9]

25 Motion of charged particles

> ## « RECALL AND CONNECT 1 «
>
> In Chapter 16, you learned about circular motion. Write an equation for the centripetal force on an object moving in a circle in terms of its speed and in terms of its angular speed.

25.2 Orbiting charged particles

1. Explain how a charged particle in a magnetic field can be made to orbit in a circular motion.

2. Derive the equation $p = Ber$ for an electron moving in a circular orbit in a magnetic field.

3. Carl Anderson took the photograph shown in Figure 25.2 in 1932. It shows the tracks of a charged particle in a magnetic field. During the motion, the particle collides with a metal target in the middle of the image.

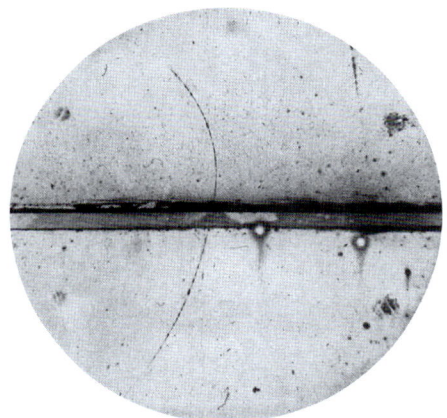

Figure 25.2

    a   Explain how the photograph shows that the particle is moving upwards. [2]

    b   The particle in the photograph was later confirmed to be a positron. A positron shares the same properties as an electron, except it is positively charged.

         Compare how the trail would appear if it were an electron with the same initial velocity entering from the same position. [2]

    c   The magnetic flux density in Carl Anderson's experiment was approximately 1.5 T.

         A positron has a kinetic energy of 60 keV.

         Calculate the radius of curvature of the positron in the 1.5 T magnetic field. [4]

[Total: 8]

> CAMBRIDGE INTERNATIONAL AS & A LEVEL PHYSICS: EXAM PREPARATION AND PRACTICE

> « RECALL AND CONNECT 2 «
>
> In Chapter 4, you learned Newton's second law relating resultant force to acceleration. Write Newton's second law in algebra in terms of acceleration and in terms of momentum.

25.3 Electric and magnetic fields

1. Derive the equation $v = \dfrac{E}{B}$ for the velocity of a particle in a velocity selector.

2. A velocity selector consists of a uniform electric field that is perpendicular to a uniform magnetic field.

    When a beam of particles with equal charges and equal masses but different particle velocities passes perpendicular to both fields, some particles will continue undeflected.

    a Explain why those particles that continue undeflected have equal velocities. You may use a labelled diagram to accompany your answer. [6]

    b A velocity selector has a magnetic field of 0.5 T.

       Calculate the electric field strength needed to produce a beam of electrons with a speed of $1.2 \times 10^7 \, \text{m s}^{-1}$. You may assume that the electrons are at their rest mass. [2]

       [Total: 8]

25.4 The Hall effect

1. How does the Hall effect produce a potential difference between the two sides of a Hall probe when it is placed in a magnetic field?

2. Calculate the Hall voltage for the germanium Hall probe:
    - Charge carrier (electrons) density = $2.3 \times 10^{13} \, \text{m}^{-3}$
    - Thickness = 3.0 mm
    - Current = 0.45 mA
    - Magnetic flux density = 300 µT.

3. A Hall probe has a depth of 2 mm. It is made of a semiconductor with a charge carrier density $2.8 \times 10^{20} \, \text{m}^{-3}$. The free charge carriers in the semiconductor of the Hall probe are electrons.

    a Derive the equation $V_H = \dfrac{BI}{ntq}$ [4]

> **UNDERSTAND THESE TERMS**
>
> - Hall effect
> - Hall voltage

b The graph in Figure 25.3 shows the Hall voltage for a number of values of current in a permanent magnetic field.

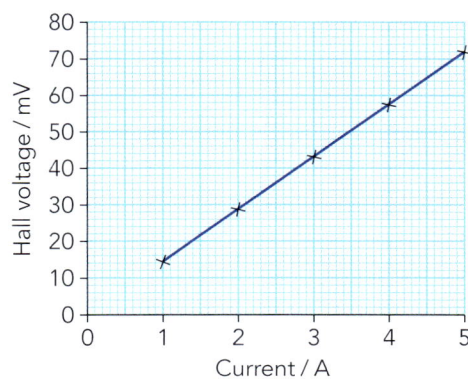

Figure 25.3

Use the graph to determine the magnetic flux density. [3]

c Explain what difference (if any) the student would see in their results if they were to reverse the direction of the current through their Hall probe. [3]

[Total: 10]

25.5 Discovering the electron

1 Explain why a single, narrow beam of electrons, when deflected by electric or magnetic fields, is evidence for the particles all having the same mass, charge and speed.

2 Calculate the charge to mass ratio for an electron. (Use data from the formula sheet.) Give a unit for your answer.

> **REFLECTION**
>
> How did you do in the longer written questions in this chapter? Did you notice how the questions were structured to give you clues as to what is on the mark scheme? What further work do you need to do to ensure that you get the majority of the marks in these questions?

SELF-ASSESSMENT CHECKLIST

Let's revisit the Knowledge focus and Exam skills focus for this chapter.

Decide how confident you are with each statement.

Now I can:	Show it	Needs more work	Almost there	Confident to move on
determine the direction of the force on a charge moving in a magnetic field	Practise applying Fleming's left-hand rule for various situations involving charged particles moving in a magnetic field.			
recall and use $F = BQv \sin \theta$	Use the equation $F = BQv \sin \theta$ to calculate sizes of forces on charged particles in magnetic fields.			
describe the motion of a charged particle moving in a uniform magnetic field perpendicular to the direction of motion of the particle	Use the terms centripetal force and acceleration in a circle to explain the shape of orbits of charged particles in magnetic fields.			
explain how electric and magnetic fields can be used in velocity selection	Draw a labelled diagram of a velocity selector. Include details of the fields and the forces on a charged particle if it is going above, below and at a selected speed.			
understand the origin of the Hall voltage and derive and use the expression: $V_H = \dfrac{BI}{ntq}$	Write out the steps in the derivation of the expression: $V_H = \dfrac{BI}{ntq}$ Include a diagram of the Hall probe being used and give an example of a calculation involving the equation.			

25 Motion of charged particles

CONTINUED

Now I can:	Show it	Needs more work	Almost there	Confident to move on
understand the use of a Hall probe to measure magnetic flux density	Write a procedure for a practical to measure the magnetic flux density of a uniform magnetic field with a Hall probe.			
plan and structure long-form responses	After self-assessing exam questions, reflect on whether the sequence in which you wrote your answer was the most logical way to make your explanation.			

26 Electromagnetic induction

KNOWLEDGE FOCUS

In this chapter you will answer questions on:
- observing induction
- explaining electromagnetic induction
- Faraday's law of electromagnetic induction
- Lenz's law
- everyday examples of electromagnetic induction.

EXAM SKILLS FOCUS

In this chapter you will:
- show that you understand the 'give' command word and can answer 'give' questions.

If you are asked to 'give' an answer in a question, the answer will likely only be worth one or two marks. You will need to either recall knowledge/information that you have been taught, or identify a significant piece of information given to you in the question.

| Give | produce an answer from a given source or recall/memory |

26 Electromagnetic induction

26.1 Observing induction

1. An e.m.f. is induced if a straight wire conductor is moved relative to a magnetic field. What is the change to the induced e.m.f. if:

   a a larger magnetic flux density is used

   b the conductor is moved in the opposite direction

   c the conductor is moved at a slower speed

   d the polarity of the magnets are reversed?

2. A simple generator can be modelled in a laboratory.

   a A model generator produces a p.d. of 4 V when turned at 600 revolutions per minute.

   Predict the output p.d. when it is turned at 750 revolutions per minute. [1]

   b In the laboratory the generator produces less p.d. than your answer to part **a**.

   Suggest why this might be. [3]

   c The model generator uses a pair of permanent magnets to create a magnetic field in one plane.

   Real world generators use magnets set at all directions around the rotating coil. This produces a higher output p.d. for the same magnetic field strength, for the same number of turns in the coil, and the same speed of rotation.

   Explain why. [2]

   [Total: 6]

> **UNDERSTAND THESE TERMS**
> - Fleming's right-hand (generator) rule
> - magnetic flux
> - magnetic flux linkage

> **« RECALL AND CONNECT 1 «**
>
> In Chapter 11, you learned the difference between p.d. and e.m.f. What is the difference between p.d. and e.m.f.?

> **REFLECTION**
>
> When you are studying a new topic, think about the possible links to previous topics. For example, if you do not have a good knowledge of electrical circuits, resistors and capacitors, then you may find these questions on electromagnetic induction quite difficult. What techniques could you use to help identify gaps in your knowledge?

26.2 Explaining electromagnetic induction

1. Write an explanation of electromagnetic induction.
2. State the direction of the induced currents in Figure 26.1.

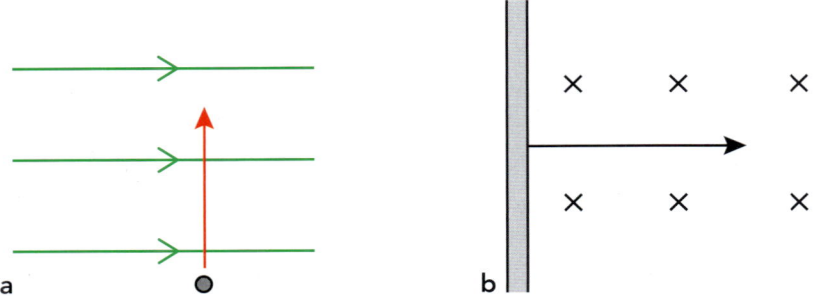

Figure 26.1: a A wire being moved upwards through a magnetic field to the right. **b** A wire being moved to the right through a magnetic field into the page

3. Copy and complete the table.

Magnetic flux / Wb	Magnetic flux density / T	Area of coil / m²
	0.50	2.5×10^{-3}
1.0×10^{-5}		0.20
1.5×10^{-3}		7.5×10^{-3}
	6.0	4.0×10^{-6}

4. Use the information in the table to calculate the magnetic flux linkage in coils A, B and C.

Coil	Cross-sectional area	Number of turns	Magnitude of magnetic field	Orientation
A	40 mm²	200	500 mT	perpendicular to the direction of the magnetic field lines
B	12 cm²	3600	120 µT	30° to the direction of the magnetic field lines
C	1.3 m²	20 000	1.6 T	45° to the direction of the magnetic field lines

5   A search coil (Figure 26.2) can be used to measure magnetic flux density.

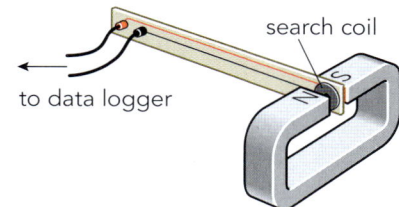

Figure 26.2

The coil is moved rapidly through 90° within a magnetic field. The needle on a micro ammeter connected to the coil is seen to move.

a   Explain why the needle is seen to move. [2]

b   The coil is then rotated back at the same speed through the same 90 degrees.
    State what the student now sees on the ammeter. [1]

c   The student observes that the search coil will also produce the same effect when held at 90° to the field and moved straight out of the field.

    Describe a procedure that the student could follow to use this technique to measure the magnetic flux density of the field.

    Include the apparatus that they should use and explain any techniques or modifications that they can make to ensure their measured magnetic flux density is accurate. [6]

[Total: 9]

26.3 Faraday's law of electromagnetic induction

1   Link each part of the written definition of Faraday's law of electromagnetic induction to the algebraic relationship.

    The magnitude of the induced e.m.f. is directly proportional to the rate of change of magnetic flux linkage.

    $$E \propto \frac{\Delta(N\Phi)}{\Delta t}$$

> **UNDERSTAND THIS TERM**
> - Faraday's law of electromagnetic induction

2   A magnet is dropped through a small flat coil of wire.
    This is shown in Figure 26.3a.

    The e.m.f. induced across the wire is recorded by a data logging voltmeter.

    Figure 26.3b shows a graph of these results.

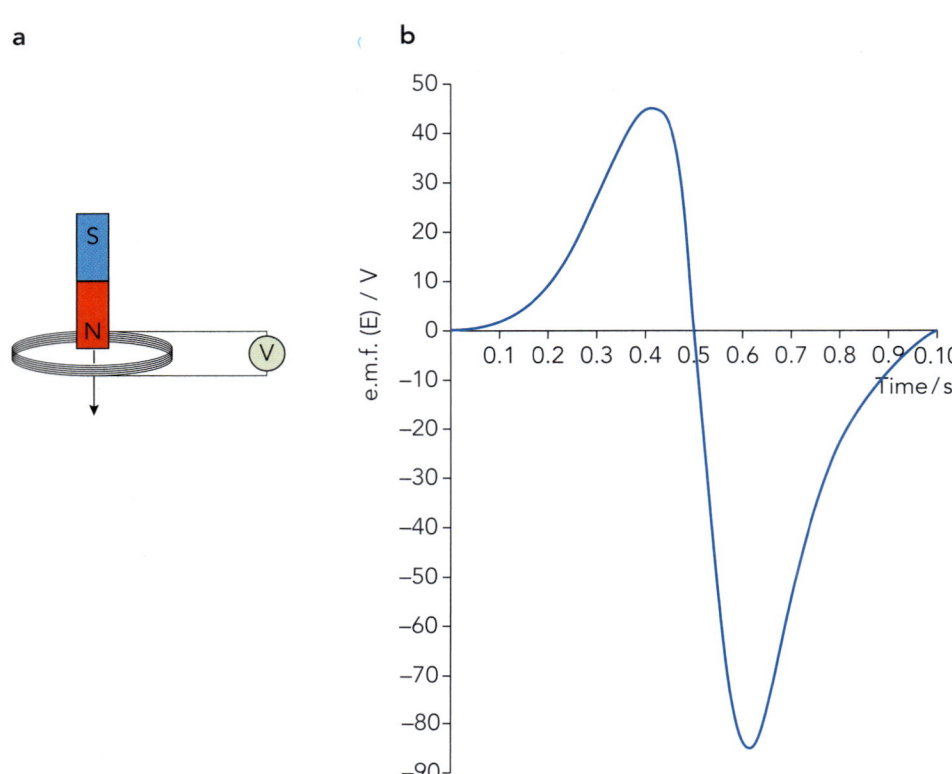

Figure 26.3

a   State what is meant by magnetic flux linkage. [1]
b   Describe and explain the shape of the graph. [4]
c   Use the graph to calculate the total change in magnetic flux as the magnet enters the coil. [2]
d   A second experiment is conducted with three times the number of coils. Explain what changes the students would see in their graphs. [2]

[Total: 9]

26.4 Lenz's law

1   How does Lenz's law change Faraday's law of electromagnetic induction into an equation?
2   Explain why Lenz's law is a consequence of the law of conservation of energy.

UNDERSTAND THIS TERM

- Lenz's law

3 a Explain why an induced e.m.f. will be in the opposite direction to the direction of change in the magnetic field that produced it. [1]

  b A long copper cylinder is positioned vertically so that objects can be dropped into it and these objects will fall through the centre of the cylinder.
    A steel block is dropped through the cylinder and timed using light gates.
    The same steel block is then magnetised and dropped through the cylinder again.
    After being magnetised, the steel block takes longer to fall through the cylinder than before.
    Use Faraday's law and Lenz's law to explain these observations. [4]

[Total: 5]

26.5 Everyday examples of electromagnetic induction

1 How is an alternator different from a dynamo?
2 Why will a transformer not work if the input supply is d.c.?
3 Figure 26.4 shows a side view of a coil being rotated continuously at a constant speed in a magnetic field.

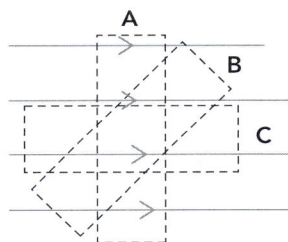

Figure 26.4

  a Give the position of the coil at which the induced e.m.f. is a maximum. [1]
  b The generator produces an alternating current.
    Suggest a change could be made to give an output of direct current. [1]
  c A demonstration transformer allows you to change the number of turns on the secondary output coil and the frequency of the input a.c. current.
    i   State the law by which an e.m.f. is induced on the secondary coil in a transformer. [1]
    ii Give the change in the output e.m.f. if the number of turns on the secondary coil is doubled. [1]
    iii Give the change in the output e.m.f. if the frequency of the input a.c. current is halved. [1]

[Total: 5]

> **CAMBRIDGE INTERNATIONAL AS & A LEVEL PHYSICS: EXAM PREPARATION AND PRACTICE**

REFLECTION

How confident do you feel about your understanding of the command words 'state' and 'give'? Could you explain the difference between them to a friend?

SELF-ASSESSMENT CHECKLIST

Let's revisit the Knowledge focus and Exam skills focus for this chapter.
Decide how confident you are with each statement.

Now I can:	Show it	Needs more work	Almost there	Confident to move on
define magnetic flux as the product of the magnetic flux density and the cross-sectional area perpendicular to the direction of the magnetic flux density	Write out a definition of magnetic flux in words and in algebra.			
recall and use $\Phi = BA$	Calculate the magnetic flux for a range of situations.			
understand and use the concept of magnetic flux linkage	Use the expression $N\Phi = BAN$ for situations involving a linked field, i.e. each turn of the coil has the same magnetic flux through it, and so it is linked N times.			
understand and explain experiments that demonstrate: • that a changing magnetic flux can induce an e.m.f. in a circuit • that the direction of the induced e.m.f. opposes the change producing it • the factors affecting the magnitude of the induced e.m.f.	Use elaborate interrogation to explain how we can show that: Moving a magnet relative to a coil of wire induces an e.m.f. The direction changes if either the poles or the direction of movement changes. The induced e.m.f. depends upon the rate of change of flux linkage.			

CONTINUED

Now I can:	Show it	Needs more work	Almost there	Confident to move on
recall and use Faraday's and Lenz's laws of electromagnetic induction	Write out Faraday's and Lenz's laws of electromagnetic induction in both words and algebra and practise using it to explain and make calculations with situations involving electromagnetic induction.			
show that I understand the 'give' command word and can answer 'give' questions	Go through the 'give' questions in this chapter and make sure you understand why that command word was chosen.			

27 Alternating currents

KNOWLEDGE FOCUS

In this chapter you will answer questions on:
- sinusoidal current
- alternating voltage
- power and alternating current
- rectification.

EXAM SKILLS FOCUS

In this chapter you will:
- practise answering questions that contain multiple command words.

A large number of the more complex exam questions rely on using multiple command words in the question such as 'describe' and 'explain', or 'suggest' and 'explain'. This type of question usually carries higher marks. To successfully answer these questions you will need to make sure you cover both command words in your answer. You may need to plan your answer to make sure you are covering both command words equally. There are a number of these more complex questions in this chapter which will give you practice at answering these questions.

27 Alternating currents

27.1 Sinusoidal current

1. Sketch a graph of a sinusoidal alternating current with a time period of 40 ms, and peak current of 0.40 A.
2. Write an expression for the current at time *t* related to the peak current and the time period.
3. Determine the magnitude of the current of a 60 Hz a.c. supply 32 ms after it is initially switched on.

   The peak current is 0.90 A. **[Total: 2]**

> **UNDERSTAND THIS TERM**
> - sinusoidal

27.2 Alternating voltages

1. Sketch a graph of a sinusoidal alternating p.d. with a time period of 300 µs, and peak p.d. 20 kV.
2. Write an expression for the p.d. at time *t* related to the peak p.d. and the time period.
3. Explain how a cathode ray oscilloscope can be used to give accurate readings of p.d. and time period for alternating current signals.
4. An electrician uses a portable graphing oscilloscope to measure the p.d. output at a terminal in a building. Figure 27.1 shows the graph they produce.

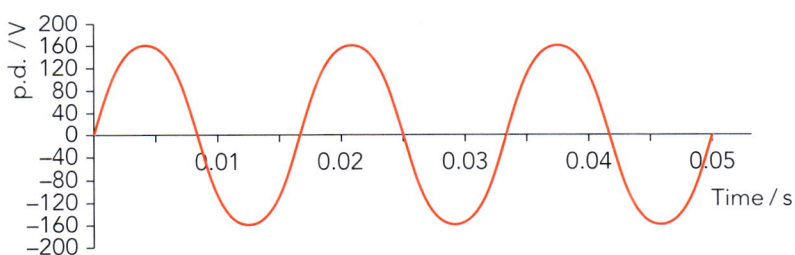

Figure 27.1

> **UNDERSTAND THESE TERMS**
> - period
> - frequency
> - peak value

a. Calculate the angular frequency of the alternating p.d. [3]
b. Determine the p.d. at time 0.015 s. [1]
c. The electrician finds a fault in the wiring where there is a short circuit caused by a misplaced component. The effective resistance of the component is 320 ohms. Calculate the peak power dissipated in the wire. [2]
d. Describe and explain how your answer to part **c** will be different to the average power dissipated through the component. [3]

[Total: 9]

> **« RECALL AND CONNECT 1 «**
>
> Think back to Chapter 8, where you learned the three equations for electrical power. Write out the three equations for electrical power.

27.3 Power and alternating current

1. Copy and complete this table:

$V_{r.m.s.}$	V_0
230 V	
	160 V
440 kV	
	47 kV

2. Use an algebraic argument to explain why the mean power in a resistive load is half the maximum power for a sinusoidal alternating current.

3. A variable frequency power supply has a peak p.d. of 24 V.

   a. Calculate the r.m.s. p.d. [1]

   b. The supply is now used to drive a current through a resistor of 22 ohms. Calculate the average power output. [2]

   c. Figure 27.2 shows an alternating current signal. Sketch a graph of I^2 against t. [4]

   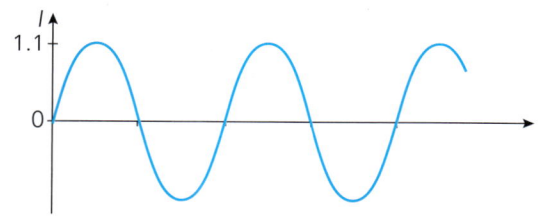

   Figure 27.2

   d. The frequency of the power supply is now doubled. The peak p.d. is not altered. Describe and explain the change to the power output of the circuit. [2]

   [Total: 9]

UNDERSTAND THIS TERM
- root mean square (r.m.s.) value

27.4 Rectification

1. **a** Draw a circuit diagram that could be used to rectify an a.c. supply using just one diode.

   (Giving a half-wave rectified output.)

   b Draw a circuit diagram that could be used to rectify an a.c. supply using more than one diode.

   (Giving a full-wave rectified output.)

2. A student makes a circuit to rectify an a.c. supply using one diode. The student researched the maximum current for their silicon diode, which is 50 mA. If the current is above this value for even a very short period of time, the silicon will melt.

   The student calculates that the maximum p.d. they should use is 2.0 V a.c.

   a The silicone diode melts.

   Suggest an error that the student may have made in their calculations. [2]

   b Suggest a change that the student can make to reduce the likelihood of the diode melting. [1]

   The student then uses a bridge rectification circuit.
   Figure 27.3 shows the p.d. against time graph that this produces.

   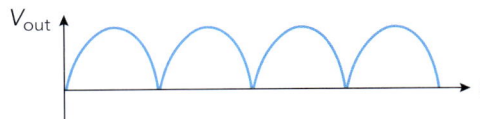

   Figure 27.3

   The student add a capacitor in parallel with the load resistance of the circuit.

   c Sketch a line on a copy of the axes in Figure 27.4 to show the new shape of the rectified signal. [1]

   Figure 27.4

   d Describe and explain the effect of:
   - **i** increasing the capacitance of the capacitor [2]
   - **ii** increasing the resistance of the circuit. [2]

   [Total: 8]

> **UNDERSTAND THESE TERM**
> - rectification
> - half-wave rectification
> - full-wave rectification

> **CAMBRIDGE INTERNATIONAL AS & A LEVEL PHYSICS: EXAM PREPARATION AND PRACTICE**

REFLECTION

There are questions in this chapter that include both 'describe' *and* 'explain' as command words. You will need to make sure you include *both* the description *and* the explanation in your answers to these questions. Did your answer cover both command words? How confident do you feel that you understand the command words 'describe' and 'explain' and the difference between them? What techniques could you use to make sure you don't forget to answer any command words in questions that contain more than one?

SELF-ASSESSMENT CHECKLIST

Let's revisit the Knowledge focus and Exam skills focus for this chapter.

Decide how confident you are with each statement.

Now I can:	Show it	Needs more work	Almost there	Confident to move on
understand and use the terms period, frequency and peak value as applied to an alternating current or voltage	Practice analysis of graphical representations of a.c. currents and a.c. potential differences.			
use equations of the form $x = x_0 \sin \omega t$ representing a sinusoidally alternating current or voltage	Calculate p.d.s and currents at given times in their sinusoidal cycles.			
recall and use the fact that the mean power in a resistive load is half the maximum power for a sinusoidal alternating current	Calculate average powers if given peak power for a sinusoidal a.c. current.			
distinguish between root mean square (r.m.s.) and peak values and recall and use $I_{r.m.s.} = \frac{I_0}{\sqrt{2}}$ and $V_{r.m.s.} = \frac{V_0}{\sqrt{2}}$ for a sinusoidal alternating current	Identify when peak values or r.m.s. values are given or expected in questions or answers and convert between them.			
distinguish graphically between half-wave and full-wave rectification	Make a set of sketch graphs to show half-wave and full-wave rectification.			
explain the use of a single diode for the half-wave rectification of an alternating current	Write explanations with a set of diagrams to explain half-wave rectification with a single diode.			

CONTINUED

Now I can:	Show it	Needs more work	Almost there	Confident to move on
explain the use of four diodes (bridge rectifier) for the full-wave rectification of an alternating current	Write an explanation with a set of diagrams to explain full-wave rectification with four diodes in a bridge circuit.			
analyse the effect of a single capacitor in smoothing, including the effect of the value of capacitance and the load resistance	Compare graphs of full-wave rectification both with and without a capacitor for smoothing the output. Use your knowledge about capacitors and resistors to explain the effect of changing either the capacitor value or the resistance value in the circuit.			
answer questions that contain multiple command words	Write out plans for answers for as many questions with multiple command words as you can.			

Exam practice 7

This section contains past paper questions from previous Cambridge exams, which draws together your knowledge on a range of topics that you have covered up to this point. These questions give you the opportunity to test your knowledge and understanding. Additional past paper practice questions can be found in the accompanying digital material.

The following question has an example student response and commentary provided. Once you have worked through the question, read the student response and commentary. Are your answers different to the sample responses?

1 a An electron is travelling at speed v in a straight line in a vacuum. It enters a uniform magnetic field of flux density 8.0×10^{-4} T. Initially, the electron is travelling at right angles to the magnetic field, as illustrated in Fig. 1.1.

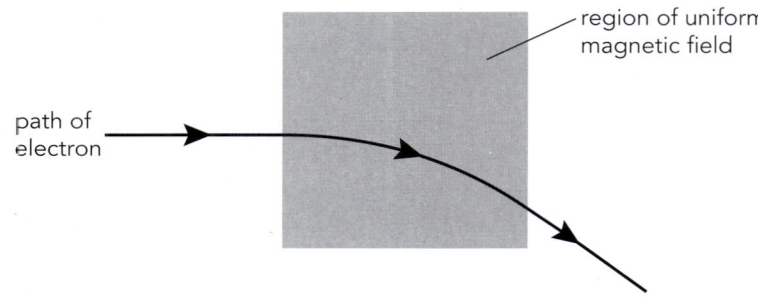

Fig. 1.1

The path of the electron in the magnetic field is an arc of a circle of radius 6.4 cm.

    i State and explain the direction of the magnetic field. [2]

    ii Show that the speed v of the electron is 9.0×10^6 m s^{-1}. [3]

b A uniform electric field is now applied in the same region as the magnetic field.

The electron passes undeviated through the region of the two fields, as illustrated in Fig. 1.2.

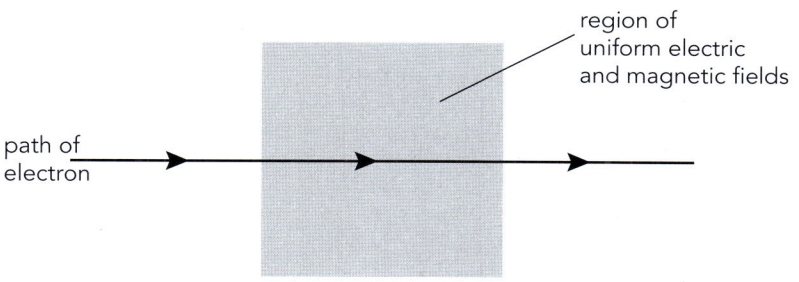

Fig. 1.2

    i On Fig. 1.2, mark with an arrow the direction of the uniform electric field. [1]

    ii Use data from **a** to calculate the magnitude of the electric field strength. [2]

c The electron in **b** is now replaced by an α-particle travelling at the same speed v along the same initial path as the electron.

Describe and explain the shape of the path in the region of the magnetic and electric fields. [2]

[Total: 10]

Cambridge International AS & A Level Physics (9702) Paper 42, Q9, June 2020

Example student response			Commentary
a	**i**	You use Fleming's left-hand rule to work it out. The field is into the page.	This is correct, but to get the second mark they need to show exactly what orientation the left hand is being used in by either stating that they know the force is downwards on the electron, or that (because the electron is negative) the current is towards the left of the page. **This answer is awarded 1 out of 2 marks.**
	ii	Electron moves in a circle, so magnetic force is the centripetal force so: $Bev = \dfrac{mv^2}{r}$ $v = \dfrac{Ber}{m}$ $v = \dfrac{8 \times 10^{-4} \times 1.6 \times 10^{-19} \times 0.064}{9.11 \times 10^{-31}}$	The student has recognised a common synoptic link, that is, making a force equal to the centripetal force. They have then shown all the steps in their working for full marks on a 'show' question, including the unit conversion on the radius and finding the data of the mass of an electron from the formula sheet. **This answer is awarded 3 out of 3 marks.**
b	**i**	arrows upwards	The student has mistaken the instruction to mean the *direction* of the force on the charged particle. Otherwise, they may have mistaken the field direction as the same as the direction of the force on this charged particle. Remember that the direction of the electric field is the same as the direction of a force on a positive test charge. **This answer is awarded 0 out of 1 mark.**

Example student response	Commentary
ii $F = EQ$ $\dfrac{mv^2}{r} = EQ$ $\dfrac{9.11 \times 10^{-31} \times 9.0 \times 10^{62}}{0.064 \times 1.6 \times 10^{-19}} = E$ $E = 7200$ NC^{-1}	The student has the correct answer, but there is a simpler way to answer the question, using the equation for the speed of a particle in a velocity selector: $v = \dfrac{E}{B}$ The student is actually quite lucky because electric fields do not cause particles to move in circular paths but in parabolic ones. (See Chapter 21, Uniform electric fields.) But, in this special case, the electric field force is equal to the magnetic field force, which would make the particle describe a circular path. *This answer is awarded 2 out of 2 marks.*
c The alpha particle would be deflected downwards, because the magnetic force depends on the mass, and so the downwards force will be greater than the upwards force. The upwards force is also increased because the charge is bigger and electric field force depends on charge, but it isn't as big an increase as in the magnetic field.	To get the marks, the student needed to recognise that for the velocity selector, the speed only depends on the ratio of the two field strengths. In fact, neither of the two forces depends upon mass (although accelerations do). The forces both depend on charge but in the same proportion, so this proportional change cancels out. Again, the student would have made this whole question a lot simpler if they had recognised that the question was about a velocity selector and applied the equation: $v = \dfrac{E}{B}$ *This answer is awarded 0 out of 2 marks.*

2   Now that you have read through the sample response and commentary for question **1**, think about a similar topic and write a similar exam question that asks students to apply the same understanding and skills.

The following question has an example student response and commentary provided. Once you have worked through the question, read the student response and commentary. Are your answers different to the sample responses?

3   A bridge rectifier contains four diodes. The output of the rectifier is connected to a resistor R, as shown in Fig. 3.1.

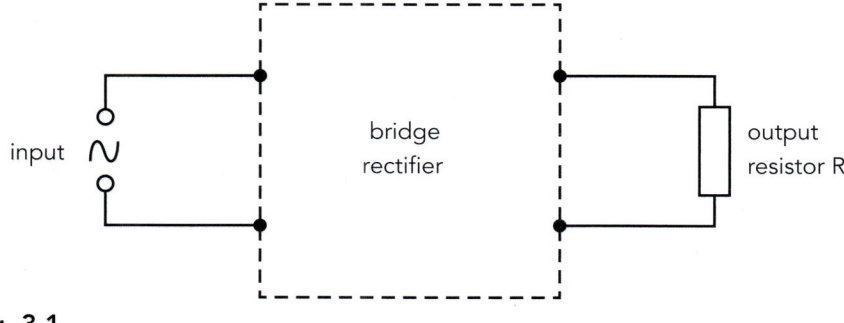

Fig. 3.1

The variation with time t of the input e.m.f. E to the rectifier is given by the expression
$$E = 15\cos(210t)$$
where t is measured in seconds and E in volts.

The variation with time t of the potential difference V across resistor R is shown in Fig. 3.2.

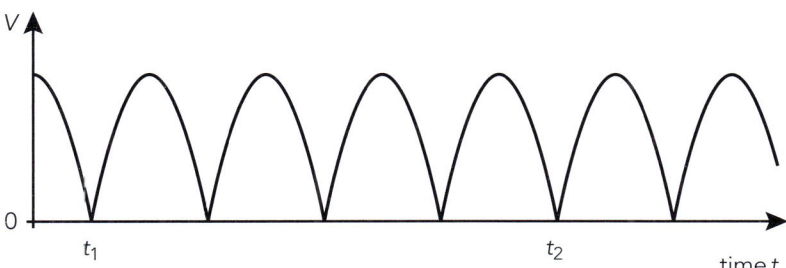

Fig. 3.2

Determine:

a the maximum potential difference V_{MAX} across resistor R [1]

b the time interval, to two significant figures, between time t_1 and time t_2. [3]

[Total: 4]

Cambridge International AS & A Level Physics (9702) Paper 41, Q10, June 2019

Example student response	Commentary
a 15 V	The student has correctly recognised that the equation given in the question is in the form: $x = x_0 \sin \omega t$ This could have been difficult, but the student has recognised that it is only worth one mark, so there is not much to be done. *This answer is awarded 1 out of 1 mark.*
b $\omega = 210$ rad s^{-1} $\dfrac{2\pi}{210} = T = 0.030$ s $t_1 - t_2 = 0.12$ s	The student has correctly used the expression to give them the time period. To get the final mark, they needed to multiply the time period by 2 rather than by 4. They have then counted the number of peaks in between the two times indicated. And so multiplied by 4. However, as this is rectified a.c. a full wave consists of two peaks, and so the time between the two points is two full time periods. *This answer is awarded 2 out of 3 marks.*

Now you have read the commentary to the previous question, here is a similar question that you should attempt. Use the information from the previous response and commentary to guide you as you answer.

4 Fig. 4.1 shows four diodes and a load resistor of resistance 1.2 kΩ, connected in a circuit that is used to produce rectification of an alternating voltage.

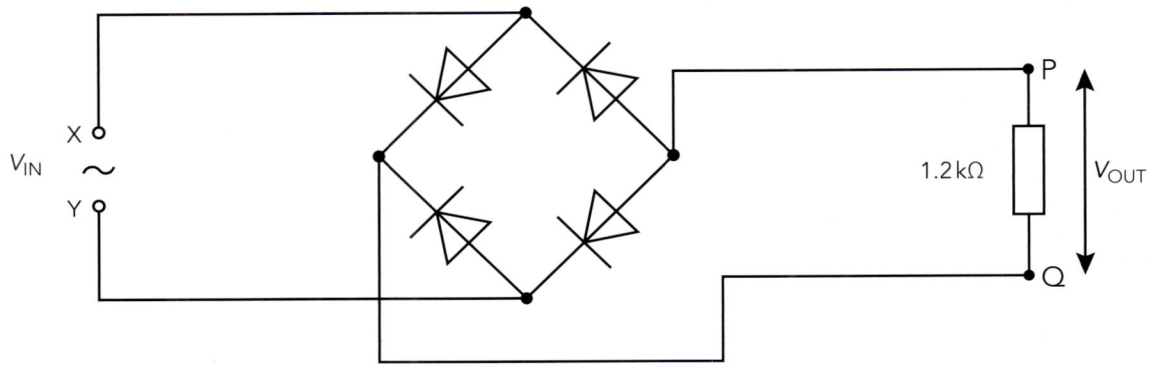

Fig. 4.1

a **i** State what is meant by rectification. [1]

   ii State the type of rectification produced by the circuit in Fig. 4.1. [1]

b A sinusoidal alternating voltage V_{IN} is applied across the input terminals X and Y. The variation with time t of V_{IN} is given by the equation:

$$V_{IN} = 6.0 \sin 25\pi t$$

where V_{IN} is in volts and t is in seconds.

   i On Fig. 4.1, label the output terminals P and Q with the appropriate symbols to indicate the polarity of the output voltage V_{OUT}. [1]

   ii The magnitude of the output voltage V_{OUT} varies with t as shown in Fig. 4.2.

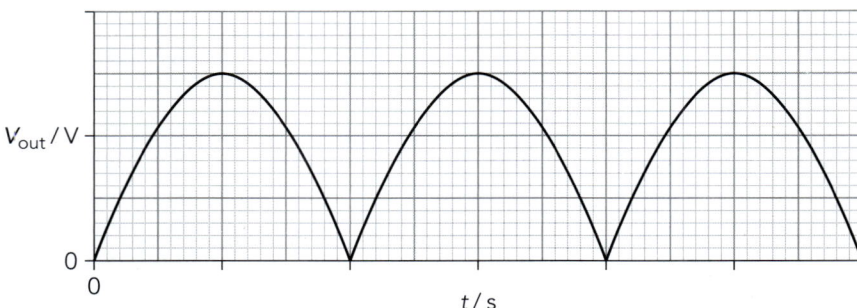

Fig. 4.2

On Fig. 4.2, label both of the axes with the correct scales. [3]

c The output voltage in **b** is smoothed by adding a capacitor to the circuit in Fig. 4.1.

The difference between the maximum and minimum values of the smoothed output voltage is 10% of the peak voltage.

    i On Fig. 4.1, draw the circuit symbol for a capacitor showing the capacitor correctly connected into the circuit. [1]

    ii On Fig. 4.2, sketch the variation with t of the smoothed output voltage. [2]

    iii Calculate the capacitance C of the capacitor. [3]

[Total: 12]

Cambridge International AS & A Level Physics (9702) Paper 41, Q5, June 2022

28 Quantum physics

KNOWLEDGE FOCUS

In this chapter you will answer questions on:
- modelling with particles and waves
- particulate nature of light
- the photoelectric effect
- threshold frequency and wavelength
- momentum of Photons
- line spectra
- explaining the origin of line spectra
- photon energies
- the nature of light: waves or particles?
- electron waves
- revisiting photons.

EXAM SKILLS FOCUS

In this chapter you will:
- further practise answering 'calculate' questions.

You have practised answering more complex 'calculate' questions throughout this book. This chapter gives you practise answering 'calculate' questions on a more complex topic. In a 'calculate' question, it is not sufficient to just write the final answer. It is important to write down all the steps in the calculation that leads to a solution or all the steps in your thinking. You should aim to write a model answer. When you are asked to show how to reach an approximate answer, you are strongly advised to write down the exact answer before rounding to the approximate answer.

| Calculate | work out from given facts, figures or information |

28.1 Modelling with particles and waves and
28.2 Particulate nature of light

1. What is the relationship between power, intensity and surface area?

2.
   a. What is the origin of the electronvolt as a unit of energy?
   b. Work out the energy transferred to an electron when it passes through a 9 V cell.
   c. Work out the kinetic energy gained by an electron when it is accelerated by a potential difference of 9 V. Express the energy in both eV and J.
   d. Work out the energy of a photon of gamma radiation that has a wavelength of 7×10^{-12} m. Express your answer in both eV and J.

3. This table lists values for the energy, frequency and wavelength of photons associated with different parts of the electromagnetic spectrum.
   Copy the table below and work out the missing values.

Electromagnetic radiation	Energy / eV	Energy / J	Frequency / Hz	Wavelength / m
gamma rays		1.989×10^{-12}		
X-rays			3×10^{19}	
UV				1×10^{-7}
visible	2.26×10^{-1}			
IR		3.978×10^{-21}		
microwaves			3×10^{10}	
radio waves			3×10^{5}	

4. The distance to the Moon is found by timing the return trip of a pulse of light with a frequency of 5.64×10^{14} Hz. A laser with a power output of 1.15 GW fires pulses of light lasting 100 ps.
   a. Calculate the energy of each photon. [2]
   b. Calculate the energy of each pulse of laser light. [2]
   c. Calculate the number of photons fired in each pulse. [1]

   [Total: 5]

5. An electron is accelerated from rest by a potential difference of 500 V.
   a. Calculate the kinetic energy it gains (in joules). [2]
   b. Calculate its final speed. [2]

   [Total: 4]

6 A charge can be accelerated through a potential difference.

Copy and complete the table by working out the missing values.

Particle	Mass / kg	Relative charge	Voltage	Kinetic energy / J	Speed / m s⁻¹
electron	9.1×10^{-31}	1	100 V		
proton	1.67×10^{-27}	1		1.6×10^{-14}	
electron	9.1×10^{-31}	1			8.39×10^{6}
alpha particle	6.643×10^{-27}	2	3 MV		
uranium ion	3.95×10^{-25}	5		8.0×10^{-10}	

> **UNDERSTAND THESE TERMS**
> - photoelectric effect
> - photon
> - Planck's constant
> - electronvolt (eV)

28.3 The photoelectric effect

1 a Describe a simple experiment to demonstrate the photoelectric effect in a school laboratory using a mercury discharge lamp, zinc metal and an electroscope.
 b Why does placing the mercury lamp closer causes the leaf to fall more rapidly?
 c Why does placing a sheet of glass between the lamp and the zinc stop the leaf from falling?
 d Why will this demonstration not work with a bright filament lamp?

28.4 Threshold frequency and wavelength

1 The kinetic energy of photoelectrons cannot be measured directly, so a device for investigating the photoelectric effect is shown in Figure 28.1. In normal operation, the emitted electrons have to do work against a 'stopping voltage'. If the electrons reach the anode, a current is recorded. The stopping voltage is increased so that the electrons only just fail to reach the anode, and the electrons have transferred all their kinetic energy doing work against the field.

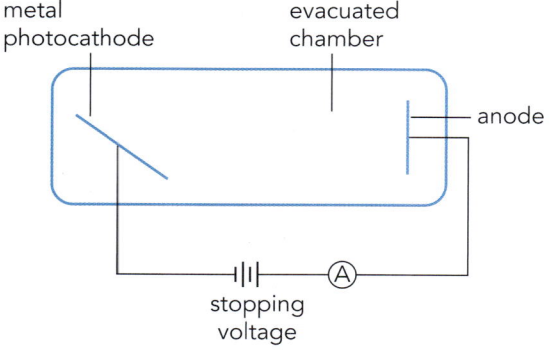

Figure 28.1

Wavelength / nm	Stopping voltage / V
189.7	0.653
172.5	1.307
158.2	1.960
146.0	2.614
135.6	3.267

a   What do you need to do with the data in the table to plot a graph of stopping voltage versus photon frequency? Plot the graph.

b   Write down the relationship between the kinetic energy of an electron and work done on it when it is accelerated by a potential difference.

c   Write down Einstein's photoelectric equation but express it in terms of the stopping voltage.

d   Use the equation and your graph to work out the threshold frequency below which no photoelectrons will be emitted.

e   Use the threshold frequency to find the work function.

f   Sketch a new graph on the same axes showing the results you would expect if the experiment was carried out on a metal with a lower work function.

2   Electromagnetic radiation of wavelength 200 nm is incident on a piece of gallium metal whose work function is 4.32 eV.

a   Calculate the energy of the photon. [2]

b   Calculate the maximum energy of the photoelectrons released from the metal. [1]

c   Calculate the maximum speed of the photoelectrons. [3]

[Total: 6]

3   Monochromatic light of a particular wavelength was shone onto different pieces of metal. Photoelectrons were emitted for all the metals except platinum.

a   Write down Einstein's photoelectric equation in terms of the kinetic energy of photoelectrons.

b   Based on the equation you wrote, describe what you would expect a graph of the maximum kinetic energy of the emitted photoelectrons against the work function to look like.

c   Make a copy of the table below and use the data to work out the kinetic energies of the photons used in the experiment. Assume that the incident photons have the same energy as the work function of platinum.

Metal	Work function / eV	Photoelectron kinetic energy / eV
lead	2.26	
magnesium	3.66	
iron	4.81	
lithium	2.9	
platinum	5.12	0.00

d   Use your answers to c to plot a graph of the maximum kinetic energies of the photons versus the work function.

4 Figure 28.2 shows the kinetic energy of photoelectrons as a function of frequency for lead.

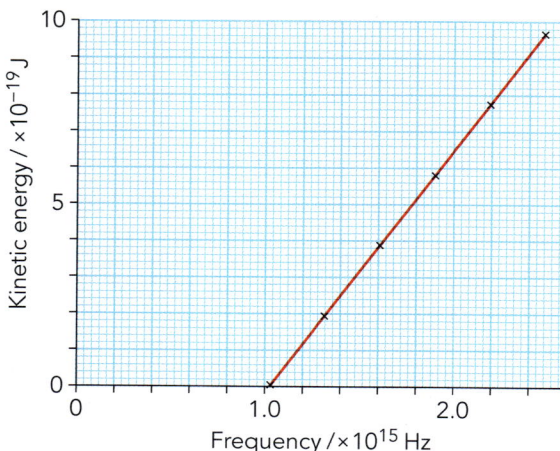

Figure 28.2

a Determine the threshold frequency using information from Figure 28.2. [1]
b State the threshold energy. [2]
c Calculate the work function and express your answer in terms of both J and eV. [2]
d Sketch the graph you would expect if lead were replaced with a metal with a lower threshold frequency. [2]

[Total: 7]

> **UNDERSTAND THESE TERMS**
> - threshold frequency
> - threshold wavelength

28.5 Momentum of photons

1 The Sun has a surface temperature of 5778 K. The solar constant is 1362 W m^{-2}. The radius of the Earth is 6371 km.

a The peak wavelength of sunlight is 501.9 nm. Assume that all photons from the Sun have this wavelength. What is the energy of an individual photon?
b What is the momentum of an individual photon?

c The brightness of a star gets less as the distance from it increases. The solar constant measures the amount of solar radiation (power received per square metre) at a distance of 1 astronomical unit (AU) from the Sun. 1 AU has a value of 1362 W m^{-2}. Use this information to work out the number of photons per square metre that reach the Earth every second.

d The Earth's radius is 6371 km. Use this information to work out the number of photons that reach the half of the Earth that is illuminated at any one time.

e Work out the total momentum of all the photons that reach the Earth in any given second. (Assume that there is no reflection.)

f Work out the radiation pressure from the Sun and compare it with atmospheric pressure (which is 10^5 Pa).

2 A solar sail is an extremely thin mirror.

  a Assume that sunlight is monochromatic so that all photons have a frequency of 6×10^{14} Hz. Calculate the energy of each photon. [1]

  b The brightness of the Sun above our atmosphere is 1362 W m^{-2}. Calculate how many photons will pass through every square metre per second. [1]

  c A solar sail is launched with a surface area of 81 m^2 perpendicular to the sunlight. Calculate how many photons will be incident on the solar sail. [1]

  d Calculate the momentum sunlight would exert on the sail. [2]

  e Discuss why scientists believe a solar sail could reach speeds approaching the speed of light. [2]

  [Total: 7]

28.6 Line spectra and
28.7 Explaining the origin of line spectra

1 What is the technical term for the splitting of light into its components?

[Total: 1]

2 Define energy levels/states.

> ≪ **RECALL AND CONNECT 1** ≪
>
> Think back to Chapter 5. Write down the equation for kinetic energy and then show that it can be expressed in terms of momentum $E = \dfrac{p^2}{2m}$.

UNDERSTAND THESE TERMS

- emission line spectrum
- absorption line spectrum

UNDERSTAND THESE TERMS

- quantised
- transition

28.8 Photon energies

1   Figure 28.3 shows part of the energy level diagram for an imaginary atom. The arrows represent four transitions **a–d** between energy levels.

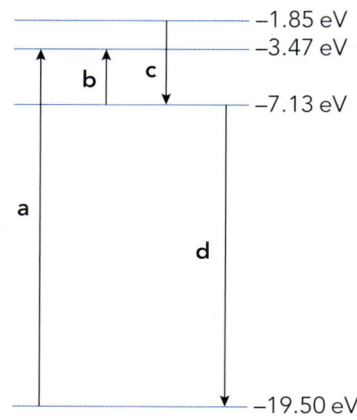

Figure 28.3

Copy the table below. Complete it for each transition by:

i   calculating the energy of the photon in eV [2]
ii calculating the energy of the photon in J [2]
iii calculating the frequency of the photon [2]
iv calculating the wavelength of the photon [2]
v   stating whether the transition contributes to an emission or absorption line. [2]

[Total: 10]

	i Energy (eV)	ii Energy / 10^{-19} J	iii Frequency / 10^{14} Hz	iv Wavelength / nm	v Emission or absorption?
a					
b					
c					
d					

UNDERSTAND THIS TERM

- ground state

REFLECTION

There are lots of calculate questions in this chapter. Are you generally scoring all the available marks in calculate questions? If not, try to identify why you are dropping marks so you can avoid making similar mistakes in the exam.

28.9 The nature of light: waves or particles?

UNDERSTAND THIS TERM
- de Broglie wavelength

1. An electron is accelerated from rest through a potential difference V.

   Show that the de Broglie wavelength of the electron after the acceleration is $\lambda = \dfrac{h}{\sqrt{2meV}}$, where m is the mass of the electron and e is its charge. **[Total: 3]**

2. a Show that an electron accelerated from rest through a potential difference V gains a velocity of $v = \left(\dfrac{2eV}{m}\right)^{\frac{1}{2}}$. [1]

   b Show that an electron will reach a speed of $4.19 \times 10^7 \, \text{m s}^{-1}$ if it is accelerated through a potential difference of $5\,\text{kV}$. [1]

   c Show that the de Broglie wavelength of this electron is $1.74 \times 10^{-11}\,\text{m}$. [1]

   d These electrons are passed through graphite with an atomic spacing of $10^{-10}\,\text{m}$. Show that they will be diffracted through an angle of almost $10°$. [1]

   [Total: 4]

3. A charged particle can be accelerated using a potential difference. If their de Broglie wavelength is small enough, a charged particle can be diffracted by matter. The table below shows various such accelerating voltages for an electron passing through graphite with atomic spacing of 10^{-10} m. The first row shows the resulting speed and wavelength and diffraction angle.

   a Make a copy of the table and work out the missing values.

Accelerating voltage / kV	Electron speed/ m s⁻¹	Electron wavelength / m	Diffraction angle / °
5.0	4.19×10^7	1.74×10^{-11}	10.01
7.5			
10.0			
12.5			
15.0			

   b What is the relationship between the values in the different columns?

28.10 Electron waves

1. Explain how the wavelengths of a proton and an electron moving with the same kinetic energy would compare. **[Total: 4]**

2. A helium nucleus is accelerated by a potential difference so that it reaches the speeds listed in this table.

Speed / 10^7 m s^{-1}	Wavelength / 10^{-15} m
1	
2	
3	
4	
5	

   a. Copy the table and then, for each speed, calculate the de Broglie wavelength for the helium nucleus.

   b. Draw the graph of wavelength against speed. Remember to include a line of best fit.

28.11 Revisiting photons

1. An electron undergoes a transition from an atomic energy level of -2.3 eV to -3.9 eV. Determine the wavelength of the emitted photon. **[Total: 3]**

REFLECTION

Have you spotted the connections between different concepts in this or earlier chapters? Would it be helpful to develop a mind map to show these links? Do you think finding these connections helps you to better understand the subject?

SELF-ASSESSMENT CHECKLIST

Let's revisit the Knowledge focus and Exam skills focus for this chapter.

Decide how confident you are with each statement.

Now I can:	Show it	Needs more work	Almost there	Confident to move on
understand that electromagnetic radiation has a particulate nature	Recall two phenomena that demonstrate that photons act like particles.			

CONTINUED

Now I can:	Show it	Needs more work	Almost there	Confident to move on
understand that a photon is a quantum of electromagnetic energy	Describe the evidence for a photon having energy both as a particle and as a wave.			
recall and use $E = hf$	What is the energy of a photon that has a frequency of 6×10^{14} Hz?			
use the electronvolt (eV) as a unit of energy	Define the electronvolt and show that 3.8×10^{-19} J = 2.4 eV.			
understand that a photon has momentum and that the momentum is given by $p = \dfrac{E}{c}$	Describe a situation where light could like be used to exert a force on something.			
understand that photoelectrons may be emitted from a metal surface when it is illuminated by electromagnetic radiation	Describe a demonstration involving a mercury lamp, metal and an electroscope.			
understand and use the terms threshold frequency and threshold wavelength	Sketch a graph of the kinetic energy of photoelectrons against frequency and label threshold frequency.			
explain photoelectric emission in terms of photon energy and work function energy	What energy would a photoelectron have if a photon has 3.4 eV and the work function of a metal was (a) 2.3 eV (b) 3.4 eV (c) 4.5 eV?			
recall and use $hf = \Phi + \dfrac{1}{2}mv_{max}^2$	Relate this to the principle of conservation of energy.			
explain why the maximum kinetic energy of photoelectrons is independent of intensity, whereas the photoelectric current is proportional to intensity	What would happen to the maximum kinetic energy of photoelectrons if the intensity of light was increased, but the photons were below the threshold energy? Explain your answer.			

CONTINUED

Now I can:	Show it	Needs more work	Almost there	Confident to move on
understand that the photoelectric effect provides evidence for a particulate nature of electromagnetic radiation, while phenomena such as interference and diffraction provide evidence for a wave nature	Describe interference and diffraction to emphasise that it is due to the superposition or interaction of wavelets or wavefronts.			
describe and interpret qualitatively the evidence provided by electron diffraction for the wave nature of particles	Describe what effect speeding up a particle has on its wavelength and then describe the demonstration of them being diffracted by graphite.			
understand the de Broglie wavelength as the wavelength associated with a moving particle	Recall the equation for momentum and what momentum a body has when it is stationary.			
recall and use $\lambda = \dfrac{h}{p}$	Show that the wavelength of an electron moving at 10% the speed of light has a wavelength = 2.43×10^{-11} m.			
understand that there are discrete electron energy levels in isolated atoms (such as atomic hydrogen)	Sketch a typical energy-level diagram. Where do the energy levels get progressively closer together – at the top or the bottom?			
understand the appearance and formation of emission and absorption line spectra	Describe how emission and absorption line spectra are formed in terms of photons and the transition of electrons between energy levels.			
recall and use the relation $hf = E_1 - E_2$	Show that it would require a photon of 1.8×10^{-18} J to promote an electron between the -19.6 eV and the -8.2 eV energy levels.			
answer a variety of 'calculate' questions	What is the difference between the 'show (that)' and 'calculate' command words?			

29 Nuclear physics

KNOWLEDGE FOCUS

In this chapter you will answer questions on:
- balanced equations
- mass and energy
- energy released in radioactive decay
- binding energy and stability
- randomness and radioactive decay
- the mathematics of radioactive decay
- decay graphs and equations
- decay constant λ and half-life $t_{1/2}$.

EXAM SKILLS FOCUS

In this chapter you will:
- further practise answering 'identify' questions.

It is important to revisit command words in different topics so that you gain practice answering questions across many different topics in physics. In this chapter you will practise your understanding of the command word 'identify', which you practised in Chapter 3. In an 'identify' question, you need to provide an answer from a number of possibilities. These possibilities may be found within the question stem, or they may be in your answer to a previous question part. For example, in this chapter, you sketch decay curves in one question part then identify which curve is associated with the biggest and smallest decay constant. The 'identify' part of a question is usually worth one mark, but they are often followed by 'and explain' or 'and justify'. Remember to answer each command word in a question in your response.

Identify	name/select/recognise

29.1 Balanced equations

1. Figure 29.1 shows a graph of neutron number against proton number.

   Identify what particle is being emitted or absorbed in each of the examples. **[Total: 5]**

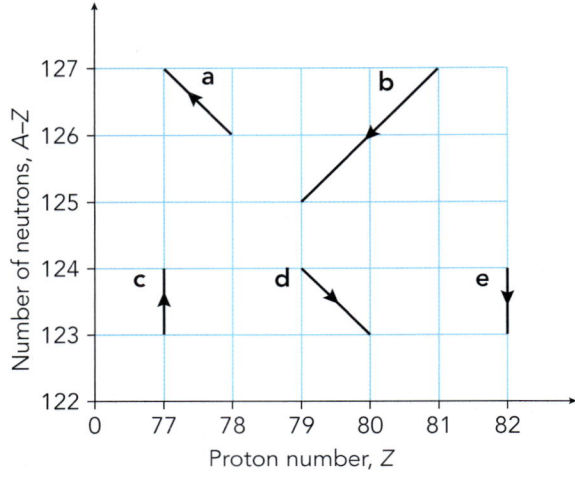

Figure 29.1

2. Determine balanced nuclear reactions for the following decays:

   a. A nucleus of thorium-232 $\left(^{232}_{90}\text{Th}\right)$ decays by α emission to form an isotope of radium, Ra. **[3]**

   b. A nucleus of caesium-137 $\left(^{137}_{55}\text{Cs}\right)$ decays by β⁻ emission to form an isotope of barium, Ba. **[3]**

   c. A nucleus of sodium-22 $\left(^{22}_{11}\text{Na}\right)$ decays by β⁺ emission to form an isotope of neon, Ne. **[3]**

   [Total: 9]

≪ RECALL AND CONNECT 1 ≪

Think back to the previous chapter. State **three** pieces of evidence provided by the photoelectric effect that supports the particle nature of electromagnetic radiation.

29.2 Mass and energy and
29.3 Energy released in radioactive decay

1. Copy and complete Table 29.1, which lists the masses of several nuclides.

    Work out the combined mass of all the nucleons and then use this information to find the mass defect and the binding energy for each nuclide.

    The first one has been done for you.
    - A proton is 1.007276 u.
    - A neutron is 1.008665 u.
    - 1 u = 1.660539×10^{-27} kg.

Element	A	Z	N	Mass of nucleus / u	Combined mass of nucleons / u	Mass defect / u	Binding energy / $\times 10^{-18}$ J
$^{4}_{2}$He	4	2	2	4.00150	4.031882	0.030382	4.53
$^{12}_{6}$C				11.99670			
$^{16}_{8}$O				15.99052			

    Table 29.1

    UNDERSTAND THESE TERMS
    - mass defect
    - binding energy

2. This question provides practice of converting between different units of mass.

    Copy and complete Table 29.2.

Nuclide	Mass of nuclide / u	Mass of nuclide / 10^{-27} kg	Mass of 1.0 mole / g
helium-3	3.016029		
iron-56		92.851994	
thorium-233	233.041582		

    Table 29.2

3. A nucleus of plutonium-239 ($^{239}_{94}$Pu) decays by alpha emission into an isotope of uranium, U.

    a. Determine the nuclear decay equation for the alpha decay of plutonium-239. [2]

b Using the data in Table 29.3, determine the energy released in this decay. [2]

Particle	Mass / u
plutonium-239	239.052163
unidentified isotope of uranium	235.04393
alpha particle	4.002602

Table 29.3

c If this energy were released over the course of a year, determine the power output for one mole of plutonium-239. [2]

[Total: 6]

29.4 Binding energy and stability

1 Table 29.4 lists some nuclides. The proton number and mass of the nucleus are included for each nuclide.

Nuclide	Proton number	Number of neutrons	Mass of nucleus / 10^{-27} kg	Mass defect / 10^{-27} kg	Binding energy / 10^{-12} J	Binding energy per nucleon / 10^{-13} J
helium-3	4	1	5.008238	0.007188	1.0742	3.58
lithium-6	3		9.988353			
iron-56	26		92.882210			
krypton-92	36		152.647077			
uranium-236	92		391.963154			
plutonium-239	94		396.955727			

Table 29.4

- The mass of a proton is $1.6726223 \times 10^{-27}$ kg.
- The mass of a neutron is $1.6749288 \times 10^{-27}$ kg.

a Copy and complete Table 29.4 by using the given information to find the binding energy per nucleon for each nuclide. You may find it helpful to find the mass defect and binding energy as intermediate steps.

b Sketch a graph of binding energy per nucleon versus nucleon number and comment on its shape.

c Use this curve to explain why fusion takes place to the left of iron (Fe) and fission to the right of iron.

2   When U-235 absorbs a neutron, it becomes the highly unstable isotope U-236, which then decays into two daughter nuclei.

Table 29.5 shows the masses of the particles involved in the nuclear reactions.

Particle	Mass / u
neutron	1.008665
Kr-92	91.926156
Ba-142	141.916430
U-235	235.043930
U-236	236.045568

Table 29.5

a   Calculate the energy released when a U-235 nucleus absorbs a neutron in the reaction:

$${}^{1}_{0}n + {}^{235}_{92}U \rightarrow {}^{236}_{92}U$$ [3]

b   Calculate the energy released when U-236 undergoes fission in the reaction:

$${}^{236}_{92}U \rightarrow {}^{142}_{56}Ba + {}^{92}_{36}Kr + 2{}^{1}_{0}n$$ [3]

c   Calculate the total energy released in the two steps of the process. [1]

d   Calculate the total energy released when 1 kg of U-235 undergoes fission. [2]

[Total: 9]

3   The proton–proton cycle in stars is one of the processes by which hydrogen fuses into helium. This is when four protons fuse to produce a He-4 nucleus plus two positrons.

a   Determine the balanced nuclear reaction for the proton–proton cycle. [2]

b   Use the data in Table 29.6 to show that approximately 27 MeV is released when four protons fuse to produce a He-4 nucleus plus two positrons. [4]

Particle	Mass / u
electron	0.000 548 6
proton	1.007 825 0
helium nucleus	4.001 506 2

Table 29.6

c   The luminosity (power output) of the Sun is 4×10^{26} W.

Calculate how many kilograms of hydrogen is turned into helium every second. [2]

d   The mass of the Sun is 1.989×10^{30} kg. Assume that only hydrogen is fusing in the Sun via this reaction.

Calculate what percentage of the Sun's mass has undergone hydrogen fusion in the 4.6 billion years it has existed. [1]

[Total: 9]

> **UNDERSTAND THESE TERMS**
> - binding energy
> - nuclear fission
> - nuclear fusion

29.5 Randomness and radioactive decay and 29.6 The mathematics of radioactive decay

> **« RECALL AND CONNECT 2 «**
> Think back to Chapter 6. State the law of conservation of momentum.

1   Explain why nuclear decay is:

   a   spontaneous [2]

   b   random. [2]

[Total: 4]

2   Table 29.7 gives some data for three different nuclides.

   a   Copy and complete the table by working out the missing values.

Nuclide	N_0	A_0	λ	Elapsed time	N (after elapsed time)	A (after elapsed time)
U-222	23 000	1.14×10^{10} s^{-1}	4.95×10^{5} s^{-1}	2.7 µs		
Pb-203	7000		1.34×10^{-2} h^{-1}	113 h		
Th-232	1350		4.93×10^{-11} y^{-1}	13×10^{7} y		

Table 29.7

   b   For each nuclide divide N_0 by your value of N after the elapsed time. Do the same for the activity (divide A_0 by A). What do you notice about these ratios? Is this surprising?

> **UNDERSTAND THESE TERMS**
> - activity
> - count rate

29.7 Decay graphs and equations and
29.8 Decay constant λ and half-life $t_{\frac{1}{2}}$

1. Carbon-14 has a decay constant of 1.21×10^{-4} years^{-1}.

   a. Copy and complete this list with the number of undecayed nuclei for the times shown.

Time / years	0	2000	4000	6000	8000	10 000
N	500.0	392.6				

   b. Plot a graph of undecayed nuclei, N, against time and use it to find the half-life.

   c. Confirm that this is the correct value from the relationship between half-life and decay constant.

> **UNDERSTAND THESE TERMS**
> - exponential decay
> - half-life
> - decay constant

2. Copy and complete Table 29.8 and, for each nuclide, find the number of protons or neutrons and either the missing half-life or decay constant expressed in the units shown.

   Take care with units (y = years).

	Z	N	Half-life	Decay constant	Decay constant / s^{-1}
H-5	1		8.60×10^{-23} s	s^{-1}	
Th-218		128	s	6.3591×10^6 s^{-1}	6.3591×10^6
Fe-64	26		2.00 s	s^{-1}	
Pu-238		144	y	7.904×10^{-3} y^{-1}	
U-238	92		4.47×10^9 y	y^{-1}	
Pt-190		112	y	1.066×10^{-12} y^{-1}	3.379

   Table 29.8

3. Different isotopes of thorium undergo beta-minus decay with the half-lives shown in Table 29.9.

   a. On the same set of axes, sketch and label the curve of *undecayed nuclei*, N, against *time* for each isotope, starting with a value of $N_0 = 100$ in each case. [4]

   b. Identify which curve is associated with the biggest and smallest decay constant and justify your answer. [2]

   [Total: 6]

Isotope	Half-life / minutes
Th-233	22.3
Th-235	7.1
Th-236	37.5

   Table 29.9

4 Different isotopes of thorium have the decay constants shown in Table 29.10, and each sample starts with a different number of undecayed nuclei, N_0.

   a Write the equation that relates activity to the number of undecayed nuclei. Write the equation (exponential function) for the number of undecayed nuclei as a function of time.

   Try and combine them to derive an equation for activity as a function of time.

   b Copy and complete Table 29.10 by working out the activity for the times shown.

Isotope	N_0	Decay constant / min^{-1}	0 min	10 min	20 min	30 min	40 min	50 min
Th-233	3217	0.031 083	99.993	73.279	53.702			
Th-235	1024	0.097 626						
Th-236	5410	0.018 484						

Table 29.10

   c Plot activity as a function of time for each isotope on the same axes. Label each curve.

   d What is the relationship between the decay constant and the steepness of each curve?

   e Work out the half-life for each isotope. What is the relationship between the half-life and decay constant?

   f All the isotopes started with the same activity. What do you notice about the relationship between the initial number of nuclei N_0 and the decay constant λ in order to accomplish this?

5 The decay of uranium-235 to lead-207 takes place with a half-life of 704 million years. Geologists use the ratio of these two nuclides to date rock samples.

   a Identify which nuclide is the parent and which is the daughter. [1]
   b Determine the fraction of the sample that is undecayed uranium-235 nuclei when the daughter–parent ratio is 1 : 1.7. [1]
   c Determine the age of the rock sample for a daughter–parent ratio of 1 : 1.7. [2]

   [Total: 4]

6 a Outline a method for measuring the half-life of a radioactive isotope like U-238, which has a half-life of 4.468×10^9 years. [3]
   b Determine the fraction of this isotope that remains in a particular sample of the isotope after a time of 0.7 half-lives have passed. [2]

   [Total: 5]

29 Nuclear physics

> **REFLECTION**
>
> How did you find the 'identify' questions in this chapter? Did you spot the question that also asked you to justify your answer? Do you feel you could confidently explain the meaning of the 'identify' command word to a friend?

SELF-ASSESSMENT CHECKLIST

Let's revisit the Knowledge focus and Exam skills focus for this chapter.

Decide how confident you are with each statement.

Now I can:	Show it	Needs more work	Almost there	Confident to move on
understand the equivalence between energy and mass as represented by $E = mc^2$ and recall and use this equation	The average mass of a person is 63 kg. Show that if that mass was turned into energy according to Einstein's equation, it would power a 900 W microwave oven for 196 billion years.			
represent simple nuclear reactions by nuclear equations	Thorium-233 has a proton number of 90. Show the equations for alpha, beta-plus and beta-minus decays.			
define and use the terms mass defect and binding energy	Write the definition of the mass defect and binding energy. How are they related? Check your answers. Write the definitions on a flash card.			
sketch the variation of binding energy per nucleon with nucleon number	Sketch the graph with additional information: maximum nucleon number, typical values of the binding energy per nucleon, and the nuclide with the biggest value.			
explain what is meant by nuclear fusion and nuclear fission	Define nuclear fusion and nuclear fission.			

CONTINUED

Now I can:	Show it	Needs more work	Almost there	Confident to move on
explain the relevance of binding energy per nucleon to nuclear reactions, including nuclear fusion and nuclear fission	Turn the plot of binding energy per nucleon versus nucleon number upside down and use it to explain the energy released in nuclear fusion and nuclear fission.			
calculate the energy released in nuclear reactions using $E = \Delta mc^2$	Show that when four protons (1.00797 u) fuse to become a helium nucleus (4.00151 u) about 28 MeV is released.			
understand that fluctuations in count rate provide evidence for the random nature of radioactive decay	Describe what causes fluctuations in the activity of a radioactive substance.			
understand that radioactive decay is both spontaneous and random	Define spontaneous and random and explain why this applies to radioactivity.			
define activity and decay constant, and recall and use $A = \lambda N$	How does increasing the decay constant affect the activity for a given value of N?			
define half-life	Define half-life in terms of the decay constant and a plot of activity versus time. If the decay constant were doubled, what would happen to the half-life, and how would that change a graph of activity versus time?			
answer a variety of 'identify' questions	Identify which equation I would need to use in order to calculate the gravitational force between two masses.			

30 Medical imaging

KNOWLEDGE FOCUS

In this chapter you will answer questions on:
- the nature and production of X-rays
- X-ray attenuation
- improving X-ray images
- computerised axial tomography
- using ultrasound in medicine
- echo sounding
- ultrasound scanning
- Positron Emission Tomography (PET).

EXAM SKILLS FOCUS

In this chapter you will:
- understand what is needed to get full marks in difficult 'describe' questions.

Questions that ask you to describe complex processes, such as those involved in medical imaging, can be difficult. The first exam skills question in this chapter is a good example.

| Describe | state the points of a topic / give characteristics and main features |

When revising, decide which details you need to memorise. Make a set of concise but detailed bullet points.

Evidence suggests that repeatedly answering questions and recalling facts is better than just re-reading or highlighting. As you work through the chapter, make a note of what you need to memorise for this topic and think about how you will do this.

30.1 The nature and production of X-rays

1   a   Name the parts labelled **i–vi** in Figure 30.1, a simplified diagram of an X-ray tube.

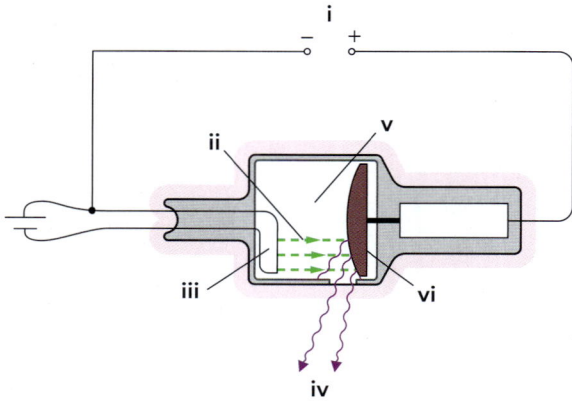

Figure 30.1

   b   How are X-rays produced in an X-ray tube?

2   In an X-ray tube, electrons are produced from a cathode by thermionic emission.

   These are accelerated through a large potential difference. They then collide with a metal target and decelerate. Photons of high frequency electromagnetic radiation are produced.

   a   The current through the hot metal filament is increased by a factor of 1.5. Describe and explain the change in the intensity of the emitted X-ray beam. [3]

   b   These photons are emitted in random directions. Explain how an X-ray machine produces a collimated beam. [2]

   c   Show that the maximum kinetic energy of electrons accelerated through 80 kV is approximately 1.3×10^{-14} J. [2]

   d   Dental X-rays involve scans near the brain. These need to be less ionising than medical X-rays.

   Suggest a possible difference between the operation of a medical vs dental X-ray. [2]

   [Total: 9]

UNDERSTAND THESE TERMS

- collimated beam
- intensity

REFLECTION

Did you notice that the regions of the electromagnetic spectrum X-rays and gamma rays overlap in the orders of magnitude of their wavelengths? This is because X-rays and gamma rays are defined by their origin rather than their wavelengths. This is another example of where our definitions in physics have to be very precise. What 'memory' techniques will you use to make sure you can recite key details with precision so you do not lose simple marks?

30.2 X-ray attenuation

> **« RECALL AND CONNECT 1 «**
>
> In Chapter 29, you learned about using exponential functions and half-lives to make calculations of how the activity of radioactive nuclides change over time. Half thickness in attenuation works very similarly to this.
>
> A radioactive nuclide has a half-life of 6 hours. Calculate the fraction which is left after 24 hours.

1   a   Copy and complete these sentences.

The decrease in the intensity of X-rays as they pass through matter is called ....

Intensity is defined as the .... per ....

The intensity decreases .... with the distance it travels into the matter.

The thickness of material that decreases the intensity of X-rays to 50% of their incident intensity is called its ....

     b   Write an equation for the attenuation of X-rays in the matter.

     c   Calculate the half thickness of a material with an attenuation coefficient of $0.17\,\text{mm}^{-1}$.

2   As X-rays pass through matter, they are attenuated.

     a   Explain what is meant by the attenuation of X-rays. [2]

     b   A dental X-ray has an initial intensity of $6.0\,\text{W}\,\text{m}^{-2}$. This is passed through a patient's cheek and then their teeth, where it falls onto a photographic plate.

Use the data in Table 30.1 to calculate the intensity of an X-ray beam after passing through 4.6 mm of soft tissue and then 7.8 mm of bone. [4]

Tissue	Half thickness / mm
soft tissue	5.8
bone	1.2

Table 30.1

[Total: 6]

> **UNDERSTAND THESE TERMS**
>
> - attenuation
> - attenuation (absorption) coefficient

30.3 Improving X-ray images

1   a   Why are contrast media sometimes injected into soft tissues before an X-ray scan?

     b   Why are image intensifiers used in fluoroscopy?

     c   How does an image intensifier work?

2   X-rays can be used to produce images of internal organs in the body.

   a   During a routine X-ray scan of a kidney, a contrast medium is added to some of the tissues. Explain why. [3]

   b   The attenuation coefficients of materials are approximately proportional to the cube of the average proton number of the atoms within the material. Table 30.2 shows some average proton numbers of tissues in the body and in the contrast medium.

Substance	Average proton number
soft tissue	7
bone	14
contrast medium	55

Table 30.2

   i   Bone has an attenuation coefficient of $0.60\,\text{cm}^{-1}$ for 100 keV X-rays. Calculate the attenuation coefficient for soft tissue and for the contrast medium. [2]

   ii Calculate the ratio:
   $$\frac{\text{intensity of X-ray beam after travelling through 0.60 cm contrast medium}}{\text{intensity of X-ray beam after travelling through 0.60 cm soft tissue}}$$
   [2]

   iii Comment on your answer to part ii. [2]

   [Total: 9]

> **UNDERSTAND THESE TERMS**
> - contrast (of an image)
> - image intensifiers
> - contrast media

30.4 Computerised axial tomography

1 a   Why would a CAT scan not be used before a routine procedure on a pregnant person?

   b   What are two advantages of a CAT scan over a simple X-ray scan?

2   Computerised axial tomography (CAT or CT) uses fan-shaped X-rays to create 'slices' of the human body. These are combined in a computer to give an accurate 3D image of the body.

Give reasons why the number of CAT scans a patient has should be kept as low as possible. [Total: 2]

> **UNDERSTAND THIS TERM**
> - computerised axial tomography (CAT or CT)

30.5 Using ultrasound in medicine

1   a   Draw a labelled diagram of an ultrasound transducer.
    b   What is the piezo-electric crystal usually made of?
    c   What property must the material of the acoustic window have?
    d   Why is a large block of epoxy resin or other damping material behind the crystal?

2   An ultrasound transducer contains a piezo-electric crystal that produces and detects ultrasound waves.
    a   Describe how the piezo-electric effect is used to both produce and detect ultrasound waves. [6]
    b   The frequency of the ultrasound waves should match the natural frequency of the piezo-electric crystal. To do this, the optimum size of a piezo-electric crystal is half the wavelength of the ultrasound waves. Explain why. [2]

[Total: 8]

> **UNDERSTAND THESE TERMS**
> - piezo-electric crystal
> - piezo-electric effect

> **REFLECTION**
>
> There is a lot of detail to learn and remember in this topic. How good are you at remembering details? Were you able to successfully remember all the details needed to gain all 6 marks in the difficult 'describe' question 30.5.2a? Five good memorisation techniques are: self-quizzing, spaced practice, interleaved practice, self-explanation and elaborative interrogation. Use the internet to find out what they all mean. Do you use these techniques? Which one(s) work best for you?

30.6 Echo sounding

1   Copy and complete this table:

Density / $kg\,m^{-3}$	Speed of sound in medium / $m\,s^{-1}$	Acoustic impedance / $kg\,m^{-2}\,s^{-1}$
1000	1500	
	1450	1.34×10^6
1780		4.20×10^6
1600	4000	

2   Calculate the distance to a boundary for an ultrasound wave which returns 44 μs after it has been emitted. The speed of sound in the medium is $4000\,m\,s^{-1}$.

3   Impedance matching is used to ensure that the maximum intensity is transmitted through the outer layer of skin covering the body.

    Use the data in Table 30.3 to justify why an impedance matching gel is used.

Use a calculation of reflected intensity with and without impedance matching gel. [Total: 6]

Material	Acoustic impedance / ×10⁶ kg m⁻² s⁻¹
air	0.0004
skin	1.71
gel	1.65

Table 30.3

> **UNDERSTAND THESE TERMS**
> - acoustic impedance
> - impedance matching

30.7 Ultrasound scanning

1. What is the difference between an A scan and a B scan?

2. An A scan is used to investigate a liver for fatty deposits. The ultrasound passes through fat, muscle, and then liver tissue.

   Figure 30.2a shows an A scan graph for someone with a normal, healthy liver.

   Figure 30.2b shows an A scan graph for someone with fatty deposits on their liver.

   The peaks have been numbered for you to reference in your answers. Presume that there is no immediate reflection from the skin. For both graphs, the first peak is the voltage on the transducer as the peak is sent.

   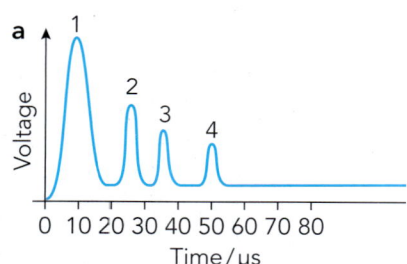 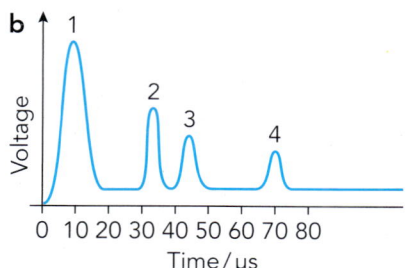

   Figure 30.2

   a Describe what information a radiographer can gain from the subsequent smaller peaks. [2]

   b Table 30.4 shows are the speeds of ultrasound in the three tissues shown in the scans.

Tissue	Speed of sound in medium / m s⁻¹
fat	1450
muscle	1590
healthy liver	1640

   Table 30.4

Explain how the scan shows that the second patient has a larger percentage of fat in their liver. Presume that the physical size of the liver is the same for both patients. [3]

c   Suggest one other difference in the body of the person with fatty deposits on their liver compared with the person with a healthy body. [1]

d   Calculate the thickness of the muscle layer in a patient with a healthy liver. [3]

[Total: 9]

30.8 Positron Emission Tomography

1   a   Why are radiotracers used in a PET scan?

   b   Why is the radioactive nuclide attached to a glucose based molecule?

   c   The radioactive nuclide fluorine-18 has a half-life of 2 hours. Explain why this is suitable.

2   In PET scans, a radiotracer is injected into the body. It is absorbed in varying amounts by the organs of the body. Positrons are emitted, which annihilate when they meet electrons producing a pair of photons with equal and opposite momentum.

   a   Explain why the annihilation of an electron–positron pair produces a pair of photons with equal but opposite momentum. [3]

   b   Describe the detection of the pair of photons and explain how the data collected can be used to give a location of the electron–positron annihilation. [3]

   c   PET scans are particularly useful for detecting tumours. Tumours have an abnormally large metabolic activity. Explain how these are shown in a PET scan. [3]

[Total: 9]

> **UNDERSTAND THESE TERMS**
> - radiotracer
> - line of response

> **« RECALL AND CONNECT 1 «**
>
> In Chapters 15 and 29, you learned to write and balance nuclear equations for a range of decays.
>
> Write a nuclear equation for carbon-10 as it decays to boron-10.
>
> Carbon has 6 protons, and boron has 5.

SELF-ASSESSMENT CHECKLIST

Let's revisit the Knowledge focus and Exam skills focus for this chapter.

Decide how confident you are with each statement.

Now I can:	Show it	Needs more work	Almost there	Confident to move on
explain how X-ray beams are produced and controlled	Make a detailed set of notes about the safe operation of X-ray tubes and practise recalling them.			
explain how ultrasound is produced and detected	Make a presentation about how piezo-electric crystals are used in an ultrasound transducer to produce and detect ultrasound waves and present it to a friend or family member.			
explain how ultrasound images are produced, revealing internal structures	Use annotated diagrams to explain how ultrasound waves can be used to make images of the internal structure of the body.			
describe how conventional and CT scan X-ray images are produced	Make a comparison table about how X-rays are used in conventional X-rays and CT scans.			
explain the principles of positron emission tomography	Make a detailed set of notes about how PET scans are used to image the internal structures of the body, including details about how matter and antimatter interact from Chapter 15.			
understand what is needed to get full marks in difficult 'describe' questions	Review past paper exam questions and their mark schemes for all the key descriptions in this chapter, memorise the key details.			

31 Astronomy and cosmology

KNOWLEDGE FOCUS

In this chapter you will answer questions on:

- standard candles
- luminosity and radiant flux intensity
- stellar radii
- the expanding Universe.

EXAM SKILLS FOCUS

In this chapter you will:

- understand what is meant by the term 'estimate' and why it is useful.

Physicists often use estimates. For example, they round numbers to make calculations quicker and easier. This is an excellent way of 'sense-checking' calculations. In this chapter, you will be asked questions about redshift. You may be asked how fast a distant galaxy appears to be moving away from us. If you get a speed that appears to exceed the speed of light, you will know you have made a mistake. In other calculations, you may not have all the information you need to solve a problem, so you make 'educated guesses' or estimates for the missing information.

31.1 Standard candles

1. Astronomers use different techniques to work out the distance to stars and galaxies.

   This includes the use of standard candles.

   a. Define the term *standard candle*. [1]
   b. Explain how a Cepheid variable acts as a standard candle. [2]
   c. State what is special about type 1A supernovae that allow them to be used as standard candles. [1]

   [Total: 4]

> **UNDERSTAND THESE TERMS**
> - luminosity
> - standard candle

« RECALL AND CONNECT 1 «

Think back to Chapters 17 and 22. The equation for radiant flux density is known as 'an inverse square law'. These type of laws are important in physics. Name any other inverse square laws that you have met.

REFLECTION

It is sometimes difficult to know where to start with a calculation. One effective technique is to write down the values and associated symbols (e.g. $L = 3.83 \times 10^{26}$ W) as well as the symbol for the value you are looking for. Do you have a better method, and can you explain it to a friend?

31.2 Luminosity and radiant flux intensity

1. You have been asked to give a talk to non-scientists about how astronomers work out the distance to stars and galaxies.

   a. Explain that a light-year is not a measure of time, and show how far 4.2 light-years is in km.
   b. What two assumptions do astronomers make when relating the brightness of a star to its luminosity?
   c. Describe a quick demonstration to show that radiant flux intensity follows an inverse square. You can use a bright filament lamp and a light meter.

31 Astronomy and cosmology

2 a Write the equation for radiant flux density (the one that relates luminosity, radiant flux density and distance to a star).

b Table 31.1 has some data for six fictional stars.

The luminosity is given in terms of the solar luminosity $L_⊙$ ($L_⊙ = 3.83 \times 10^{26}$ W).

Copy and complete the table by using the equation for radiant flux density to work out the missing values.

Name of the star	Distance / light-years	Radiant flux density / W m^{-2}	Luminosity / $L_⊙$
Helios	1.58×10^{-5}	1362.1	
Sophie	2.73		2.50
Hendrix		3.89×10^{-9}	1100.00
Giovanni	17.2		5.07
Rumaisa		1.45×10^{-8}	1.54
Yusra	65.0	2.61×10^{-8}	

Table 31.1

> **UNDERSTAND THESE TERMS**
> - light-year (ly)
> - radiant flux density

31.3 Stellar radii

1 a What are the two factors the luminosity of a star depends on?

b Table 31.2 has some data for five fictional stars. The luminosity is given in terms of the solar luminosity $L_⊙$ (where 1 $L_⊙ = 3.83 \times 10^{26}$ W).
Copy and complete the table by using the Stefan–Boltzmann law to work out the missing values and record them on a copy of the table.

Name of the star	Temperature / K	Stellar radius / km	Luminosity / $L_⊙$
Helios	5800	6.89×10^5	
Aries	4500	8.81×10^6	
Gemini α	3000		0.6
Gemini β		1.00×10^6	27.3
Hedwig	6000	3.74×10^5	

Table 31.2

2   The surface temperature of the Sun is 5800 K and the wavelength of light at peak intensity is 500 nm.

   a   Use the black body spectrum provided (Figure 31.1) to estimate the wavelength of light at the peak intensity for the red dwarf star Proxima Centauri. [1]

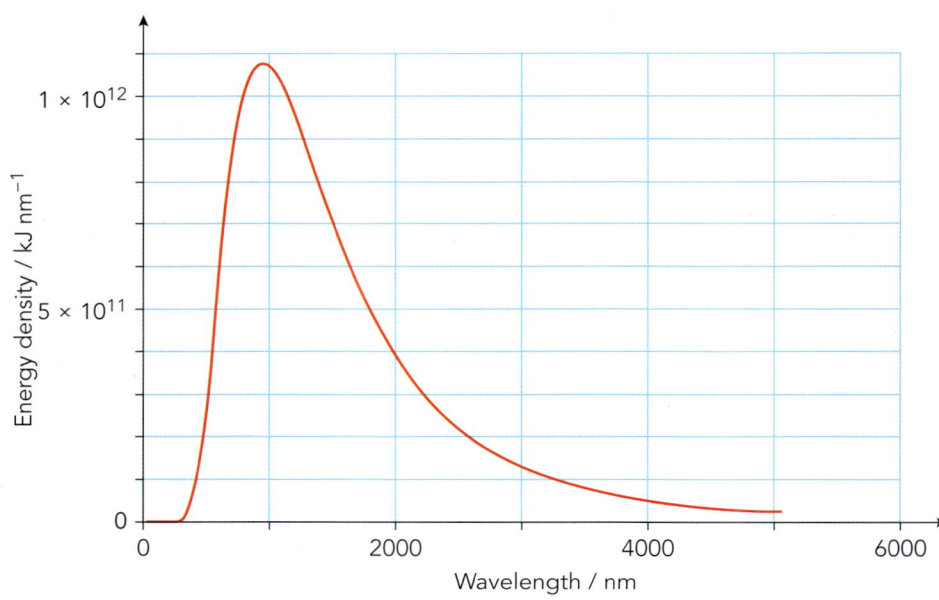

Figure 31.1

   b   Use this estimate and the information provided for the Sun to calculate the surface temperature of Proxima Centauri. [2]

   c   Astronomers have measured the radiant flux intensity of Proxima Centauri as 3.25×10^{-11} Wm^{-2} and its distance from our solar system as 4.246 light-years.
   Use this information to show that its luminosity is 6.6×10^{23} W. [2]

   d   Use the Stefan–Boltzmann law to calculate the radius of Proxima Centauri. [3]

[Total: 8]

UNDERSTAND THESE TERMS

- Wien's displacement law
- Stefan–Boltzmann law

《 **RECALL AND CONNECT 2** 《

Think back to Chapter 12. Write down an explanation of the Doppler effect. Name **two** things that are not affected by the speed of the source.

31.4 The expanding Universe

1. One of your friends says 'The Big Bang was an explosion that took place 13.8 billion years ago.'
   a. Which part of this statement is correct, and which part is incorrect?
   b. How do we know from the spectrum that galaxies are moving away from us (receding)?
   c. What is the evidence for the Big Bang theory?
   d. How can we use Hubble's law to conclude that the universe started as a Big Bang?

2. Astronomers have measured the redshift of the Sombrero galaxy as 0.003 416.

   This is the fractional change in the wavelength of the observed light.
   a. Use this information to calculate its recession speed. [1]
   b. The experimental value for the Hubble constant H_0 is about $2.4 \times 10^{-18}\,\text{s}^{-1}$.
      Use this information to calculate the distance to the Sombrero Galaxy in light-years. [3]
   c. Another astronomer wants to check the data.
      An emission line measured on Earth is 656.4 nm. Calculate the wavelength that an astronomer should expect the same line to have in the light detected from the Sombrero galaxy. [2]

   [Total: 6]

3. a. Describe the cause of the redshift in the light arriving from distant galaxies. [2]
   b. Table 31.3 shows data for a fictional universe. It shows galaxies at different distances and how fast they are moving away from the Milky Way.

Distance / 10^{21} m	Velocity / 10^5 m s^{-1}
0.0	0
4.7	2.7
6.6	3.6
8.5	4.7
16.1	8.9
18.0	9.9
18.9	10.5
20.8	11.5

   Table 31.3

   Plot a graph of velocity against distance to each galaxy for this fictional universe. [3]
   c. Use the graph you plotted to estimate the Hubble constant. Make your working clear. [2]
   d. Calculate the age of this fictional universe. [2]

   [Total: 9]

> **UNDERSTAND THESE TERMS**
> - Big Bang theory
> - redshift
> - Hubble's law

> **REFLECTION**
>
> Do you feel you understand the term 'estimate' and what is expected from an estimated answer? How did you do in the estimate questions in this chapter? If you didn't score as well as you could have, how could you improve your approach when tackling similar questions?

SELF-ASSESSMENT CHECKLIST

Let's revisit the Knowledge focus and Exam skills focus for this chapter.

Decide how confident you are with each statement.

Now I can:	Show it	Needs more work	Almost there	Confident to move on
understand the term luminosity as the total power of radiation emitted by a star	Explain the term luminosity in terms of the power output of a lamp.			
recall and use the inverse square law for radiant flux intensity F in terms of the luminosity L of the source: $F = \dfrac{L}{4d^2}$	Write down the formulae and practise expressing it in terms of radiant flux density F, luminosity L and distance to the star d.			
understand that an object of known luminosity is called a standard candle	Write a definition of the term standard candle, with two examples.			
understand the use of standard candles to determine distances to galaxies	Rearrange the inverse square law for radiant flux intensity in terms of distance.			
recall and use Wien's displacement law $\lambda_{max} \propto \dfrac{1}{T}$ to estimate the peak surface temperature of a star	Write down Wien's displacement law and use a reference star such as our Sun to find the surface temperature of 10 other stars given their peak wavelength.			
use the Stefan–Boltzmann law $L = 4\pi\sigma r^2 T^4$	Write down the Stefan–Boltzmann law and practise rearranging it in terms of the radius of a body r and its temperature T.			

CONTINUED

Now I can:	Show it	Needs more work	Almost there	Confident to move on
use Wien's displacement law and the Stefan–Boltzmann law to estimate the radius of a star	Use Wien's displacement law to find the temperature of a star given the peak wavelength or reading it from a black body spectrum. Rearrange the Stefan–Boltzmann law in terms of the radius of a star r and substitute values for luminosity L and surface temperature T to find the radius of the star.			
understand that the lines in the emission spectra from distant objects show an increase in wavelength from their known values	Write down the expression for the Doppler effect.			
understand what is meant by the term 'estimate' and why it is useful	Estimate the luminosity of the Sun without using a calculator given that the radiant flux density is about 1400 Wm^{-2} and sunlight takes about 8 minutes to reach us. Round any values where necessary.			

Exam practice 8

This section contains past paper questions from previous Cambridge exams, which draws together your knowledge on a range of topics that you have covered up to this point. These questions give you the opportunity to test your knowledge and understanding. Additional past paper practice questions can be found in the accompanying digital material.

The following question has an example student response and commentary provided. Once you have worked through the question, read the student response and commentary. Are your answers different to the sample responses?

1   Polonium-211 ($^{211}_{84}$Po) decays by alpha emission to form a stable isotope of lead (Pb).

   a   Complete the equation for this decay:

   $$^{211}_{84}\text{Po} \rightarrow \text{......}\text{Po} + \text{......}\alpha$$ [2]

   b   The variation with time t of the number of unstable nuclei N in a sample of polonium-211 is shown in Fig. 1.1.

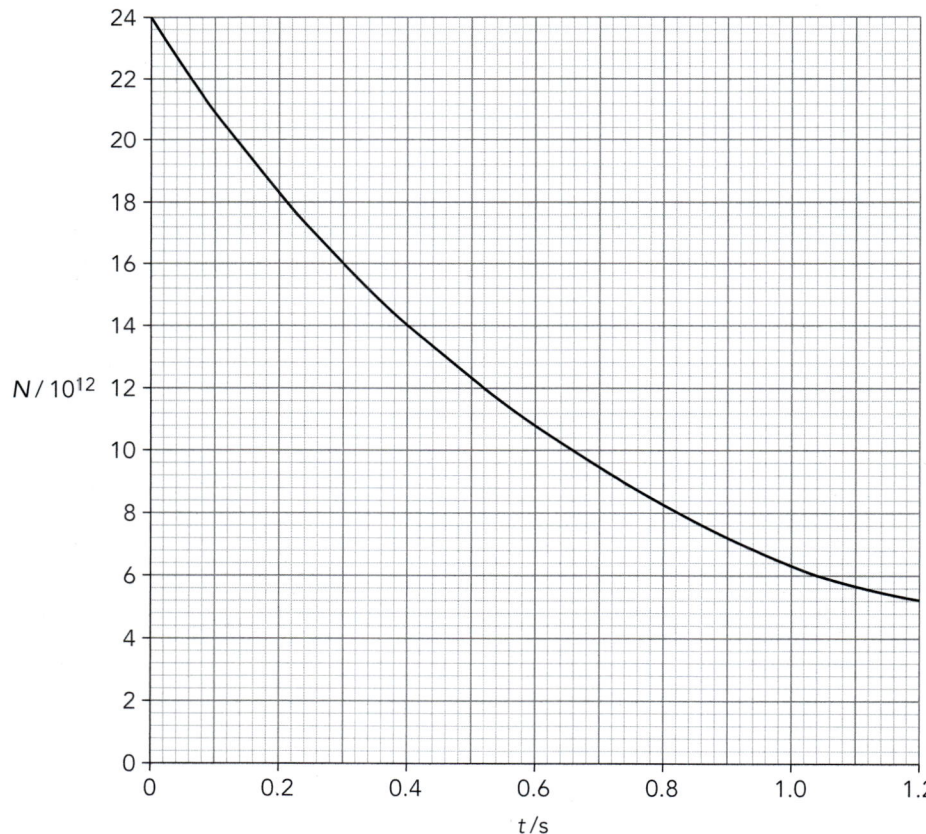

Fig. 1.1

Exam practice 8

At time $t = 0$, the sample contains only polonium-211.

    i   Use Fig. 1.1 to determine the decay constant λ of polonium-211. Give a unit with your answer. [2]

    ii   Use your answer in **b i** to calculate the activity at time $t = 0$ of the sample of polonium-211. [1]

    iii   On Fig. 1.1, sketch a line to show the variation with t of the number of lead nuclei in the sample. [2]

c   Each decay releases an alpha particle with energy 6900 keV.

    i   Calculate, in J, the total amount of energy given to alpha particles that are emitted between time $t = 0.30$ s and time $t = 0.90$ s. [3]

    ii   Suggest why the total amount of energy released by the decay process between time $t = 0.30$ s and time $t = 0.90$ s is greater than your answer in **c i**. [1]

[Total: 11]

Cambridge International AS & A Level Physics (9702) Paper 42, Q9, March 2022

Example student response			Commentary
a		$^{211}_{84}\text{Po} \rightarrow ^{207}_{82}\text{Po} + ^{4}_{2}\alpha$	The student's answer is correct. *This answer is awarded 2 out of 2 marks.*
b	i	$t_{\frac{1}{2}} = 0.52$ s $\lambda = \dfrac{0.693}{0.52} = 1.333$ s	The value is correct, but the correct unit is s^{-1}. *This answer is awarded 1 out of 2 marks.*
	ii	$A = \lambda N$ $A = 1.333 \times 24 \times 10^{12}$ $A = 3.19 \times 10^{13}$ Bq	The student's answer is correct. *This answer is awarded 1 out of 1 mark.*

Example student response	Commentary
iii 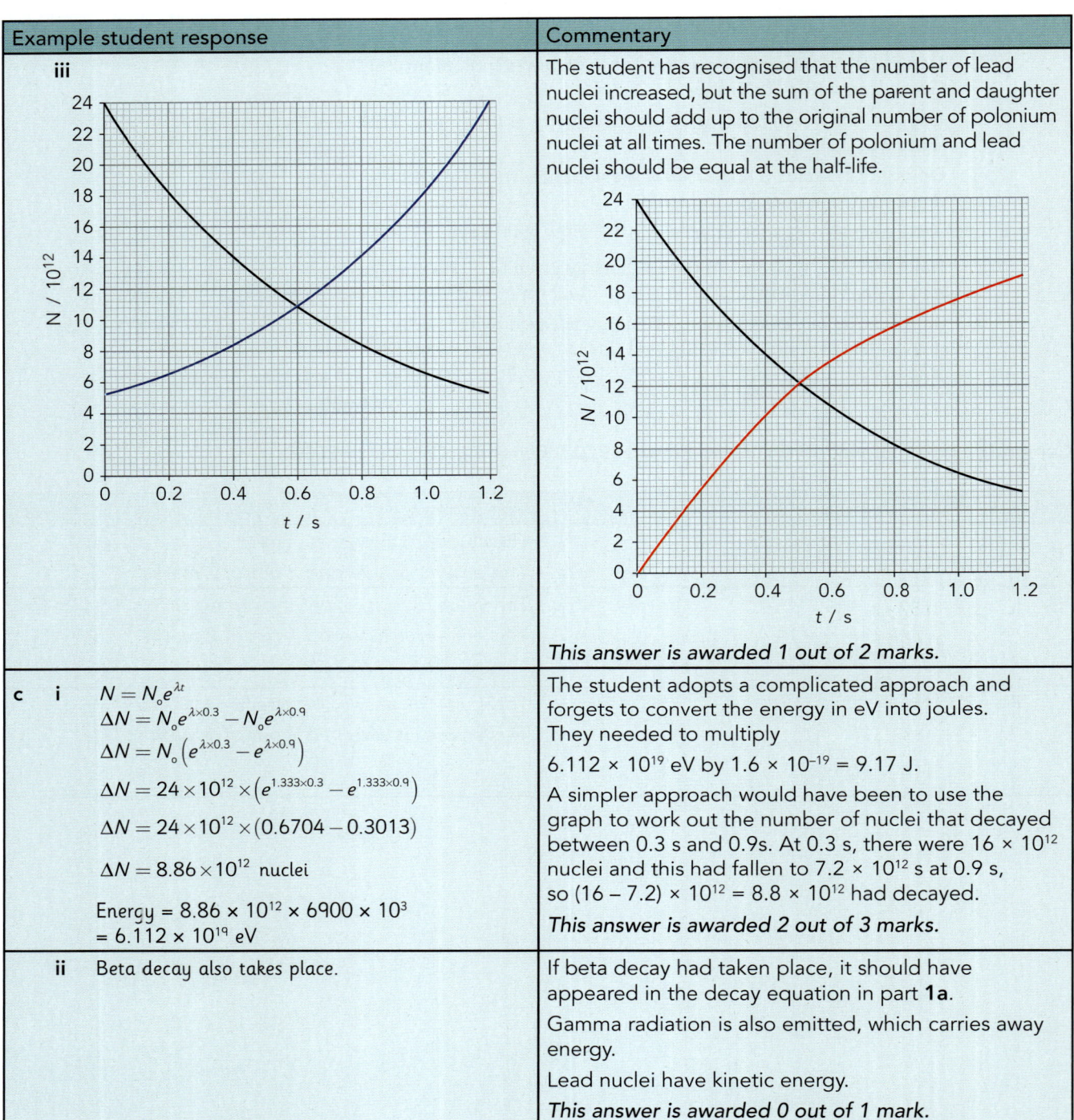	The student has recognised that the number of lead nuclei increased, but the sum of the parent and daughter nuclei should add up to the original number of polonium nuclei at all times. The number of polonium and lead nuclei should be equal at the half-life. *This answer is awarded 1 out of 2 marks.*
c i $N = N_o e^{\lambda t}$ $\Delta N = N_o e^{\lambda \times 0.3} - N_o e^{\lambda \times 0.9}$ $\Delta N = N_o \left(e^{\lambda \times 0.3} - e^{\lambda \times 0.9} \right)$ $\Delta N = 24 \times 10^{12} \times \left(e^{1.333 \times 0.3} - e^{1.333 \times 0.9} \right)$ $\Delta N = 24 \times 10^{12} \times (0.6704 - 0.3013)$ $\Delta N = 8.86 \times 10^{12}$ nuclei Energy $= 8.86 \times 10^{12} \times 6900 \times 10^3$ $= 6.112 \times 10^{19}$ eV	The student adopts a complicated approach and forgets to convert the energy in eV into joules. They needed to multiply 6.112×10^{19} eV by $1.6 \times 10^{-19} = 9.17$ J. A simpler approach would have been to use the graph to work out the number of nuclei that decayed between 0.3 s and 0.9s. At 0.3 s, there were 16×10^{12} nuclei and this had fallen to 7.2×10^{12} s at 0.9 s, so $(16 - 7.2) \times 10^{12} = 8.8 \times 10^{12}$ had decayed. *This answer is awarded 2 out of 3 marks.*
ii Beta decay also takes place.	If beta decay had taken place, it should have appeared in the decay equation in part **1a**. Gamma radiation is also emitted, which carries away energy. Lead nuclei have kinetic energy. *This answer is awarded 0 out of 1 mark.*

Now you have read the commentary to the previous question, here is a question on a similar topic that you should attempt. Use the information from the previous response and commentary to guide you as you answer.

2 a i State what is meant by nuclear binding energy. [2]

ii On Fig. 2.1, sketch a line to show the variation with nucleon number A of the binding energy per nucleon E of a nucleus. [2]

Fig. 2.1

b In one type of nuclear process, deuterium $\left(^{2}_{1}H\right)$ undergoes the reaction

$$^{2}_{1}H + ^{2}_{1}H \rightarrow ^{3}_{2}He + ^{1}_{0}n$$

i State the name of this type of nuclear process. [1]

ii Explain, with reference to your line in **a ii**, why this reaction results in the release of energy. [2]

c Table 2.1 shows the masses of the particles involved in the reaction in **b**.

particle	mass / u
$^{1}_{0}n$	1.008 665
$^{2}_{1}H$	2.014 102
$^{3}_{2}He$	3.016 029

Table 2.1

Calculate the energy released when 1.00 mol of deuterium undergoes the reaction. [5]

[Total: 12]

Cambridge International AS & A Level Physics (9702) Paper 41, Q8, June 2022

The following question has an example student commentary and answer provided. Work through the question first, then compare your answer with the sample answer and commentary. How different were your answers to the example student answers? Are there any areas where you feel you need to improve your understanding?

3 **a** **i** Explain how X-rays are produced for use in medical diagnosis. [3]

  ii State why X-ray images are taken of multiple sections of the body during computed tomography (CT) scanning. [1]

b An X-ray image is taken of the structure shown in Fig. 3.1.

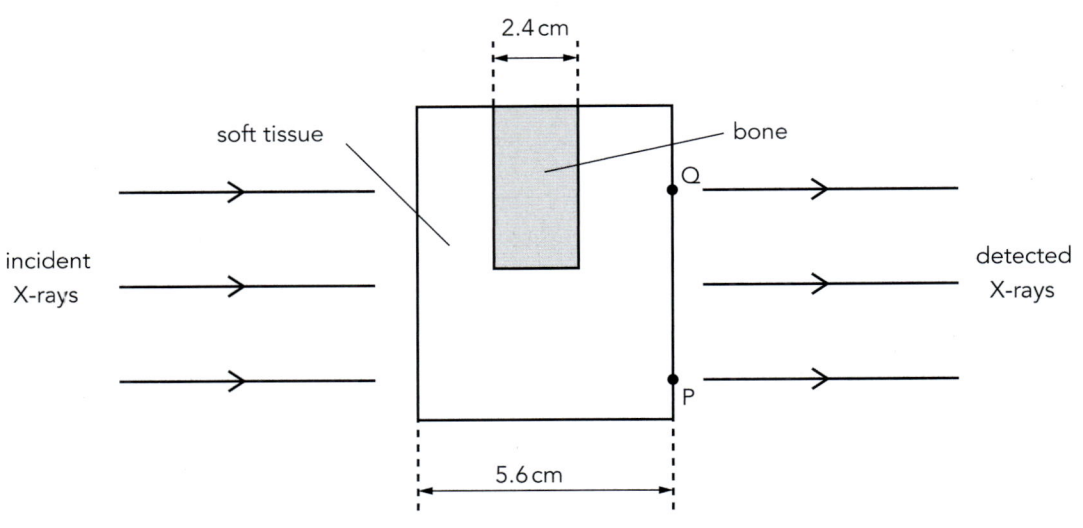

Fig. 3.1

The linear attenuation coefficient of bone is 3.4 cm⁻¹.

The linear attenuation coefficient of soft tissue is 0.89 cm⁻¹.

The incident X-rays are parallel and have a uniform intensity I_0 across the structure.

Determine, in terms of I_0, the intensity of the detected X-rays from:

  i point P [2]

  ii point Q. [2]

c Explain, with reference to your answers in **b**, whether the X-ray image of the structure in Fig. 3.1 has good contrast. [1]

[Total: 9]

Cambridge International AS & A Level Physics (9702) Paper 41, Q9, June 2022

Exam practice 8

		Example student response	Commentary
a	i	High speed electrons are incident on a metal target. When they hit it, they slow down. X-rays are emitted when the electrons decelerate.	The student gets 2 marks for saying that the electrons hit the metal target and that they are emitted when electrons decelerate. To get the third mark, they need to talk about how they get to the high speed in the first place. Which is to say they are 'accelerated by a high potential difference'. *This answer is awarded 2 out of 3 marks.*
	ii	These 'slices' of the body can be compiled into a three dimensional image.	This is absolutely correct and is plenty of detail for a 'state' question. *This answer is awarded 1 out of 1 mark.*
b	i	$I = I_0 e^{-\mu x}$ $I = I_0 e^{-0.89 \times 5.6}$ $I = 0.0068 I_0$	This is correct working. The student doesn't need to give a final answer as they are asked to leave it in terms of I_0. They have selected the correct attenuation coefficient and the correct distance from the information in the text and diagram. *This answer is awarded 2 out of 2 marks.*
	ii	$I = I_0 e^{-\mu x}$ $I = I_0 e^{-0.89 \times 5.6} e^{-3.4 \times 2.4}$ $I = 1.96 \times 10^{-6} I_0$	The student needed to reduce the effective width of the soft tissue by the width of the bone. Their equation would become: $I = I_0 e^{-0.89 \times 3.2} e^{-3.4 \times 2.4}$ Here unfortunately they have effectively combined the attenuation due to the bone with the attenuation due to the whole width of the limb. This isn't quite correct although they have the right idea. *This answer is awarded 0 out of 2 marks.*
c		Good contrast means there will be sufficient difference in intensity to see an image. So yes there is good contrast because the intensity of the X-ray through the soft tissue is much greater than the X-ray through the bone.	This scores the mark. The important point was to make sure they made a comparison and then a conclusion. *This answer is awarded 1 out of 1 mark.*

Now you have read the commentary to the previous question, here is a similar question that you should attempt. Use the information from the previous response and commentary to guide you as you answer

4   a   Explain the principles of the detection of ultrasound waves for medical diagnosis. [4]

    b   By reference to specific acoustic impedance, explain why there is very little transmission of ultrasound waves from air into skin. [3]

[Total: 7]

Cambridge International AS & A Level Physics (9702) Paper 42, Q5, June 2020

Practical skills for A Level

> **KNOWLEDGE FOCUS**
>
> In this chapter you will answer questions on:
> - planning and analysis
> - planning
> - analysis of the data
> - treatment of uncertainties
> - conclusions and evaluation of results.

> **EXAM SKILLS FOCUS**
>
> In this chapter you will:
> - develop an approach to questions that ask you to design, evaluate or improve practical work.

Spend time memorising apparatus and techniques rather than specific methods. In general, there are only a few quantities that we need to measure in physics and only a few pieces of apparatus that we use to do that. If you are asked to design an experiment, you will probably be given a relationship to test. So, think about the quantities you need to change, measure or keep the same, and then tell the examiner how to do that and what apparatus to use.

Practical skills for A Level

P2.1 Planning and analysis

1. Write a plan for a simple practical in which you need to measure the average speed of an object over a short distance. Write no more than three sentences. Include the quantities you are going to measure, the apparatus you are going to use to make the measurements, and how you will analyse the data.

> **REFLECTION**
>
> How confident were you when answering this question? Measuring average speed is a simple example of an experiment – most questions where you are asked to write plans can be just as simple as that if you work systematically.

P2.2 Planning

1. Suggest a suitable instrument to measure each of these quantities and their approximate values.

    a diameter of a copper wire ~0.3 mm
    b length of an interrupt card for a light gate ~10 cm
    c mass of a ball bearing ~1 g
    d temperature of melting ice, ~273 K
    e potential difference across a diode ~0.7 V

2. The period of a mass–spring system is given by the equation:

    $$T = 2\pi\sqrt{\frac{m}{k}}$$

    where,

    T is the time period of the oscillator,

    m is the mass,

    k is a constant related to the stiffness of the springs.

    Design a laboratory experiment to test the relationship between T and m.

    Explain how your results could be used to determine values for k.

    You should draw a diagram showing the arrangement of your equipment. In your account you should pay particular attention to:

    - the procedure to be followed
    - the measurements to be taken
    - the control of variables
    - the analysis of the data
    - any safety precautions to be taken.

    [Total: 15]

> **UNDERSTAND THESE TERMS**
>
> - independent variable
> - dependent variable
> - control variable

P2.3 Analysis of the data

1. Rearrange each of these equations into the form $y = mx + c$, making the bold, blue term the gradient.

   a. $E = V + \mathbf{I}r$

   b. $E = \dfrac{\mathbf{F}L}{Ax}$

   c. $\mathbf{h}f = \Phi + E_{K_{max}}$

   d. $v^2 = \dfrac{\mathbf{G}M}{r}$

2. Copy and complete this table by stating:
   - which graph should you plot for each relationship
   - the meaning of the gradient
   - the y-intercept.

Relationship	Graph	Gradient	y-intercept
$y = mx + c$			
$y = ax^n$			
$y = ae^{kx}$			

3. A protactinium generator can be used in a laboratory to investigate the exponential decay of radioactive isotopes.

   a. Before conducting the experiment, the background count rate was measured. Explain what the experimenters should do with this value to ensure that the value of the activity, A, was as accurate as possible. [1]

b The activity of a sample of a radioactive isotope is measured over a period of time.

The table shows the results.

t / s	A / cpm
0	677
30	489
60	345
90	253
120	153
150	125

    i   Plot a graph of $\ln A$ against t. [5]
    ii   Use the graph to determine a value for the decay constant k. [2]
    iii Calculate an experimental value for the half-life of protactinium. [3]

c The protactinium generator contains radioactive uranium held in a solution within a sealed bottle.

The bottle can be agitated, and then some protactinium is isolated in an organic layer.

Protactinium itself is a beta emitter and has a very short half-life.

Uranium is an alpha emitter and has a half-life in the order of billions of years.

Identify **two** safety precautions for working with the protactinium generator. [2]

[Total: 13]

« RECALL AND CONNECT 1 «

Think back to Chapter P1. How do you estimate uncertainties before you have taken any measurements? And how do you calculate uncertainties after you have taken repeated measurements?

P2.4 Treatment of uncertainties

« RECALL AND CONNECT 2 «

Think back to Chapter P1. What is the difference between a systematic, zero and random error?

CAMBRIDGE INTERNATIONAL AS & A LEVEL PHYSICS: EXAM PREPARATION AND PRACTICE

1   A student is measuring the specific heat capacity of some metal blocks. Each block has a mass of 1.000 ± 0.001 kg. The table shows the results for one of the blocks.

Energy transferred to the block / J	Temperature / °C
0 ± 50	27 ± 0.5
1400 ± 50	29 ± 0.5
3000 ± 50	30 ± 0.5
4400 ± 50	32 ± 0.5
5300 ± 50	33 ± 0.5
6700 ± 50	34 ± 0.5
8100 ± 50	36 ± 0.5

a   Calculate the value of specific heat capacity and its absolute uncertainty for a result using the final row of the data result of this experiment. [3]

b   Explain which measurement should be improved. Justify your answer. [2]

c   i   Plot a graph of energy transferred against temperature. [4]
    ii Use the graph to calculate the specific heat capacity of the metal. [3]
    iii Add error bars to your graph and use them to estimate the uncertainty of your result. [4]

d   The final value of specific heat capacity will always be a little too high.
    Explain why taking repeated measurements and calculating the average will not improve this experiment. [4]

[Total: 20]

P2.5 Conclusions and evaluation of results

1   Here are some hypotheses and a sketch graph of the results.

Justify whether the evidence supports or invalidates each hypothesis by describing whether the graph supports the hypothesis or not.

a 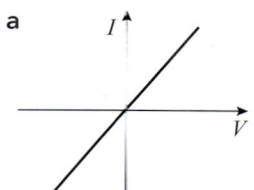   b 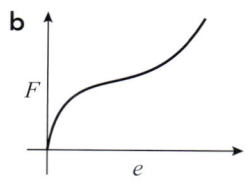   c 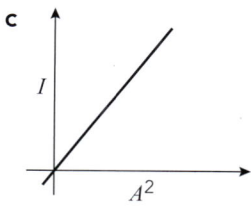   d

Hypothesis	Sketch graph of results
a Potential difference is proportional to current for a range of values of V.	
b Force is proportional to extension.	
c Intensity is proportional to amplitude squared.	
d Gravitational field strength is inversely proportional to distance.	

UNDERSTAND THESE TERMS

- uncertainty
- worst acceptable line

SELF-ASSESSMENT CHECKLIST

Let's revisit the Knowledge focus and Exam skills focus for this chapter.

Decide how confident you are with each statement.

Now I can:	Show it	Needs more work	Almost there	Confident to move on
develop a systematic approach to carrying out experiments, including planning, setting up apparatus, investigating and recording results, analysing data and writing conclusions	Review all of the exam skills from this chapter and the AS practical skills chapter, make a revision checklist for each skill and ensure that you can recognise and apply them quickly in exams.			
plan an investigation to test a relationship or investigate a problem, identifying the dependent, independent and control variables	Practise many practical exam questions, and answer each question in the same logical format.			
use logarithms and logarithmic graphs	Plot log graphs for exponential relationships and log–log graphs for power law equations. Analyse the graphs by determining the value and significance of the gradients and the intercepts.			
combine uncertainties, extending work from Practical Skills at AS Level	Calculate uncertainties for a range of complex experiments.			
plot error bars on graphs and find uncertainties in gradients and intercepts	Use uncertainties to add error bars to graphs and use these bars to give accurate lines of best fit and worst fit and calculate the percentage difference between them.			
develop a systematic approach to questions that ask me to design, evaluate or improve practical work	Use mark schemes on practical papers to write yourself a checklist of the things to include in design, evaluating, or improving practical questions.			

> Acknowledgements

The authors and publishers acknowledge the following sources of copyright material and are grateful for the permissions granted. While every effort has been made, it has not always been possible to identify the sources of all the material used, or to trace all copyright holders. If any omissions are brought to our notice, we will be happy to include the appropriate acknowledgements on reprinting.

Cambridge International copyright material in this publication is reproduced under licence and remains the intellectual property of Cambridge Assessment International Education.

Cambridge Assessment International Education bears no responsibility for the example answers to questions taken from its past question papers which are contained in this publication.

Thanks to the following for permission to reproduce images:

Cover image scanrail/Getty Images, Figure 25.2 Anderson, Carl D. (1933). 'The Positive Electron'. *Physical Review* 43 (6): 491–494. DOI:10.1103/PhysRev.43.491